SPIDERWEB CAPITALISM

Spiderweb Capitalism

How Global Elites Exploit Frontier Markets

Kimberly Kay Hoang

PRINCETON UNIVERSITY PRESS

PRINCETON AND OXFORD

Published by Princeton University Press
41 William Street, Princeton, New Jersey 08540
99 Banbury Road, Oxford OX2 6JX
press.princeton.edu

First paperback printing, 2024
Paperback ISBN 978-0-691-23125-9
Cloth ISBN 978-0-691-22911-9
ISBN (e-book) 978-0-691-22910-2

British Library Cataloging-in-Publication Data is available

Editorial: Meagan Levinson and Jacqueline Delaney
Jacket/Cover Design: Karl Spurzem
Production: Erin Suydam
Publicity: James Schneider and Kathryn Stevens
Copyeditor: Annie Gottlieb

This book has been composed in Adobe Text Pro

CONTENTS

ACKNOWLEDGMENTS

This book has taken me quite literally all around the world and into some of the most privileged spaces that I could ever have fathomed as a first-generation college graduate from a refugee and working-class background. As a young kid growing up, I understood that our society was stratified by class. In my imagination wealthy people lived in well-manicured homes in gated communities, walled off from the rest of us. However, my journey doing the research for this book taught me that there is a kind of stratospheric wealth invisible and hidden in some of the most elite social circles that span the globe.

Conducting research on wealthy people is an extremely difficult task, and while many social scientists have been able to make great inroads into seeing how wealthy individuals live, consume, and make sense of their wealth in relation to those less fortunate, few systematically study how the rich make and protect not only their money, but also their reputations. As someone who did not attend an elite prep school or an Ivy League college, or work in a prestigious financial firm upon graduating from college, I was very much an outsider trying to crack open doors that are hidden and walled off from people like me. This is by far the most difficult and ambitious research I have ever conducted. Not only was getting access to wealthy individuals around the world highly challenging, but then trying to connect the dots of their relationships with one another in tangled and layered webs felt like being caught inside a 3D maze with no clear way in or out.

This book would not be possible without the people who let me into their social and business networks, took the time to let me interview them, and made crucial introductions to others in their network. They not only shuttled me around the world with them into spaces that would otherwise be off limits to me, but they also spent a great deal of time explaining their strategies and dilemmas as they navigated markets in new frontiers. Studying highly educated elites who are so specialized in their respective areas was at times intimidating, and I often wondered what value I could add as a sociologist.

However, over time, the interviews I carried out with so many people helped me to see that few people had the luxury of time to connect the dots of the complex nodes in these massive webs. I am grateful to all the people who were both patient and at times incredibly harsh, because they opened another world for me to study, analyze, and explain to other outsiders.

I am deeply grateful for the financial or intellectual support of my academic community at the University of Chicago. When I arrived at UChicago, my colleagues pushed me to think about a "big idea project" that was "more ambitious theoretically and empirically" than my first book. This was both intimidating and exciting. Pre-tenure, this felt like a high-risk, high-reward endeavor. But as much as they pushed me intellectually, I received an extraordinary amount of support from four different department chairs, Elisabeth Clemens, Karin Knorr Cetina, Linda Waite, and Andreas Glaeser, who all helped me find the courage to resist the inner pressure to produce quick results with less rigorous data and analysis and instead slow down to work on a big idea project. I also felt a great deal of support from my deans, David Nirenberg and Amanda Woodward, who both were supportive of the project in its early stages and provided financial support to backstop the external grants I received.

This project is an academic project shaped by being in conversation with my colleagues and students at the University of Chicago. I am grateful to Andrew Abbott, Patrick Bergemann, Karin Knorr Cetina, Edward Laumann, Jonathan Levy, John Levi Martin, Kristen Schilt, Amanda Sharkey, Forrest Stuart, Jenny Trinitapoli, Robert Vargas, and Geoffrey Wodtke, who all read various drafts of this manuscript and have been extraordinarily generous with critical feedback that helped push my theorizing in important ways. I am especially grateful to the curious and fearless undergraduate research assistants who worked with me at various stages of the research process: Khoa Phan Howard, Lucas Penido, Gaurav Kalwani, Kevin Petersen, Quinn Nguyen, Emily Zhu, Lena Breda, Nikhilesh Chitlangia, Zhi Rong Tan, Yunhan Wen, Pallavi Anand, Richard Wu, and Ana Guerrero. Brian Fenaughty read the entire book manuscript, provided sharp feedback, and was an invaluable conversation partner in my final stages of writing. The staff at Global Studies, especially Lee Price, kept a warm and welcoming environment when I needed to hide out and write in the early mornings before students trickled onto campus.

In 2020, I had the privilege of holding a book workshop where Jennifer Carlson, Greta Krippner, and Sida Liu each generously read a rough draft of the full manuscript and provided incredibly valuable written feedback, which pushed me to deepen my analysis and clarify the book's theoretical contribution across multiple fields. In addition, Terence Halliday and Hannah Appel both read the full manuscript and provided generous critical comments. Hana E. Brown and Jennifer Jones have been my steadfast writing crew, meeting biweekly for over ten years now. They have read everything I have ever written, from the most half-baked ideas to polished drafts in the final stages of revising, and their friendship has sustained me during some of the most challenging times with this project.

The research for this book was costly, and I would like to acknowledge several institutions and organizations that awarded me with generous grants and fellowships supporting my research. The field research would not have been possible without the generous support of the Fulbright Global Scholar Award and the Social Science Research Council Transregional Research Junior Scholar Fellowship: InterAsian Contexts and Connections. At the University of Chicago, I received support from the Center for the Study of Gender and Sexuality, the David Hoeft Award for Newly Tenured Faculty, the Center for International Social Science Research, an Albion W. Small Grant, along with grants from the University of Chicago's Centers in Hong Kong and Paris. Together those awards helped to cover the costs of travel, hotels, and meals so that I could both carry out interviews and connect the different people involved in building these complex capital webs. Given the extraordinary demands on my time with respect to teaching, service, and directing the Global Studies program, I am grateful for the American Council of Learned Societies Fellowship that enabled me to take a research leave to complete the final draft of this book.

In the field, I was fortunate to have the support of many institutions and people. I thank all of those in Vietnam at Vietnam National University, the Southern Institute of Sustainable Development Office of International Cooperation, Hoa Sen University, and Fulbright University Vietnam. In Myanmar, I thank the Embassy of the United States of America, the Ministry of Foreign Affairs of the Republic of the Union of Myanmar, and the Yangon School of Political Science for their support of this project.

Fieldwork and writing can be incredibly lonely endeavors, and I am grateful to the many friends who not only provided me with company, but often served as sounding boards as I talked through some of my emergent findings. Heartfelt thanks to Danny Phan, Rita Nguyen, Jamie Jo Eslinger, Tuyen Hoang, Karida Brown, Michael Rodriguez-Muñiz, Diana Castillo, Tiffany Chew, Jessica Cobb, Lauren Beresford, Chi Ha, Mimi Vu, Dana Doan, Anh-Minh Do, Sonny Swe, Thao Nguyen, Crystal Lam, Marcus Chen, Nathalie Pham, Sylvia

Saw McKaige, Mimi and Man Lam, and many others who have chosen to remain anonymous—you know who you are, and I am deeply grateful.

I had the privilege of presenting this book to numerous audiences, who provided me with the opportunity to try out my ideas and challenged me to deepen my analysis. These include audiences at Princeton University, Harvard University, Northern Illinois University, University of Arizona, University of Southern California, University of Illinois Chicago, Cornell University, University of Virginia, University of North Carolina at Greensboro, Purdue University, Columbia University, the American Bar Foundation, University of California, Los Angeles, Ohio State University, University of Maryland, University of Illinois at Urbana-Champaign, and the University of Wisconsin-Milwaukee. Portions of this book also appear in the journals *American Sociological Review* and *Gender & Society*—where I benefited from the anonymous reviewers.

I am most grateful to Meagan Levinson, my editor at Princeton University Press, for her support and expert editorial advice as she pored through the entire book manuscript. At a time when several presses push authors to simplify their books for a general audience, I especially appreciated Meagan's approach, which respects the intelligence of readers and leaves room for nuance and complexity. Meagan understood the intellectual project and did not push me to make this a superficial book about how rich people think, behave, or spend their money. I am also indebted to Christie Henry, the director at Princeton University Press, who not only provided me with financial support to defray the costs of childcare during the height of the COVID-19 pandemic, but also took the time to write the most generous email, which gave me the second wind to finish this book. Jacqueline Delaney and the entire press team at Princeton Press have been a dream team to work with.

Lastly, I want to thank my husband, Robert Vargas, a brilliant social scientist, my fiercest champion, and the love of my life. This project pushed the boundaries of our love to all sorts of new places and opened my eyes to a whole new set of exponential possibilities when it comes to managing a dual-career household. During the height of the COVID-19 pandemic we welcomed our daughter, Evelyn, into this world. In those early months, when we were without help, Robert took care of both of us while I worked to complete this manuscript. The time we spent sheltering in place as a little family is time I will cherish forever. I love the two of you and this little family of ours with every fiber of my being. Evelyn, mommy loves you, and I hope that I will live long enough to watch you grow and slay in your own way. ∞ xoxo ∞

Ho Chi Minh City, Vietnam

It was 5:00 p.m., the sun was setting, and the air was beginning to cool down after a blazing hot afternoon. I managed to grab a taxi at the height of rush hour in the downtown business district just as the sea of people were descending from their offices.

I was on my way to meet Alan Tang[1]—the chief executive officer of one of Vietnam's largest asset management firms with over $2 billion of assets under management. Alan was one of a small but growing number of individuals who have become extremely wealthy in Vietnam's rapidly growing foreign investment market.

At the time, I thought Alan was probably one of the most important people I could interview for this book. He was the key player in the market and essential to unlocking so many questions about how global elites manage risky investments in frontier markets like Vietnam and Myanmar. I had spent months trying to get an interview with him. By this time, I had already interviewed several of his employees as well as his firm's in-house counsel. Prior to this meeting, he had stood me up once and asked to reschedule two other times, so I could not be late. I had thirty minutes to get ten blocks, which would not have been a problem if not for the traffic.

I found myself anxiously staring at my watch as I sat in bumper-to-bumper traffic. Looking out the window, I could not help but feel a tinge of panic at the sight of this city, taken over by motor vehicles creating new traffic jams on the old roads constructed primarily for thousands of motorbikes. By 5:10, I started to panic in earnest and so pushed the taxi driver to get me there faster. He pressed his way through the traffic, and at one point he even followed the lead of several other cars and drove up on a sidewalk to get ahead.

At 5:25 p.m. the cab was two blocks from the hotel, and I calculated that it would probably be safer and faster for me to get out and run. I grabbed some cash out of my bag to pay him and leaped out of the taxi and set off running in a work dress and heels.

When I arrived, my watch read 5:32 p.m. Fuck, I thought to myself. I am late. I nervously wiped the sweat off my forehead as I took in the sound of a live piano coming from the bar. The mood was much calmer and the pace less frantic inside the lounge of one of the city's most luxurious hotels. After a quick scan, I found Alan seated comfortably in an armchair, wearing a gray pin-striped suit of material certainly thicker than the dress I was wearing. Clearly, he was not deterred by the traffic, humidity, dirt, or noise outside as he was being waited on in this cool, air-conditioned space. Instead, his eyes were glued to his phone as he rapidly typed away, looking cool as a cucumber.

I straightened out my dress and nervously walked to his table. "Hi Alan, I'm Kimberly. I hope I didn't keep you too long."

He looked up from his phone and said to me, "I was just wrapping up another meeting here. Have a seat." Alan called over the waitress, who asked me if I would prefer coffee, tea, or wine. I told her that I'd just have what he's having. The waitress pulled out a cold bottle of French Chablis that was sitting over ice and proceeded with an extremely generous pour.

As Alan wrapped up the exchange on his phone, I pulled out my cheat sheet on him with all of the background information I could find on the internet. I knew that Alan had spent more than fifteen years managing a firm that had grown from a small single managed fund of USD$5 million to one with listings on the London, Canadian, and Hong Kong stock exchanges. He is an active participant in the World Economic Forum and holds two honorary doctorate degrees. He has lived and worked in the United States, Canada, France, and most recently Hong Kong.

He was a big name in the local finance community, and nearly every-one I met had a story to tell about how they thought he made his money. A combination of jealousy, envy, and mystery surrounded Alan as those around him in Vietnam fueled rumors that Alan's investment strategies involved theft, money laundering, and corruption. Several people speculated that his source of capital was the Triad in Hong Kong—a well-known Chinese mafia group. But if Alan's reputation was so terrible in Vietnam, how was he able to continue raising so much money from some of the most reputable investors abroad, all of whom claim to do intensive due diligence checks on their partners?

Before I could even take the first sip of my wine, Alan wasted no time and said, "Kimberly, right? Yeah, you are famous here in Vietnam. You wrote the book about the sex industry. I heard many stories about you working as a hostess. I have friends who know you from those days. You're a brave girl." I nervously took a sip of wine, realizing that Alan had done his due diligence on me. He went on to tell me that he had skimmed the introduction of my book *Dealing in Desire*. He told me that he respected the ways that I had to get my hands dirty to dig deep for that book. Before I could even divert the conversation to the topic of my new book project and why I wanted to interview him, he cut to the chase, saying, "I know you know how we do business in Vietnam. So tell me, how I can help you?"

I responded by telling Alan that I was back in Southeast Asia doing research for a new book project about foreign investment in frontier markets. As a sociologist, I am primarily interested in understanding how people like him finesse risky frontier markets. The first thirty minutes of our conversation were quite boring. Alan gave me his well-rehearsed public relations spiel about his humble beginnings as a small fund and the hustle to survive in this market. He told me the same story I'd heard probably 100 times from other folks that I'd interviewed about Vietnam's market potential as one of the fastest-growing markets in the region. He was just here riding the wave of Vietnam's rapidly growing economy.

I politely nodded my head, and when he finished, I asked him, "As I understand it, bribery and corruption are par for the course here in Vietnam and also in Myanmar, another market I am studying. . . . So how are you able to raise funds from investors who have to comply with strict laws around bribery and corruption?"

Alan stopped, put his glass of wine down on the table, looked me dead in the eyes and asked me, "So you want to know my trade secrets?"

No, I explain to him. I am not a journalist interested in writing up a story about any one person. I am an academic, here to interview hundreds of people to understand broader patterns, processes, and practices of how different people finesse these markets.

He condescendingly replied, "There is a saying in the business world. Those who cannot do, teach. The first thing I tell all of my employees is, take your fancy Ivy League degrees and leave them at the door." He went on to tell me how business school professors waste so much time teaching students how to build predictive models to forecast or calculate market risks or performance. But that was all "bullshit" because there are too many unpredictable variables in Vietnam.

I pressed him on what mattered, and he told me two things that would change the entire course of my research. First, he said, "To make money anywhere in Asia, you need to master the art of 'playing in the gray.'" That is a craft. The people who can play in the gray, he explained, know how to finesse the very boundary between legal and illegal activity. They are front-running the market and the law—getting ahead of the formal regulatory process by starting to build or operate without the proper permits, registration, or tax receipts, but with the tacit protection of officials who are often lubricated by gifts or bribes. That is what makes this a frontier or emerging market.

Second, he told me, "Behind every chief executive officer (CEO) is a chairman." The chairmen are people in this world who are so rich they never appear in newspapers or on public lists like *Forbes*. These ultra-high-net-worth individuals (UHNWIs) "have what I call 'fuck you' money. . . . For them these markets are just one square on their roulette table." The CEOs on the ground, he explained, "are just the face of the deal . . . sure, we make good money, but we are also the 'fall guys' who bear all of the risks." The chairmen effectively are "nowhere and everywhere and are accountable to no one" as they hide behind layers and layers of companies in capital webs spun around the world.[2]

This interview planted a few seeds that would alter not only my research questions, but my entire methodological approach as I worked to uncover a massive web of people and institutions who coordinate capital investments all around the world—by mastering the game of playing in the gray.

SPIDERWEB CAPITALISM

Introduction

SPIDERWEB CAPITALISM

In 2016, an anonymous source leaked 11.5 million financial documents commonly known as the Panama Papers. These pages, which had been kept from the public eye by attorney-client privilege, connected over 140 ultra-wealthy individuals—including Vladimir Putin, the King of Saudi Arabia, and China's top leader Xi Jinping—across 50 countries to offshore companies in 21 tax havens, such as the Cayman Islands, Panama, and the British Virgin Islands, to name a few.[1] The 2015 investigation of the 1Malaysia Development Berhad [1MDB] company revealed that $4.5 billion of Malaysian public pension funds had been siphoned off into the personal accounts of the country's former Prime Minister, Najib Razak, and the Malaysian financier, Taek Jho Low. This was not a self-contained event that occurred somewhere "over there" in a small Southeast Asian country. During an investigation into 1MDB, Goldman Sachs, headquartered in New York and one of the largest global financial institutions, admitted to conspiring in a scheme to pay over $1 billion in bribes to officials in Malaysia and Abu Dhabi to obtain lucrative business deals.[2] This fraud not only involved conspirators from the United States but also had impacts on its politics, as Low channeled the funds into the accounts of his associates, including the Haitian-American rapper Pras Michél, who funneled the money into two Super PACs, "Black Men Vote" and "Trump Victory," to lobby US Presidents Obama and Trump.[3]

1

Such offshore scandals provide a glimpse into the deep, intertwining web of licit and illicit markets, and reveal the extent to which global finance structures have produced an economic "black hole," wherein a very small group of privileged political and economic elites move and manage money through offshore shell corporations. These are paper companies without active business operations that are set up solely for the purpose of holding funds, managing another entity's financial transactions, legally reducing tax liabilities, and obscuring the true owner of an asset onshore.[4] Journalists and scholars alike have attempted to chart these complex networks in the wake of various scandals, but the players are notoriously difficult to track. In *Spiderweb Capitalism,* I uncover the mechanics behind the invisible, mundane networks of people connected through hidden and complex webs—lawyers, accountants, company secretaries, and fixers—who facilitate illicit activities by conducting transactions across multiple sovereignties. Through a close examination of the emerging markets of Vietnam and Myanmar, I illustrate how offshore entities are used to connect economic elites from around the world with political elites and their brokers from less developed economies in hidden networks of global capitalism.

This book centers on one primary question. How do global elites capitalize on risky frontier markets? The answer, as I will show, is by playing in the gray. To theorize the process of playing in the gray, the goal of this book is threefold: (1) to uncover the structure of the networks, which I refer to as spiderweb capitalism, (2) to examine the people who make and move money around the world through offshore vehicles, and (3) to reveal how elites finesse the gray space between legal and illegal practices to establish significant social and political connections that allow them to exploit new frontiers.

Uncovering the Puzzle

To tell this story, I begin in two countries—Vietnam and Myanmar—that attract the kinds of investors looking for high risk and high returns. This group of investors draws on old strategies developed in the West and uses them to front-run the political and legal systems in frontier markets with weaker regulatory structures.

In April 2016, with support from the Fulbright Global Scholars program and the Social Science Research Council, I packed my bags and moved to Southeast Asia, where I planned to make Ho Chi Minh City (HCMC), Vietnam, and Yangon, Myanmar, my home bases for the next eighteen months. And then, more quickly than I could have imagined, my plans changed dramatically. As I followed the data, I discovered a much larger puzzle that tied HCMC and Yangon to Hong Kong and Singapore and then stretched even farther, connecting them to a broader system of offshoring.

Having spent over ten years in and outside of Vietnam carrying out research for my first book, *Dealing in Desire,* I had made several connections that would be vital to the discoveries for this second book. I included Myanmar because several of my former contacts had moved to Yangon and set up offices there, looking to expand into an even newer frontier, and their move helped facilitate my engagement with Myanmar. From there, I was introduced to Xuan Liu, the CEO of an asset management firm with offices in Vietnam, Myanmar, Hong Kong, and Singapore. Xuan took me under his wing as his personal assistant and graciously taught me a great deal about both Vietnam's and Myanmar's foreign investment climate. The time I spent in Xuan's office was critical, because the job taught me how to speak in a new technical financial language which, in turn, helped me identify relevant questions to ask investors.

My early days of working in the firm also aided my understanding of the politics in what anthropology professor Karen Ho calls the "front office" and the "back office."[5] By following Xuan around, I was able to witness the front-office work he carried out, which, for the most part, involved relational work with potential investors and state officials outside the firm. Xuan relied on employees in the back office to deal with the technical work of executing the deals he had sourced. Xuan introduced me to his team as a researcher interested in studying foreign investment in Southeast Asia and as an assistant who would help with whatever he needed at the moment. I signed a nondisclosure agreement (NDA), with the plan that anything I would write about the firm I would first run by the relevant parties within the firm. After this, Xuan introduced me to his management team, which meant I now had access to the back office.

While I gained some understanding by completing low-level tasks in the back office, I learned the most during the semi-structured interviews I conducted outside of the office. These meetings took place with office employees during their lunch breaks and over happy hours at nearby bars. And the person to whom I owe a great deal of gratitude was a lawyer, Tuyen, who served as the firm's in-house counsel. Tuyen was born in Vietnam but had spent many years living abroad in Canada and spoke fluent English.

During our first lunch meeting Tuyen asked me if I knew what a special purpose vehicle or holding company was. I did not. As I would later uncover, these were the keys to unlocking so many of my questions about how his firm helps global elites exploit frontier markets. A special purpose vehicle, he explained, is a paper company set up offshore—for his businesses, "offshore" meant Hong Kong or Singapore. That paper company is a holding company, whose primary purpose is to own the subsidiary company onshore in Vietnam or Myanmar. Since all of this was new to me, I asked him to explain it to me in laymen's terms. He gave me this example.

Ultra-high-net-worth individuals (UHNWIs) have investments all around the world. They are often wary of going into risky markets with high levels of corruption because that could have both criminal and reputational repercussions. So they make investments in a special purpose vehicle or holding company set up in Singapore or Hong Kong. That paper company in Hong Kong or Singapore would then turn around and, on paper, own a stake in local firms with actual business operations in Vietnam or Myanmar, but no one would know that the UHNWI had an investment in Vietnam or Myanmar. If something were to go wrong with an investment onshore, there is a legal firewall with the offshore vehicle that protects all of their other assets. For example, if they get issued a back tax by the Vietnamese state, the state cannot put a lien on other investments they have in South Korea, Thailand, or Romania. Each investment has its own paper company that keeps all their investments separate from one another. These practices are technically legal, but they are gray and purposefully opaque. Offshore companies are incorporated in a jurisdiction other than where the beneficial owner resides or where the business operations take place, making them hard to locate and trace.

After six months of living in Vietnam and Myanmar, the data led me to Singapore and Hong Kong, where I was flush with the contact information of lawyers, bankers, company secretaries, accountants, and fund managers who were based there but who specialized in onshore investments in Vietnam and Myanmar. The shift to include four countries in my project design felt overwhelming, but once I got to Hong Kong and Singapore, a whole other world opened up to me. The relocation led to many more interviews, in which I learned that the parent companies in Hong Kong and Singapore were part of a much larger group of shell companies incorporated in the British Virgin Islands (BVI), Panama, the Cayman Islands, Samoa, and Seychelles. This first view of spiderweb capitalism was incredibly daunting. I had to find a way to follow the story as it was unfolding before me, and as I would come to learn, few people could trace these massive webs.

The financial professionals who set up these vehicles were so specialized in their respective domains that they knew very little about how the entity they had set up or controlled was connected to the parent companies abroad. In fact, as one lawyer explained to me, "Not knowing what happens above in BVI or Panama or how bribes are carried out in Vietnam or in Myanmar creates legal firewalls around them so that no one person is implicated in the whole process." By following the narratives, I came to realize that the investments in Vietnam and Myanmar were not isolated within those countries. Ownership and investment vehicles did not move from Country A to Country B. Rather, they were embedded in a global network of subsidiaries where only a tiny number of people had complete access to the full picture of capital ownership structures between country A and Countries C through F in a web-like supersystem. As a result, my entire ethnographic research puzzle grew much larger in scope.

I started to wonder: Who were the different specialists involved with constructing various parts of these financial webs? What roles did financial professionals working on small parts of the larger portfolios play in setting up these structures? How were small markets like Vietnam and Myanmar interconnected in a broader ecosystem of global capitalism? The professor in me wanted to know why we as scholars have failed to capture this story. The answers to these smaller questions are critical to understanding the art of playing in the gray. Because, as it turns out, there are a group of ultra-rich elites who hide behind multiple layers of highly specialized financial professionals that know exactly how the money moves. The chairmen, as Alan and Xuan both call them, employ C-suite executives, asset managers, private wealth managers, bankers, lawyers, accountants, company secretaries, fixers, and nominees. All these specialists together *make* markets by setting up obscure webs of capital networks through offshore funds, enabling them to move money around the world without having to abide by the rules of any one sovereignty.

Spiderweb Capitalism and Playing in the Gray

Spiderweb capitalism is a system which features a complex web of subsidiaries that are interconnected across multiple sovereignties and are virtually impossible to identify. Offshore financial centers have enabled both economic and political elites—who in less developed economies are often one and the same—to secure exclusive and quasi-legal opportunities for the private accumulation of wealth. The web is so complex and involves so many layers and actors that it becomes challenging to trace. Every strand of the web is connected by networks of financial, legal, executive, and public relations professionals all of whom are all hidden from one another as they purposefully obfuscate their relations with other parts of the web. The big spiders are the UHNWIs who control the web. But those spiders use "agents" or "fixers" to cover close connections to transactions that would be considered "dirty" or corrupt. Those agents are smaller spiders who provide the connective silk between massive global webs and smaller ones on new frontiers. The smaller spiders are high-net-worth individuals (HNWIs) who are highly compensated to carry out the groundwork in building out these capital webs on behalf of UHNWIs. I argue that spiderweb capitalism explains the heretofore puzzling and rapid rise of foreign capital in markets with low levels of trust and cooperation, using complex structures of offshore investment vehicles.

But mapping out a picture of the web is simply not enough. I then dig deeper to understand *how* this web gets constructed in the first place. The strategies, I argue, involve a meticulous endeavor of playing in the gray, which involves exploiting the gray area between legal/illegal, developed/ undeveloped, clean/corrupt, democratic states/predatory states. The gray space between these dichotomies is key to deepening our understanding of a paradox in investment: international financial institutions and global governance bodies have bought the economic mantra that development can only occur in economies with strong rule of law, which makes investment safe for international capital—yet this is a case where economic growth is sustained under weak rule of law.

By mapping the structure and uncovering the people and processes that create this web, I illustrate how global capital is increasingly untethered from single nation-states as rich people and their financial advisors use offshore structures to gain access to investments, procure business licenses, and then sanitize gray money for investment on global stock exchanges. The goal of this book is to provide a window into the complex networks created by financial professionals who move money across borders, shift legal geographies through offshore vehicles ("enab[ling] economic elites to select the legal spaces that will govern their own transactions"[6]), forge interpersonal ties with political elites, and make money out of playing in legal, financial, and political gray zones.[7]

––––

Barriers to Unraveling Spiderweb Capitalism

This ethnographic journey to study both the architecture and the people involved in spiderweb capitalism has led me to question why we have not uncovered capital markets as interconnected in this way before. While the frontier markets are certainly new areas for spiders to expand their webs, the strategies have been in use since the late 1800s.[8] Three important barriers have limited our ability to study and theorize these webs: (1) those who are interested in offshore finance only study one piece of the puzzle; (2) our overreliance on economists who primarily use quantitative and network tools limits a deeper analysis of how real people make markets in messy, irrational, and unpredictable ways; and (3) powerful institutions, by virtue of being powerful, are intimidating to study—and costly in time and resources, as these individuals are exceptionally hard to access.[9]

Let me start with the problem among scholars. Just as financial professionals are specialized, so too are academics. Legal scholars focus primarily on the role of lawyers in writing legal code and shifting legal geographies.[10] Economists often imagine that developed markets are rational and operate with a clear set of rules, regulations, and legal systems, "as elites demand some sort of organization of enduring and stable prestige."[11] In contrast, undeveloped markets feature widespread corruption, where tactics of sabotage are "used to secure some special advantage or preference."[12] To the extent that they examine the world of offshoring, economists focus on taxation and profit-shifting methods.[13] Political scientists and sociologists have not been able to develop a way of looking at financial markets outside of a lens of nation-states—or First World/Third World, Global North/South.[14]

The lack of a truly interdisciplinary approach means that we are not only focusing too much on one piece of this larger puzzle, but we are also looking in the wrong places. Virtually no scholar links the roles of lawyers, bankers, wealth managers, accountants, fixers, and company secretaries, who all play smaller roles within the larger web of investments, outside of a First/Third World or a global cities lens. The kinds of cross-country comparisons advanced by political scientists further eclipse our ability to look at how these states are in fact interconnected through offshore webs.

Sociologist Saskia Sassen shifted the lens away from nation-states to a focus on global cities as a result of the growth of global markets for finance and the reduced role of governments in regulating international economic activity.[15] New York, London, Tokyo, Frankfurt, and Paris emerged as key geographic sites known for their concentrated command points in organizing the world economy.[16] Cities, Sassen argues, serve as important nodes and command posts for the coordination of highly specialized financial markets that are crucial for fueling the expansion of global markets.[17] Unlike nation-states that compete with each other, these cities constitute a system that ultimately contributes to the growth of developed nations. What is most powerful about Sassen's framework is the attention to other spatial units and scales in a context of privatization and deregulation.[18]

We tend to study finance and capital either within a single state, or as they flow across states, because historically this was what mattered. To the extent that countries extracted wealth from other countries, this was largely carried out through political dominance and colonialism. But since the 1990s, globalization allowed the proliferation of companies to operate on a global scale to maximize profits, and the creation of offshore accounting allowed global elites in a variety of businesses to employ financial professionals to help set up legal structures across the globe. Consequently, the state-based model for understanding economic flows now appears partial at best. The approach I take in this book makes legible the complex web of financial elites who hide behind thick webs in a labyrinth of what Robert Reich calls "paper entrepreneurialism."[19] This arrangement gives financial agents in New York or London the ability to carve out legal and financial spaces offshore that are unaccounted for by both state regulatory bodies and academic research.[20]

The second barrier to uncovering webs of capital has to do with our over-reliance on economists for the answers. Even economists themselves know and rightly state that there are "systematic inconsistencies in international financial statistics because there are more liabilities than financial assets reported" in global cities where the world's financial centers dominate.[21] In his book *The Hidden Wealth of Nations* economist Gabriel Zucman argues that 8 percent of the world's financial wealth is held offshore, which costs states $200 billion in lost tax.[22] Nicholas Shaxson argues that over half of all bank assets, one-third of foreign direct investments, and 85 percent of international banking is routed offshore.[23] Ronen Palan and others similarly invoke the invisibility of offshore funds by articulating how offshore jurisdictions allow U/HNWI's and multinational corporations (MNCs) to be "elsewhere" and "ideally nowhere" through legal spaces that are created to bypass regulations.[24] Economic sociologist Cristobal Young draws inspiration from astrophysics and refers to the large amounts of money that wealthy elites place offshore as "black holes" that "[create] anomalies in international financial accounting statistics."[25] "Just as black holes distort light and gravity in ways astronomers can detect, tax havens distort international accounting statistics in ways that leave a visible trace of their existence and size."[26] But, it is not enough to know that there is money missing somewhere out there in a black hole. We must find ways to understand the context and structural conditions that enable these massive gaps in accounting by looking at how real people finesse these markets.

Lastly, conventional wisdom on how the economy works has failed to account for this transformation, because few scholars have the time, training, and resources to explore global finance at its current scale. As I elaborate in the methodological appendix, this kind of research is costly and requires a massive investment of time and energy to travel around the world, trying to recruit willing research participants who will speak candidly about their practices.

This book draws on tools from sociology, anthropology, geography, law, and economics to make sense of spiderweb capitalism and the art of playing in the gray. In this kaleidoscope, the primary focus of the book might differ depending on the disciplinary lens of an engaged reader.

I argue, however, that binaries between First/Third World, developed/ undeveloped, or clean/corrupt prevent us from seeing how corrupt or gray transactions in frontier markets are deeply interconnected with mature markets in democratic societies.[27] The glue that connects all of these is the special purpose vehicles and holding companies used by global elites that supersede any one sovereign nation. Offshore financial centers cater to sovereignties and wealthy individuals alike, as they simultaneously undermine some states while relying on other states to help protect the very capital that HNWIs accumulate.

For a sociologist or an anthropologist, the goal of this book is to *give global capital a face* by showing how real people construct this spiderweb. This is distinct from most accounts of global capital flows by economists, sociologists, and anthropologists. Economists often treat capital as something that is highly abstract and only moves around through a set of computers and algorithms, paying little attention to how the people who make markets are connected to one another.[28] Economic sociologists in theory should have a better account of global capitalism; they focus overwhelmingly on how people *behave* in markets—usually in one isolated corporation or firm—rather than on how they *make* markets. Similarly, an important body of work by cultural sociologists focuses on how the wealthy make sense of their wealth, their anxieties of affluence, only after they have made that money.[29] Lastly, anthropologists primarily focus on the *consequences* of global capitalism—specifically, what happens after foreign investments enters a nation and how that affects the local people, country, etc.[30]

Rather than focus on *effects* or *consequences,* this book draws inspiration from C. Wright Mills, a prominent twentieth-century sociologist who focused instead on how global elites make their money and the ways that they make meaning out of the moral dilemmas they face by having to play in the gray.[31]

At the level of practice, a law and economics lens scrutinizes the friction between dichotomies of legal/illegal, private/public, corrupt/clean to argue that these in fact co-constitute each other. There is no neat dichotomy between legal and illegal, licit and illicit. The illegal and the illicit facilitate legal and licit market making. As Hannah Appel contends, offshore structures serve as containers for both capital origination in frontier markets and the process of making the illegal life of capital legal in an entangled series of circuits that are impossible to capture quantitatively.[32]

I argue that people *make markets* though tactics of both *sabotage* and *coordination* in small intimate networks where the legal/illegal, the moral/immoral, and the licit/illicit are in fact deeply interconnected, as the illegal facilitates the legal market making.[33] By analyzing how corruption actually facilitates economic transactions in frontier markets and how that capital gets cleaned up in offshore structures and as it graduates to the public on global stock exchanges, I show how these two opposing economies, when woven together through a complicated chain of shell companies, ultimately end up as one unified system of capitalism.

To begin, we'll start by examining frontier markets, which illustrate how most capital accumulation takes off through a set of transactions that are often considered corrupt and dirty. Here, from the ground level up, entrepreneurs pushing to grow large and fast enough to attract foreign investors work to maximize their accumulation of profits through tax evasion in a complex web of bribes paid out to state officials. As small firms mature, they graduate to global stock exchanges by undergoing a process of professionalization. Concurrently, capital that was once paid out in the form of bribes is usually sanitized through legal structures in a network of shell companies in offshore financial centers. Rather than sitting idle, that money is often invested in mature markets around the world through a set of designated nominees.

Global Ethnography

This book marries ethnographic approaches with network approaches to both map out the networked institutions and describe the very content that flows through that network. By using ethnography as a tool to zoom both in and out, it becomes possible to connect the complementary interests of market actors across multiple states that appear to be at odds with one another. By carrying out a global ethnography, *Spiderweb Capitalism* brings together perspectives on offshore financial centers, shadow banking, law and legal contracts, and foreign investments in frontier and emerging markets into one place by mapping out the ways that these systems work in concert with one another.[34] Moving across scales, *Spiderweb Capitalism* reveals how these markets depend on particular relationships to the state (in the space between the licit and the illicit), and how other individuals on the ground negotiate moral dilemmas around drugs, sex/infidelity, and bribery to get inside access to the most lucrative deals.

Data collected for the book project maps a global network of financial elites throughout the world. For eighteen months during 2016–2017 I traveled over 350,000 miles, following the ownership of global capital from offshore accounts in places like the British Virgin Islands, Cayman Islands, Samoa, and Panama to special purpose vehicles or holding companies in Singapore and Hong Kong, before being invested onshore in Vietnam and Myanmar. In addition to making Yangon, Ho Chi Minh City (HCMC), Singapore, and Hong Kong my home bases, I also took several trips across the globe to follow representatives of local firms as they traveled with sell sheets to raise private investment capital, as well as "money movers" who were sourcing investment deals and deploying capital. In this way, this project provides a model for investigating field sites that are not always "grounded." What I had was almost literally a view from "up in the air," whether that was on an airplane or on the top floor of a hotel or an office building. On the ground, I was often part of an entourage that visited investment sites through curated tours in a caravan of tinted windows with security escorts. Like the foreign investors, we did not get to see or learn anything deep about what was happening to the communities around us outside the cars.

In total, I interviewed over 300 individuals, including UHNWIs and the people who manage their money, such as private wealth managers, fund managers, chairpersons, local entrepreneurs, C-suite executives, lawyers, bankers, and company secretaries. As I traveled between global cities and localized investment zones with UHNWIs and their financial professionals, I came to understand that for the super-rich investors in my study, the world is not divided into countries—rather, just rich parts and poor parts where they make their investments.[35] Yet those who study elites who are global in scope do not often empirically parse out the social strata among the wealthy.[36] It is important to differentiate between the UHNWIs and the descending hierarchy of highly compensated financial professionals (HNWIs) who manage their money—the world's top 0.1 percent and the further stratified 1–10 percent, respectively.[37]

This book makes a clear distinction between the dominant spiders (UHNWIs), who make up the 0.1 percent, and their subordinate associates, who for the purposes of this book are among the top 1–10 percent.

Subordinate spiders in the 1–4 percent are HNWIs who serve as asset managers, fund managers, lawyers, and bankers. There are also a group of subordinate spiders who are part of a professional and managerial class, who make up the 5–10 percent. This group includes accountants, company secretaries, and others who also play an important role in building out these capital webs. The key distinction between dominant and subordinate spiders has to do with ownership of capital as well as the individual's relational position and role in the network. Dominant spiders have greater network centrality and, if they wanted to, could see more parts of the capital web. However, they employ subordinate spiders who have lesser network centrality but who offer specialized services to dominant spiders to bear and mitigate the risk. Subordinate spiders see parts of the network, but never have a full view of the web.

In today's world of widening economic inequality, the winner takes all. In 2021, *Forbes* magazine defined ultra-high-net-worth individuals (UHNWI) as people with liquid assets ("money held in bank or brokerage accounts") of at least $30 million; and high-net-worth individuals (HNWI) are defined as people with liquid assets of between $1 million and $30 million.[38]

The obsession with widening inequality has captured the public imagination. The *New York Times, Wall Street Journal,* and *CNN* provide interactive features for people to insert their income to discover their rank and percentile. In October of 2018, the Economic Policy Institute published a study showing that the top 0.01 percent earned $2,756,865 a year, making the average among the top 1 percent roughly $719,000 a year, while those in the top 5 percent averaged $300,000 (see Table 1). Those in the lower half of the top 10 percent made roughly $118,000 a year as part of a professional and managerial class. These differences are significant among the group of elites for a few reasons.

The 0.1 percent come "not just [from] the obvious centers of New York, San Francisco, and London, but also [from] emerging metropolises like Mumbai, Moscow, and Shanghai."[39] While *Forbes* magazine notoriously creates lists of the world's billionaires, in the twenty-first century the majority no longer come from the Western hemisphere (see Map 1).

What Map 1 begins to hint at is the emergence of wealth in Russia, East and Southeast Asia, and the Middle East.[40] At the same time, the numbers that *Forbes* lists here are likely the most conservative. While Forbes works diligently to cover the richest individuals in the world, they often miss a large number of wealthy elites, particularly those from politically contentious countries who do not want their wealth displayed to the public. People living in in post-communist countries with less-stable governments,

TABLE 1. Income of the top 10% (Lawrence Mishel and Mulat Kassa, "Top 1.0% of Earners See Wages Up 157.8% since 1979," *Working Economics Blog*, Economic Policy Institute, December 18, 2019.)

Wage group	Average annual wages (2017 dollars)					Percent change Long-term		Percent change Great Recession			
	1979	2007	2009	2016	2017	1979–2007	1979–2017	2007–09	2009–17	2016–17	2007–17
Bottom 90%	$29,608	$34,542	$34,332	$35,838	$36,182	16.7%	22.2%	−0.6%	5.4%	1.0%	4.7%
Top 90th to 99th	$96,843	$140,739	$140,373	$151,575	$152,476	45.3%	57.4%	−0.3%	8.6%	0.6%	8.3%
90%–95%	$82,122	$110,096	$111,127	$117,817	$118,400	34.1%	44.2%	0.9%	6.5%	0.5%	7.5%
95%–99%	$115,245	$179,043	$176,932	$193,773	$195,070	55.4%	69.3%	−1.2%	10.3%	0.7%	9.0%
Upper 5%	$148,063	$286,352	$262,307	$293,608	$299,810	93.4%	102.5%	−8.4%	14.3%	2.1%	4.7%
Upper 1%	$279,336	$715,586	$603,810	$692,948	$718,766	156.2%	157.3%	−15.6%	19.0%	3.7%	0.4%
99.0%–99.9%	$241,260	$475,466	$434,834	$486,396	$492,311	97.1%	104.1%	−8.5%	13.2%	1.2%	3.5%
99.9%–100%	$622,018	$2,876,667	$2,124,597	$2,551,917	$2,756,865	362.5%	343.2%	−26.1%	29.8%	8.0%	−4.2%
Average	$38,161	$50,910	$49,571	$52,825	$53,474	33.4%	40.1%	−2.6%	7.9%	1.2%	5.0%

MAP 1. *Forbes* Magazine Map of the World's Richest (*Source:* Mapbox and *Forbes* magazine)

like Russia, China, or Vietnam, often worry that their governments could turn on them at any moment to expropriate their assets. What is clear is that owners of capital are no longer concentrated in First World nations. Moreover, politically exposed people (PEPs)—individuals in high-profile political roles, their immediate families, and their close associates—often operate behind highly compensated private wealth managers and asset managers who invest money on their behalf.

The investment deals I studied range between USD$200,000 and $450 million and represent such sectors as real estate, manufacturing, mining, technology, the service sector, and trade. A main reason investments cross such diverse sectors of the economy is that for most investors, access has less to do with expertise than with relational networks. Political relations matter for all sorts of deal brokering, and once a deal is complete, firms will hire the appropriate strategic executives to execute the day-to-day operations of running the actual business (such as managing staff and running local operations).

Importantly, this book draws on composite cases, as I purposefully do not trace a single deal from beginning to end as a way to protect my research subjects and guarantee their anonymity. After conducting interviews in Vietnam and Myanmar, I asked those key informants to introduce me to the financial professionals who helped them set up their structures in Hong Kong and Singapore. Once I got to Hong Kong and Singapore through a series of referrals, I asked those individuals about their experience working on projects in Vietnam and Myanmar that were not connected to the case I studied on the ground. In each interview, I told every interviewee that I was not interested in them as part of a case study; I was interested in identifying and fleshing out the broader patterns and practices that had been shared by several other interviewees.

This method fundamentally shifts the paradigm through which to analyze the global economy's architecture and geography by linking a set of economic relationships onshore to legal structures and foreign investors offshore. This is akin to having six different puzzles. They all have unique patterns, but the pieces themselves are the same, so by taking a few pieces from each puzzle we can reconstruct the whole picture while simultaneously blurring out individual players.

In his seminal work on the power elite, C. Wright Mills described a group of elites who were members of a socially closed subgroup that had a self-aware, corporatist social identity and a shared sense of connection with each other.[41] They knew of each other, and they protected each other. There was *Klasse für sich*—a self-aware inner circle of the upper classes that looked out for and protected itself. They closed others off from themselves and each other. And, as Mills explained, you could "find" them when you wanted to. They were reliably found at Country Club A, or they were listed as donors on the concert programs of the local symphony.

Spiderweb Capitalism is a story of a new sort of social grouping that is composed of financial actors who keep their actions secret not only from the public, but also from each other. They have highly compensated "agents" or "fixers" to cover their tracks for them. They do not seem to have a sense of social cohesion. They might have orgies and other secretive get-togethers in an effort to try to establish mutual trust, or at least mutual hostage, but they don't know whether someone out there is going to pull out a camera. To put it another way, there doesn't seem to be a "code" that serves as a basis of social solidarity.[42]

My Dealings in the Gray

Uncovering black holes starts with examining the relationships, networks, and market-making on the ground. After three months of working as Xuan's personal assistant, I found myself in a situation that was legally and morally ambiguous, or as I would later theorize it: *playing in the gray*. Having access to private meetings and exchanges among the CEOs, government officials, advisors, and foreign investors thrust me into the very world that I wanted to study. It also meant, however, that I was privy to dealings that were common practice in Vietnam. As a US citizen, this could potentially make me an accessory to criminal activity under the Foreign Corrupt Practices Act (FCPA). After consulting with lawyers at the University of Chicago, I learned that I should neither witness nor be part of any deal-making activity that might be illegal under the FCPA.

It was not always clear—and not just to me—what was legal or illegal. Indeed, many activities fell in the gray area of the law. Sometimes bribes in Vietnam were more implicit than explicit. For example, a firm might hire a consultant to help deal with government relations. The said employee might have close government ties, such as a family member or a friend, who would be crucial for gaining access to information and effectively navigating the complex regulatory terrain. Was that consultant's salary a bribe? In Vietnam the answer would be "no," because the person would bring much-needed access to vital information to the office. In the US context, however, the answer would be "yes," as demonstrated by the case in which US authorities brought criminal charges against JPMorgan Chase in Hong Kong for what the bank internally dubbed the "Sons and Daughters Program." In the end,

JPMorgan Chase agreed to pay USD$264 million "to settle charges that bank employees in Hong Kong ran a scheme to bribe Chinese officials [by hiring] friends and relatives of Chinese government leaders in exchange for investment banking business."[43]

Ethical dilemmas like those in the field and the debates that were ensuing in the academy about studying illicit activity ultimately led me to leave Xuan's firm. This came with some serious methodological limitations. I could never witness interactions firsthand, for example, and if an investee company had two or three sets of books—common practice in both Vietnam and Myanmar—I could not look at them.[44]

Upon seeking legal advice from several lawyers, both at the University of Chicago and in Southeast Asia, I was told that I would not be mandated to report what people said to me in confidence during my interviews with them outside of the deals. Still, I ultimately decided not to write about Xuan Liu or anyone in that firm, because it would be too challenging to protect their anonymity and adhere to the NDA that I signed. The time I spent there, however, give me the lay of the land and I used that information to identify the key individuals whom I recruited for interviews. Because I did not want to give up on this project altogether, I decided to carry out interviews and limit my ethnography to traveling with research subjects as they were raising money all over the world and as they were sourcing deals to deploy that capital in Vietnam and Myanmar. During the travels, I did not sit in on any meetings. Instead, I spent long plane rides, breakfasts, and after-hour drinks following up with my research participants as they recounted the events that had transpired that day. As an aside, I am not sure that staying in the firm would have made methodological sense, because I could not get close to the deal-brokering process from the back office, where activities were slow, mundane, and technical and could not teach me much about the people or relational work I was interested in studying.

While I left that firm, I faced several challenges with identifying the new set of key players in the market. Both Vietnam and Myanmar had undergone massive transformations, which meant that there were a new set of people with ties to the new regimes with access to sweetheart deals. For example, in Vietnam, there was a new prime minister, and with him came a new group of underlings who dominated several sectors of the economy. As new players in the market rose to the top of highly regulated economic sectors, old ones were going to jail on charges of corruption, and everyone in between was trying to figure out how to protect themselves and develop relations with the new political power players. As one interviewee put it, "They were all trying to figure out how to kiss up to the new person in power." At the same time, Myanmar had just elected Aung San Suu Kyi, the leader of the National League for Democracy and the first incumbent State Counselor (equivalent to prime minister), and the country was buzzing with excitement from foreign investors looking to establish themselves on this new frontier, where they hoped that the old crony way of doing business would give way to a democratic and transparent business climate.

With the generous help of three University of Chicago undergraduate research assistants, we combed through newspapers, magazines, and LinkedIn for contact information of potential research subjects. I also employed "snowball sampling"—in which I asked research participants to assist in identifying other potential interviewees and to make important introductions—from the contacts that I had made working inside the asset management firm for a short time. I spent three months interviewing everyone I could in Vietnam, including fund managers, private wealth managers in family offices, decision makers from inside corporate firms, lawyers, accountants, bankers, and anyone else working on different aspects of the deal-making process. In the interviews, without looking for it, offshoring kept coming up over and over again. In the first 100 interviews, nearly 80 percent of interviewees used the same language as Tuyen, referring to special purpose vehicles and holding companies to describe the structuring of their investments offshore in Hong Kong and Singapore through a complex subsidiary chain. That preliminary research laid the groundwork for me to identify the appropriate research questions and eventually create the framework for the research puzzle that this book works through.

The Rise of East and Southeast Asia

The turn to Southeast Asia quickly reveals that old paradigms, like "First World/Third World" and "Global North/Global South," are no longer useful for framing the global economy. Over the last twenty years, we have witnessed dramatic changes in global financial flows that raise important questions about the simultaneous rise of East and Southeast Asia and the waning economic dominance of the United States and Western Europe.[45] For instance, during the 1980s and 1990s, New York, London, and Tokyo solidified their positions as leading financial centers and dominated much of the global economy by managing disproportionate shares of the financial industry and vast numbers of financial transactions.[46]

The global financial meltdown of 2008, however, dealt a reversal of fortune to these cities, and Singapore, Shanghai, Hong Kong, and Seoul began to emerge as new centers of global finance.[47] As Aihwa Ong, Rem Koolhaas, and others note, Asian economies have since skyrocketed, with dramatic capital increases.[48] Long-term postwar growth, combined with the ascent of a global capitalist class, has changed the dynamics of intra-regional investment since 2000: whereas foreign direct investment (FDI) in Southeast Asia used to come largely from the United States and Western Europe, it now increasingly originates within East Asia.[49]

In 2012, the World Bank reported that East Asia accounted for 32 percent of global market capitalization, ahead of the United States at 30 percent and Europe at 25 percent.[50] By 2011 there were more millionaires in Asia than in the United States or Europe.[51] Concomitant with the economic rise of countries in East and Southeast Asia following the 2008 global financial crisis, formerly dominant Western countries experienced economic declines that persist today; in October 2014, for example, European banking authorities announced that twenty-four European banks had failed financial stress tests.[52]

Compared to the United States and Europe, China and Southeast Asia, in particular, have been experiencing record growth rates, thus overtaking the hegemony of the West in these emerging and frontier markets. Emerging markets are poised to become the most important markets of the twenty-first century.[53] Found in developing countries with rapid industrialization and increasing integration into the global economy, emerging markets are experiencing growth rates more than double those of advanced economies.[54] As a result, the concentration of global capital in the hands of a select few means that the world is now divided between HNWIs and poor people across developed, emerging, and frontier markets around the world. Or, as Esteva, Prakash, and Mohanty prudently dub it, *One-Third World* versus *Two-Thirds World*, where the rich and poor coexist in many countries, transcending national borders.[55]

Overview of the Book

Spiderweb Capitalism develops over three parts. The first part of the book starts by drawing out a new picture of global capital flows by tracing the "social spiders'" web. The second part zooms in on the people and institutions to reveal how financial elites (owners of capital) syndicate risk by employing a group of financial professionals to do the work of *playing in the gray* on their behalf. The primary argument here is that economic growth in less-developed economies is a consequence of tightly embedded relations between economic elites (local and foreign investors) and political elites that result in varieties of corruption and an assortment of tax structures that enable global elites to finesse these markets with impunity. Finally, the third part zooms in close on individuals working on the ground in these new frontiers who must carry out the work involved in all these transactions, and the moral dilemmas they confront as they navigate playing in the gray. These chapters are intensely relational and geared towards understanding how real people confront a set of moral dilemmas, justify their actions as they work their way through those dilemmas, and experience the life-altering consequences as they reap huge profits or experience massive losses as a result of playing in the gray.

In "Social Spiders' Tangled Webs" (chapter 1) I develop the concept of spiderweb capitalism as a metaphor for the complex network of offshore shell companies that adept players in the gray finesse. Using the analogy of social spiders, I provide a picture of how the web gets constructed, differentiating between dominant spiders (UHNWIs) and subordinate spiders (HNWIs). I use the cases of Vietnam and Myanmar to describe the variegated ways capital moves from offshore funds before arriving onshore in emerging and frontier markets for investment. What makes this different from social networks or professional ecologies is the distinctively global structure of this web, which supersedes sovereign nations.

Zooming in on people and institutions, "Spinning New Investment Deals" (chapter 2) gives global capital a face by focusing on people who work in coordination with each other to put deals together. There is a group of people who own capital and are looking to make money with it, and another group of people who put the capital to work by sourcing deals on behalf of capital owners. Those sourcing deals find local enterprises that are looking for exit opportunities to cash out their entrepreneurial endeavors. This chapter connects the dots to show how they come together. I illustrate how economic elites leverage relationships and social networks to raise capital for markets with scant data and very few facts.

"Varieties of Corruption and Bribery" (chapter 3) answers the question: "How do global elites exploit frontier markets?" by providing a continuum of *how they play in the gray* through multiple strategies of obfuscation which result in varieties of corruption. I lay out an argument about how licit and illicit activity co-constitute each other, particularly in the embedded ties that bind key political officials and economic elites (local and foreign investors) who are there to try to get inside access to the market. By unpacking the intersection of illegal and legal activities, I illustrate the ways investors obfuscate bribes to political elites to make the argument that illicit activity shapes licit investments. "Tax Strategies of Global Elites" (chapter 4) is an illustrative account of how global elites play in the gray through varied structures of taxation. The point here is to also show a continuum that coexists in the same market: early-stage investors tend to engage in *tax evasion* practices before graduating to *tax avoidance* through legal transfer pricing practices that enable them to shift profits offshore, where there is a much lower tax burden.

"Impunity in Stealth Webs" (chapter 5) differentiates between the 0.1 percent (UHNWIs, owners of capital) and the 1–10 percent (HNWIs, custodians of capital) to illustrate how UHNWIs operate with near impunity by syndicating risk to highly compensated financial professionals who construct legal barriers for the owners and shoulder all of the criminal risks associated with playing in legal gray zones.

Digging deeper into the people and the personal, "Moral Dilemmas and Regimes of Justification" (chapter 6) examines the moral dilemmas that individual investors confront as they navigate their unique place in the spiderweb. In an effort to humanize capital flows, this chapter engages the sociological literature on moral markets to examine how individuals construct morality or a sense of business ethics in a quasi-legal world where illicit and licit activity co-constitute each other. I illustrate how a group of individuals develop their moral regimes of justification to articulate the different ways that they must adjust their own moral compass in finessing these markets. "The Exit: Feast and Famine" (chapter 7) reveals what happens to an individual after a successful exit from the market and then closely examines three specific cases in which individuals lost a great deal of money—resulting from, respectively, a government ousting; theft by a foreign partner; and a hostile takeover by local partners.

Spiderweb Capitalism's conclusion outlines its policy implications and weighs in on debates related to global inequality, taxation, and the embeddedness of the political and economic spheres. It engages with the question of how to unravel chaotic and tangled webs, and invites public debate about how to create a system in which political and economic elites are not regulating their own quasi-illicit behaviors.

It is my hope that this book, inspired by C. Wright Mills, will unravel the complex web that enables elite spiders to operate with near impunity, thereby exacerbating global inequality. By focusing on how people make markets through tactics of sabotage and coordination in small intimate networks, *Spiderweb Capitalism* illuminates market-making in the early twenty-first century global economy.

1

Social Spiders' Tangled Webs

If you look closely at a US one-dollar bill, you will find what appears to be a little spider in the top right corner of the front-facing note.

Around the "spider" is a tight web spun around every edge of the front and the back of the bill. The spider and its web symbolize the state of global capitalism today. Spiders hide behind complex webs woven into every corner of the world's capital markets.

The vast and multilayered webs make spiders hard to locate and their webs challenging to untangle. Like hidden spiders, the world's ultra-wealthy are hard to access as they spin capital webs around the whole world in ways that are incredibly challenging to trace. This chapter develops the concept of spiderweb capitalism to address who the spiders are and reveal how they work in coordination with a network of financial professionals to spin multilayered webs across multiple sovereignties.

In my framework of spiderweb capitalism, there is not just one spider, but rather a community of spiders who work in concert to build out different parts of the web. Here, I draw inspiration from *Anelosimus eximius*, a species of social spiders known to live together in cooperation to construct the biggest webs in the world.[1] In these webs there are dominant and subordinate spiders, but everyone in the web serves a specific function. Some spiders build and repair the web, some subdue and organize prey, still others work to keep the place clean.[2] Communal spiders collaborate to construct, maintain, and provision their web community, cooperating in the capture of prey and feasting together.[3]

Drawing on this analogy, I build on journalist Nicholas Shaxson's work to conceptualize spiderweb capitalism, not as bounded by nation or concentrated in global cities, but rather as part of a globally interconnected web that thwarts efforts to complete our picture of international financial accounting and statistics.[4] Spiderweb capitalism, for the purposes of this book, draws inspiration from sociologist C. Wright Mills by underscoring the interlocking relations between the political and economic spheres. What Mills teaches us is that financial agents make their money by laying the legal groundwork to exploit their relationships and access to state officials to make their money. The offshore system is the secret that locks financial elites and state actors in a relationship of mutual profit. As a result, spiderweb capitalism is not going anywhere, because dismantling this system would be tantamount to asking the regulators to regulate themselves.

But simply establishing the existence of a web is not enough. It is important to unpack how the web came into being. Here I outline all of the different people that wealthy individuals must enlist to help them build out a global network; and the relationships that enable and sustain these webs. Financial webs are spun by diverse sets of social spiders who cooperate to maintain these webs and share in the financial rewards.

The dominant spiders, the UHNWIs, stay behind the scenes. The subordinate spiders in these webs, the HNWIs, are financial professionals who are highly compensated yet reap a relatively small share of the capital gains. Subordinate spiders offer specialized services which require them to have some knowledge of what others work on, but they never have a full view of the massive web. A global web of institutions, including banks, law firms, accounting firms, and corporate service providers, make up the silk thread that connects the smaller and bigger spiders to one another. The lawyers, bankers, accountants, fixers, and others working across multiple institutions spin out complex and massive webs that span all corners of the globe. Conceptually, the "prey" in spiderweb capitalism encompasses the public and all those who are snared in these capital webs. That group, however, is not the central empirical focus of this book.

The story begins by mapping out the structures offshore and the silk that connects them to investments and financial activity onshore. The view of the whole web reveals how risky frontier markets like Vietnam and Myanmar are connected to allegedly transparent and developed states in one global ecosystem that is spiderweb capitalism.

Meet Fritz: A Subordinate Spider in EverColor's Web

Fritz is a 40-year-old United States citizen who has been working for Ever-Color[5]—a wealth management firm in Hong Kong—for the past ten years. Fritz spends most of his time on planes as he commutes between Seattle, where his wife is based; Hong Kong, where EverColor's office is located; and Vietnam and Myanmar, where he oversees the firm's investments. He holds a bachelor's degree from Princeton and a law degree from a smaller private university in California. Fritz started his career working for the Private Wealth Management group of Merrill Lynch before acquiring a law degree, which allowed him to work as a mergers and acquisitions attorney for an international law firm on Wall Street.

In 2010 he moved to Hong Kong, where he served as an investment director; there, he managed a portfolio of over USD$100 million for an energy company. After that he moved to one of Hong Kong's most successful hedge funds before becoming the Chief Operating Officer, General Counsel, and Head of Investments for EverColor Capital, a new fund where he now has over $250 million in assets under management (AUM). In addition, he serves on the boards of four other investment companies based in Vietnam and Myanmar.

Fritz earns a base salary of USD$300,000 per year, along with additional bonuses which vary from year to year and are often in the millions. Fritz is part of the world's global elite.

But, by his own account, Fritz is *only* part of the top 4 percent.

Fritz is not the dominant spider in this web; he occupies an inferior position in relation to his boss, Ross.

Ross, the top spider, is an UHNWI, the founder of EverColor Capital, and the man who brought $200 million to the fund that Fritz manages. Ross brought on another $50 million from a total of six subordinate spiders—HNWIs like Fritz—bringing the total fund to $250 million. Notably, all $250 million was made through hedge funds that placed large bets against the market in the wake of the 2008 global financial crisis.

I only met Ross once, for a conversation that lasted less than thirty minutes. Not because he was particularly busy, but because, like real spiders—who use up to seven different types of silk to ensnare their prey and protect themselves from predators—Ross concealed himself behind a whole group of subordinate spiders who created barriers for those wanting direct access to him. He was never the face of any deal. Hidden behind a multilayered social web, he had foot soldiers putting his money to work for him while also safeguarding him from prying eyes. As the dominant spider of EverColor Capital, Ross paid skillful financial engineers to help design a web of capital that stretched around the globe.

During my interview with Fritz, I asked him to map out the network of EverColor's investments around the world. Nobody had a full picture of the web except for Ross. Other spiders in this web can only see the part of the web they constructed. This is what the web looked like from Fritz's view as he drew it out on a napkin in a bar where I was interviewing him (see figure 1.1).

This is how Fritz broke it down to me. The main fund is domiciled in the Cayman Islands. Half of the fund is invested in mature, predictable markets such as index funds through a New York–based firm, while USD$100 million is allocated to what he dubs risky markets in Russia, Africa, and Ukraine, and in Southeast Asia via a subsidiary fund headquartered in Hong Kong. The fund in Hong Kong has made two private equity placements—in this case, investments in real estate and retail firms—onshore in Vietnam and Myanmar, where they provide working capital to local companies to nurture expansion, with the goal of reselling them at a higher value in the future. Investors (a.k.a. limited partners) in the fund, however, do not have to travel to Vietnam or Myanmar. They rely on Fritz to manage onshore investments on their behalf.

There is a Private Placement Memorandum (PPM) Fritz refers to as "the bible" which was drafted by lawyers from a large global law firm. The "bible" governs what the Cayman Island fund will invest in and outlines the investment managers' role. The investment managers have offshore funds in the Cayman Islands with a mandate to make investments in Russia, Africa, Ukraine, and Southeast Asia. Two management agreements connect the Cayman fund and the portfolio in Hong Kong focused specifically on Southeast Asia. Fritz manages the Hong Kong fund, which has to adhere to the PPM set up in the Cayman Islands.

Importantly, the CITI-Fund Administrator is the person who takes direction from the General and Limited Partners to transfer money between banks in the Cayman Islands, New York, and Hong Kong. Company secretaries in the Cayman Islands help to set up the Cayman fund, while those in Hong Kong set up the Southeast Asia fund as well as the subsidiaries in both Vietnam and Myanmar. This way everything is set up across multiple jurisdictions offshore.

For Southeast Asia, EverColor's strategy is to go into these markets at an early stage with the hope that they will take $1 million and grow it into $5 to $10 million as a result of having inside access to deals that are not widely available to the public. However, with investments in frontier markets, the

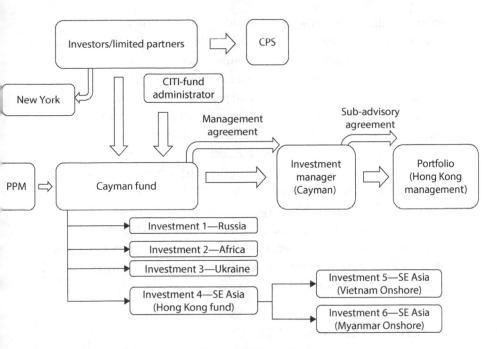

FIGURE 1.1. EverColor's Cayman, Hong Kong, and Vietnam Fund
(*Source:* Kimberly Kay Hoang)

firm's principals have a high tolerance for risk and are prepared to lose it all. Their investment strategy is akin to roulette: EverColor spreads chips across the table and only needs two or three to do well to more than make up for the losses of the rest.

The Global Elite: Super Spiders and Their Associates

On a global scale, Fritz and Ross are two people among a growing population of the world's super rich. While most accounts tend to lump the top 10 percent of the world's elite into one broad category, it is important to tease out the differences between UHNWIs and HNWIs.

We know that we now live in a world of stratospheric inequality. By most accounts, Fritz would be part of the economic elite. However, he knows he is not the dominant spider. He is close with, but not one of, the true dominant spiders, the top 0.1 percent or even 0.01 percent who maintain their dominance as the owners of capital in an economy where the return on capital outstrips the rate of growth.[6] These UHNWIs are invisible to most, veiled by the network of people like Fritz whom they rely on to invest and manage this money on their behalf. These capital owners are sometimes referred to as the "chairman/chairwoman" of a firm or fund. In my field site the financial professionals, particularly those in the banks, referred to them as "VIPs" (very important people) or PEPs with vast amounts of money to invest globally. An investment firm is called a general partner (GP), and the investors that commit capital are called limited partners (LPs). EverColor Capital would consist of a set of general partners who form investment relationships with a set of limited partners, generally consisting of pension funds, institutional accounts, and wealthy individuals. The limited partners I interviewed came from the United States, Canada, Europe (UK, France, Denmark, Germany, Switzerland, Ireland), China, Japan, South Korea, Malaysia, Thailand, Singapore, and Hong Kong. Each has a minimum of USD$5 million to invest globally. Limited partners were by far the most difficult to gain access to; they are all global citizens who claim citizenship in one or two countries but regularly travel all around the world.

Subordinate Spiders: HNWIs

If Fritz is not one of the super spiders, who is he? What I found is that Fritz is one in a long list of high-net-worth subordinate spiders who do the work of building out different parts of the web for UHNWIs like Ross. A sign that HNWIs have made it is that they have become part of the "flying class" who manage investments all around the world.

In order to map out *who* these people are and *how* they construct various parts of the web, I draw inspiration from Neil Fligstein and Doug McAdams, who make the case that in any field power is uneven and often taken for granted, which fundamentally shapes who gets what.[7] Following this logic, there are multiple and overlapping webs within a broader field. The financial professionals setting up these webs have a "diffuse understanding of what is going on in the field, i.e., what is at stake" in relation to the other, more powerful spiders in the web. However, subordinate spiders are willing to do this work because they are generously compensated for carrying out their myopic tasks.[8]

While there is a hierarchy between dominant and subordinate spiders, it's important to note that smaller spiders do not simply take orders from UHNWIs. Rather, they aim to build a connection between the super spiders and their own smaller webs constructed onshore in frontier markets, by courting UHNWIs to make minority investments in their firms, thereby forming the connective silk that links smaller webs on the frontier into larger webs around the world. Importantly, this is part of the subordinate spiders' own efforts at capital accumulation. These HNWIs work privately with their own incentive structures and may in fact bring multiple dominant spiders into their own webs as they seek capital injections. In this way, webs are connected from both ends—offshore and onshore—highlighting the agency of smaller spiders located in frontier markets, who play a significant role in building out these webs.

Together, dominant (UHNWIs) and subordinate spiders (HNWIs) occupy the most powerful positions in the broader field in relation to their prey, because they have the power to exploit spaces where rules do not yet exist.[9] Subordinate spiders in the network of professionals are often so specialized in their area of expertise that they only play one small part in a much more complex circuit, and often do not have a view of the larger web they are embedded in. All of these financial professionals play key roles in moving capital around the world through multiple offshore financial centers (OFCs), such as the Caymans, and into investments onshore. In spiderweb capitalism, the dominant spiders of the top 0.1 percent play with invisibility and impunity, while their agents who make up the top 1–4 percent reap significant rewards but also bear *all* of the criminal and civil risks for *playing in the gray*. But the subordinate spiders are diverse and are embedded in a variety of different institutions. This next section outlines the groups of subordinates I was able to identify in my effort to trace out these extensive capital webs.

PRIVATE WEALTH MANAGERS

Private wealth managers' main role is to provide financial services to wealthy clients, mainly families and individuals. Wealth managers are people who have cultivated relationships with U/HNWIs and who work for the "family office"—a privately held company that manages the day-to-day administration of investment management and wealth management for a wealthy family. They help U/HNWIs make decisions on how to invest their capital in a diverse set of vehicles, from stocks to secondary alternate investment markets (AIMs) to portfolio companies, via foreign indirect investment through fund managers or directly into growing companies. They have an extensive network of lawyers and accountants they work with to help wealthy clients set up foundations, trusts, and corporations that serve multiple ends, including tax reduction, avoidance of regulation, control of family assets, succession planning, investment, and charitable giving.[10] In my research, these were the point people for wealthy clients, and the people who surface as the face of many deals. They are key figures that enable the dominant spiders to act as invisible, hard-to-identify figures in the market. The private wealth mangers I interviewed typically made between USD$150,000 and $300,000, plus bonuses, and "carry" (or carried interest, an additional form of performance-based compensation) on successful investments.

FUND MANAGERS

Fund managers work for chairpersons and are responsible for implementing a fund's investment strategy and managing its portfolio of trading activities. The fund managers in my study were paid 1–2 percent of the fund's average assets under management (AUM). Fund managers in Singapore and Hong Kong reported earnings between USD$200,000 and $300,000 per year, while fund managers in less-developed economies like Vietnam and Myanmar reported earnings of $100,000–$150,000 per year. Fund managers who operate onshore in Vietnam and Myanmar often seek long-term capital appreciation through strategic holdings in listed and pre-IPO companies across diverse sectors of the economy. While in developed markets, fund managers may have an exit strategy with a seven-year horizon, in Vietnam and Myanmar they often hold on to their investments for seven to ten years, depending on the project.

ACCOUNTANTS/AUDITORS

Accounting and auditing firms in Vietnam and Myanmar are divided between "local" and "global" firms. Local firms charge much less and tend to service smaller firms, while the globally branded firms like Ernst & Young, PricewaterhouseCoopers (PwC), and KPMG pave the way for family-owned enterprises to undergo a process of professionalization. In general, these firms' main role is to provide accounting, audit, and advisory services. In addition, these firms provide advisory on corporate tax, international tax, company secretary services, merger and acquisition tax, and global transfer pricing services. Among the accountants I interviewed, those in Hong Kong and Singapore specialized more in tax planning and transfer pricing arrangements that kept liabilities onshore in Vietnam and Myanmar and assets offshore in Hong Kong and Singapore. Auditing firms in Vietnam and Myanmar assisted more with tax compliance onshore in

Vietnam and Myanmar and with providing firms with auditing services. Because the volume of deals was not very high in Vietnam and Myanmar, auditing firms there assisted potential investors with other services like market entry and business set-up, corporate regulatory compliance, and dispute resolution.

LAWYERS

Lawyers across all these different countries work in multiple capacities, from fund structuring to deal execution. They help to set up funds and structure investments, and they provide the ultra-wealthy and their investment managers with the most up-to-date information on changing regulations. Their work often overlaps with the work done in auditing firms as they integrate tax and corporate advice, assist with accounting for international tax complications (US requirements, Investment Company Act rules), regulatory and securities laws. Global law firms often have partners they collaborate with across different jurisdictions. For example, a large firm in Vietnam might have partner law firms in Hong Kong, London, Sydney, Chicago, Luxembourg, and Singapore. In Vietnam and Myanmar, global law firms also employ a number of local Vietnamese lawyers who are key figures with access to government officials. These firms also play an important role advising the government and in shaping trade policies. Local law firms do not have the reputation or professional prowess of global firms. However, local law firms provide key insight on how to navigate a fuzzy set of laws as well as engaging in important relational work with highly placed government officials. This work is especially important in a context with weak legal institutions, where laws are often open to multiple interpretations, and where it might be difficult to enforce a judgment of companies overseas.

BANKERS

Bankers help clients open offshore and onshore bank accounts. With new advancements in technology, much of this can be done electronically through wire transfers. Most of the bankers I interviewed saw themselves as quasi-regulators. While anyone could create an LLC, IBC (international business company), or APT (asset protection trust), not everyone could open a bank account. Following the 2008 financial crisis and all of the regulatory crackdowns on banks, bankers are now required to perform due diligence checks on all of their clients. That is, they need to verify a client's personal information (via passport, driver's license, etc.), residence or physical address, and financial statements from other bank accounts to verify the source of funds for all deposits. Depending on the type of client that comes through the door, bankers can have very different kinds of banking relationships with their clients. In general, clients who come through who are not VIPs or PEPs must abide by the strictest regulatory guidelines just to open up simple accounts for their day-to-day transactions. Those with more wealth work more closely with private bankers who advise clients on how to move money and get around capital restrictions.

COMPANY SECRETARIES

Company secretaries help investors incorporate new companies, transfer existing companies, or purchase "vintage companies." Company secretaries are concentrated in OFCs and assist clients in setting up shell companies via incorporation services, guidance on the choice of banks, providing the business with a registered office address, preparation and filing of annual returns, and attending to the issuance and transfer of shares. In some cases, they draft minutes for shareholder and director meetings, assist with the deregistration of companies, and assist clients in attending to other statutory corporate compliance issues. This group of people are among the bottom 8-10 percent who are part of a professional and managerial class. Their offices are often the least glamorous and most nondescript.

NOMINEES

Nominee directors are paper owners of shell companies set up offshore. In simple terms—a wealthy person will ask someone in their inner circle to stand on title for a company they own. The person on title legally owns the company but in practice has no idea what the business does and does not reap any of the profits from the investments. They only receive compensation for lending their name. This helps true owners of investments conceal their identities and creates a barrier of protection from tax authorities, the public, and sometimes even their spouses, whom they may be trying to hide assets from. Three pieces of paper are vital in setting up a nominee structure. The secret real owner of a company will select a nominee director and send them these three documents. The first is a "nominee director declaration," in which the nominee promises to do only what the real owner tells them. The second is "a director's resignation letter" that is left undated and lets the nominee avoid liability in the event of any trouble. The third is a "general power of attorney," by which the nominee secretly hands back all control to the real owner.[11] The nominees cited by investors in my study include a wide range of possible people, from maids and drivers to romantic partners in other countries to distant family members and friends.

FIXERS

Fixers are people primarily in charge of handling bribes on behalf of investors. They get paid a consulting fee to grease the wheels of government officials, get inside information on projects, expedite licensing and permits, etc. In some cases, they will go as far as bribing judges on the side to ensure that they win a judgment in a lawsuit. In Vietnam more than in Myanmar, they are known as the "relationship people," those who have strong and close relationships with key officials to solve problems as they arise.

This group of subordinate spiders each perform very specialized tasks in helping to build out different parts of a spiderweb. It is not enough to identify the people involved in setting up the web. We must outline the context that enables the vast expansion of these capital webs into new frontiers. This story looks at the strategies global elites use to capture new money and opportunities in Southeast Asia.

The Shift Eastward

Switzerland was the grandfather of the world's tax havens. As one of the world's largest OFCs, Switzerland has offered elites the world's biggest secrecy jurisdictions and tax havens since the mid-twentieth century.[12] While most people associate Switzerland with offshore bank accounts which elites use to protect their money, the industry has grown to offer more-complex offshore structures. These include a LLC, IBC, a foreign-based APT, and a private family foundation.

For USD$1,000–$5,000, offshore LLCs allow elites to hold an IRA account outside of the United States, hold personal investments, hold real estate, manage advanced asset protection structures such as foreign trusts, and maximize privacy. For those with an active business overseas, an IBC allows a foreign division of a US company or one owned by a US person living in the US to establish a joint venture with a non-US partner that is operated offshore. The rise in more-complex offshore structures points to the role of "pure international financial *intermediation,* which has increased substantially in recent years."[13]

However, elites from around the world have very different legal relationship with OFCs depending on the laws governing offshore monies in their own countries. For years, a number of foreign countries have attempted to penetrate Swiss banking secrecy, and until the late 2000s these attempts mostly failed. Then, under mounting pressure following the 2008 global financial crisis, the United States began to investigate high-profile Swiss bankers who were helping wealthy Americans evade taxes. The United States began to establish a set of laws and regulations that would prevent capital from going offshore.

The Foreign Account Tax Compliance Act of 2010 (FATCA) is a United States federal law that requires all foreign (non-US) financial institutions (FFIs) to search their records for customers with indicia of "US person" status, such as a US place of birth, and to report the assets and identities of such persons to the US Department of the Treasury. FATCA also requires US citizens to self-report their non-US financial assets to the Internal Revenue Service (IRS). In addition, post-2008 banking regulations now require banks to "know your customer/client" (KYC), whereby a bank must undergo a process of identifying and verifying the identity of its clients. Foreign banks are now required to KYC to limit fraud, money laundering, terrorism financing, etc. Importantly, banks also pass that requirement down to those with whom they do business. These investigations ultimately forced Switzerland to make significant concessions on banking secrecy.

An unintended consequence of these laws that govern US investors abroad is that they overlook the fact that these investors operate in a global world where they compete with elites from other countries who are not constrained by these same laws. The new rules and regulations imposed by the US government, coupled with the rise of new financial elites in other emerging markets, has led to the birth of newly moneyed elites in East and Southeast Asia, Russia, Latin America, and the Middle East with an added advantage in three consequential ways.

First, offshore funds and banks are less likely to do business with anyone who has a US mailing address or passport. This is because banks have had to pay out huge settlements for helping Americans evade taxes. In 2016, the United States cracked down on "Swiss banks suspected of helping American clients evade taxes by hiding income offshore, imposing more than $1.3 billion in penalties on 80 banks in settlements involving more than 34,000 accounts that held as much as $48 billion".[14] The Hong Kong and Shanghai Banking

Corporation (HSBC) faced similar fines of $1.9 billion in 2012 from the US for poor anti-money-laundering controls.[15] In 2015, Credit Suisse made a move to sell its US private bank and revamp its aims to focus on banking the global wealthy living in Asia who do not hold US citizenship.[16] However, that does not mean that US citizens are not opening offshore accounts. Rather, the FATCA regulations have led to a new cottage industry of *independent asset managers* who serve as intermediaries with the offshore custodial bank through named corporations, limited liability companies, or trusts controlled by US citizens. To move money offshore, investors set up shell corporations and trusts with the help of wealth managers who "not only shelter wealth from taxation but serve to 'obscure concentrations of economic power' . . . mak[ing] it difficult (if not impossible) to identify the true owners of wealth."[17]

Second, under this new regulatory regime, anyone with a US passport must declare all of their bank accounts and asset holdings overseas, making it more challenging for people from Western nations to maintain their anonymity. As a result, wealthy individuals from the Middle East and Asia have shifted their money away from the United States and Europe and toward Hong Kong and Singapore as a response to US and EU tax evasion investigations and more-stringent reporting requirements. This has given rise to new centers of wealth management. Following in Switzerland's footsteps, other small jurisdictions like Hong Kong and Singapore enable capital mobility in cross-border finance.[18]

It is important to underscore the fact that these new OFCs are not actually competing with Switzerland. Rather, "a large number of the banks domiciled in Singapore or in the Cayman Islands are nothing but branches of Swiss establishments that have opened there to attract new customers. . . . Accounts circulate from Zurich to Hong Kong by a simple game of signatures [that depend] on attacks against banking secrecy and on treaties signed by Switzerland with foreign countries."[19] A number of Swiss banks have offices in Singapore to provide discreet financial services to wealthy Chinese and Southeast Asian clients. In this way, Switzerland as a nation no longer benefits from capital inflows into Swiss banks, but these Swiss establishments do, which makes the focus on the web of people rather than the states critical as U/HNWIs have found ways to continue making money for themselves by shifting these practices to new states.

Third, a deeper look into OFCs reveals the close connections between political and economic elites in frontier and emerging markets, who use OFCs to do business with the same kinds of privacy provisions once utilized by US citizens abroad. The simultaneous rise of wealthy elites in less-developed economies has provided a new market for OFCs to stay in business. This is particularly important when tracing flows of capital into "emerging markets." During a visit to one of Switzerland's private banks, I noticed that they had brochures in their offices in Mandarin, Japanese, Korean, and even in Vietnamese. Ian, a Swiss banker, explained to me:

> It used to be the case that we worked mainly with clients from the US and Europe because that's where all the money was. But today it's really about banking the global elite. With the new banking regulations, we can afford to not bank Americans because we have more than enough business from China, Saudi Arabia, Russia, and even the smaller Southeast Asian countries like Vietnam. We bank the billionaires of Vietnam and Myanmar.

The rapid economic rise of East and Southeast Asia, coupled with the financial shift away from the West, has pushed offshore banks to develop new ways of attracting a more diverse set of global elites. This is particularly important for PEPs, because one way to pay bribes to government officials is to have a fixer pay them through nominee accounts set up in OFCs. Bankers and company secretaries could afford to turn away clients with US passports because there is enough new business generated from the elite of China, the Middle East, and Southeast Asia.

The rise of U/HNWIs in different regions of the world has led to an expansion of capital webs into new frontiers. Spiderweb capitalism is not simply a web of relations between OFCs in Switzerland, Singapore, and Hong Kong; these structures are important vehicles through which to do business in economically and politically risky markets like Vietnam and Myanmar.

New Frontiers

In recent years, China and the United States have been competing to gain a foothold in Southeast Asia. In 2015, Chinese leaders established the Asian Infrastructure Investment Bank (AIIB). In response, in an effort to moderate China's influence in the region, several Western nations (the United States, Canada, and Australia) then came together to establish the Trans-Pacific Partnership (TPP).

The rivalry between the United States and China is transparent. As the TPP website stated, "*The rules of the road are up for grabs in Asia. . . . If we don't pass this [Trans-pacific Trade Partnership] agreement and write those rules, our competitors will set weak rules of the road . . . undermining U.S. leadership in Asia.*"[20] In 2012 President Obama became the first sitting US president to visit Myanmar to "underscore his desire to reorient American foreign policy more toward the Pacific."[21] Four years later, President Obama lifted US economic sanctions on Myanmar, allowing US companies and banks to explore one of Asia's last untapped markets.[22]

Soon after taking office in January 2017, President Trump ended the TPP due to its status as an Obama legacy, leaving the other countries to renegotiate a trade agreement without the United States. But Trump is so unpredictable that the following year, in April 2018, after considerable lobbying from business executives, he proposed rejoining the TPP.[23]

In spite of President Trump's position, the first Southeast Asian leader to visit the White House under the Trump administration came from Vietnam, even though the United States had had longer strategic relations with both the Philippines and Thailand. This is because Vietnam had hired the Podesta Group—including John Podesta, the former campaign director of Hillary Clinton's presidential campaign—to lobby for the Vietnamese Prime Minister's visit to the White House. This was part of an ongoing effort to maintain trade relations and moderate China's influence in the region. Shortly after that, Trump and Canadian Prime Minister Trudeau both made stops in Vietnam in an effort to similarly counter China's influence in the region. Vietnam has been an important market for Western nations, both geopolitically, because of its close proximity to China, and economically, because it has become one of the biggest initial public offering (IPO) markets in Southeast Asia, unseating Singapore in 2018.[24] These political gestures align with investor interest in new frontiers.

At the same time, global elites have sought out ways to expand their investments into new frontiers by identifying fund managers who can facilitate the expansion of their webs past the four BRIC (Brazil, Russia, India, and China) countries for investment opportunities in new frontiers. The "next eleven" (N-11), identified by Goldman Sachs investment banker and British economist Jim O'Neill, is the name of a group of eleven countries— Bangladesh, Egypt, Indonesia, Iran, Mexico, Nigeria, Pakistan, the Philippines, Turkey, South Korea, and Vietnam—which have the highest potential of becoming the world's most important economies of the twenty-first century.[25] The GDP growth rates of these countries have dramatically outpaced those of more-developed economies. Vietnam has been growing at a rate of 6–7 percent per year, while investors had also been traveling to

Myanmar with a new sense of excitement after the democratic election of Daw Aung San Suu Kyi. At the 2016 Euromoney Conference in Myanmar, investors repeatedly referred to Myanmar as a "leapfrog" country with respect to economic development.

At the same time, local and regional news outlets continued to characterize both Vietnam and Myanmar as countries with high levels of corruption, a weak legal infrastructure, financial unpredictability, and conflicting and negative bureaucratic decision making.[26] High-profile cases of corruption serve as examples and warnings to others playing in the gray. For example, in 2017, a Vietnamese banker was sentenced to death in a fraud case that involved 51 bankers and businessmen.[27] This banking scandal led to the swift devaluation of Ocean Bank from a valuation of $500 million in 2013 to $3.5 million in 2016. As foreign businesses are poised to invest in Myanmar after decades of trade sanctions,[28] the country similarly suffers from public scandals of military, government, and business cronyism. In 2021, Myanmar's experiment with democracy came to an end with a military coup that led to the detainment of Aung San Suu Kyi and several other civilian leaders placing investment interest on pause as everyone waits to see how things will unfold under the new military regime long associated with crony capitalism.

While Vietnam and Myanmar have a great deal in common as two important frontiers, with Vietnam roughly twenty years ahead of Myanmar with respect to foreign investments, the countries have very different histories, geopolitical relations, and local politics that make each place a unique site to examine.

THE CONTEXT ONSHORE IN VIETNAM

With complex histories of Chinese colonialism, French colonialism, and US imperialism, the Vietnamese government has adopted a protectionist stance on highly regulated sectors of the economy. Within the country, state banks are the main source of internal capital allocation based on long-term *relationships with the state*; local business networks gain access to the best market sites through personal ties to the communist party.[29] Several scholars who examine Vietnamese state-society relations show that the relationships between the private and public sectors are often murky and highly contentious, as state-society relationships involve entrepreneurial practices in which public officials and private investors provide social services while simultaneously lining their pockets.[30]

Legal scholar Tu Nguyen asserts, "In a political climate in which administrative power is decentralised and diffused, the growth of non-conventional
interests and new modes of mass mobilisation convolutes the power hierarchies and blurs the line separating public and private interests."[31] Vietnam's
decentralized government has led to a great deal of internal variation related
to state-market society that is important to consider. As political scientists
Malesky, McCulloch, and Nhat explain:

> most business/government interactions [are] decentralized to the pro-
> vincial level, including business registration, environmental and safety
> inspections, labour oversight, local government procurement and land
> allocation. . . . As a result, many studies have documented that the pro-
> vincial government, more than the central government, is the relevant
> level of government when analyzing the institutional climate facing
> firms.[32]

Malesky et al.'s findings point to the possibility that multiple state-market
relations can coexist within the same nation-state, based on the investment
project's provincial location and on the relationship that both local and foreign investors have with local government officials. The varied relationships
that investors have with local officials are crucial in Vietnam, because it does
not have strong legal institutions and the law is open to interpretation at the
provincial level.

Hun Kim's research on inter-Asian circulations of capital in Ho Chi Minh
City's property market further documents how the city is being remade
through different circuits of foreign capital.[33] The rise of East Asian financial centers dramatically altered intra-regional investment, transforming
less-developed countries in Southeast Asia into a lucrative new frontier,
thus increasing inter-Asian circulations of capital. Political elites in less-
developed countries must now find ways to appeal to local entrepreneurs,
Western (US, Canadian, and Western European), and Japanese investors, as
well as investors from other parts of East/Southeast Asia.[34] At the same time,
recent global economic transformations have produced a newly competitive
landscape for Western and East/Southeast Asian investors looking to invest
in emerging markets.[35]

The competing circuits of foreign direct investment (FDI) exemplify the
ways that states experiment with different governing techniques and regulatory regimes that drive the city's development.[36] Importantly, urban planning scholar Hun Kim argues that two contradictory modes of governance—
opacity and transparency—can coexist in the same space.[37]

Advancing Kim's work by looking at this relationship from market actors' perspective, I argue that the varying degrees of legal transparency versus opacity, coupled with a decentralized government, lead to *heterogenous state-market relations* that enable crony/predatory capitalism, relationships of mutual hostage (in which the threat of mutual destruction looms because both parties have engaged in corrupt/immoral activities with each other), and developmental/bureaucratic state-market relations to coexist in the same market, based on investors' varying degrees of proximity to state officials.[38] Western investors pushing for greater transparency and formal legal contracts, and who must adhere to international anti-corruption laws such as the FCPA and the Racketeer Influenced Corrupt Organizations Act (RICO), coexist in the same market as East/Southeast Asian investors who are comfortable adhering to local styles of deal brokering where bribery is commonplace.

THE CONTEXT ONSHORE IN MYANMAR (BURMA)

Like Vietnam, Myanmar (Burma) also has a complex legacy of colonialism.[39] In 1962 Burma's parliamentary democracy came to an end following the military coup led by Ne Win, and the "Burmese Way to Socialism" became the ruling ideology, which led Burma to turn inward, resulting in four decades of economic stagnation. Between 1962 and 1990, the country experienced substantial economic and political turmoil under the military dictatorship and the internal fight for democracy. Under the military dictatorship's deprivatization, the government nationalized all economic enterprises, including banks, and in 1964, the first demonetization took place.[40] This led to capital flight from Myanmar to neighboring countries like Singapore and Hong Kong.

After the military government took over, second (1985) and third (1987) demonetization episodes occurred, which sparked violence and unrest, with demonstrations and strikes that were repressed by military troops.[41] The military regime's economic mismanagement brought about economic stagnation and several crises.[42] By 1987, the state was nearly bankrupt as a result of rising inflation, rampant unemployment, and political protests demanding democratization.[43] What soon emerged was a form of crony capitalism, a symbiotic relationship between new business elites with military ties and the state.[44] The military regime provided a small-group oligarchy—made up of business tycoons and retired generals who had connections within the military high command—with access in exchange for relationships of patronage.

In the 1990s, elections took place with overwhelming support for the National League for Democracy, but the military government, which had dubbed itself the State Law and Order Restoration Council (SLORC), did not recognize the results. Instead, the SLORC instituted a series of economic reforms, including a new set of laws that granted the formation of private banks.[45] A series of economic reforms also occurred during Myanmar's transition from state socialism to state-mediated capitalism.[46]

In Myanmar's market economy, business tycoons with close ties to the government had a monopoly on the market. Tycoons hired the sons and daughters of military generals—giving them high-level positions in their businesses—"in exchange for coveted contracts and import licenses in profitable sectors: trading, logistics, property, agro-industries, tourism, oil and retail."[47] Many of these cronies were placed on a US Sanctions List, which prohibits certain US persons or entities from making new investments in Myanmar.

In 2003, after rising political tensions, President George Bush imposed sanctions against Myanmar pursuant to the Burmese Freedom and Democracy Act (BFDA) and Executive Order 13310, banning the import of products from Myanmar and the export of financial services to Myanmar, while also freezing the assets of the renamed SLORC—the State Peace and Development Council (SPDC)—and three Myanmar foreign trade financial institutions.[48] In 2007 and 2008, President Bush extended the sanctions to a group of designated Myanmarese entities responsible for human rights violations and public corruption.[49]

Myanmar would be isolated from the Western world for nearly fifty years before it would remerge in the global economy. In November 2015, Aung San Suu Kyi's National League for Democracy (NLD) won a landslide victory in the general elections, ending almost a half century of military rule. But Myanmar's opening to the rest of the world was complicated. The cronies did not disappear. Instead, many of the resource-rich families began to reposition themselves by "bringing their sons and daughters into play, spawning a second-generation elite that is consolidating through business and marriage . . . finessing their image . . . [and] retooling entire conglomerates."[50] As investors entered this market, they confronted the fact that the most profitable businesses and industries are those with long ties to a crony past. This has meant that regional players from China, Thailand, India, South Korea, and Vietnam have been some of the first movers into this market, while Western investors constrained by the FCPA have been standing by, watching the early transition.

The Web: Connecting Onshore Investments to Offshore Vehicles

Both Vietnam and Myanmar serve as important examples of nations where state power and economic interests overlap in corruptible ways. So how do investors navigate this tricky terrain in countries mired in corruption and crony capitalism? How do investors from the United States, Canada, and Western Europe, who must adhere to laws against corruption, compete with the rise of new money from East and Southeast Asian investors that is not subject to the same set of regulatory laws pushing for greater transparency and anti-corruption/cronyism? The answer, I argue, is embedded in the mesh of offshore investment vehicles that knit together capital webs, linking markets like Vietnam and Myanmar to intermediaries in Hong Kong and Singapore, which are simply subsidiaries of companies incorporated in other sovereignties offshore. The connection between New York, Ho Chi Minh City, and Yangon lies in the web of legal contracts that bind them offshore in the BVI, Panama, Seychelles, Hong Kong, and Singapore. This *system* enables capital investments in risky markets through offshore financial centers (OFCs) that have long provided global elites with anonymity, privacy, and secrecy.

Let's take the case of foreign direct investments (FDI) in Vietnam and Myanmar, the two countries of interest not just to me but also to Fritz, where there are significant flaws in the way economists measure FDI flows. Most stories of FDI calculate the amount of FDI flowing from the source country of the capital to the destination country where capital makes its way. In less-developed economies like Vietnam and Myanmar, government statisticians who try to capture the source country of capital often assume that capital flows from nation "A" to nation "B" without any regard to the multiple countries the money passes through before arriving onshore.

The general statistics office of Vietnam provides data on source country for foreign direct investment (FDI) entering the country (see figure 1.2). The United States makes up only 8 percent of FDI going into Vietnam, while China makes up only 3 percent. A cursory look at the data makes it appear as though the majority of foreign capital entering Vietnam comes from Taiwan, South Korea, Malaysia, Japan, Singapore, Hong Kong, and the British Virgin Islands. Similar numbers also appear for Myanmar (see figure 1.3). In Myanmar, the United States does not appear anywhere in the data, while China, Hong Kong, and Singapore account for nearly 75 percent of the capital inflow into the country. While these numbers reveal the declining

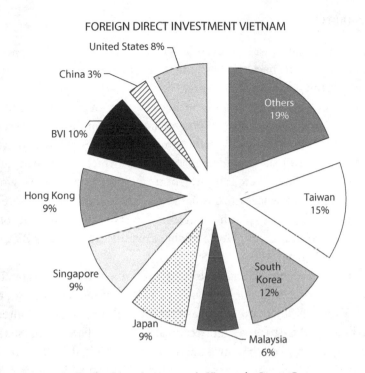

FOREIGN DIRECT INVESTMENT VIETNAM

FIGURE 1.2. Foreign Direct Investments in Vietnam by Source Country, 2016. (Illustration by author. *Source: General Statistics Office of Vietnam.*)

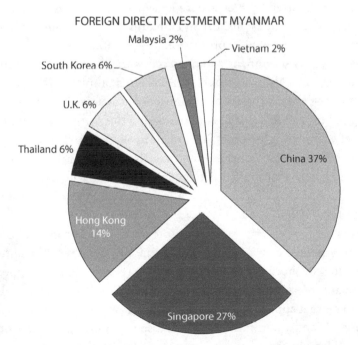

FOREIGN DIRECT INVESTMENT MYANMAR

FIGURE 1.3. Foreign Direct Investments in Myanmar by Source Country, 2016. (Illustration by author. *Source: Ministry of Planning and Finance of Myanmar.*)

significance of the West in Southeast Asia's frontier and emerging markets, they are misleading because they hide the ultimate beneficiary and original source of capital entering these markets.

However, an even closer look at this data with an eye towards offshore structures reveals that in both Vietnam and Myanmar nearly 30 percent of the foreign capital entering Vietnam comes primarily from Singapore, Hong Kong, and the British Virgin Islands: countries which are known for their offshore economies. There is no way of tracking flows of FDI in a world of webbed capitalism where the ultimate beneficiary is another offshore company. Therefore, this data is inaccurate: it does not provide an account of the source of funds coming from offshore jurisdictions such as BVI, Hong Kong, and Singapore.

I have published these charts elsewhere to make a case about capital flows *between* countries in the global South, namely between East and Southeast Asia.[51] However, it was the discovery through ethnographic and interview data that forced me to take a more critical look at the flaws in this statistical reporting. It turns out that investments from the United States sometimes ran through vehicles in Singapore while those from China were masked through Hong Kong companies offshore. Foreign investors wanting to enter into frontier and emerging markets drew on the same offshore schemes once used by Westerners by setting up *holding companies* and *special purpose vehicles* offshore in Hong Kong and Singapore to do business. They rely on financial professionals—private wealth managers, fund managers, lawyers, and/or company secretaries—to help set up offshore investment vehicles. *Special purpose vehicles*, as Brooke Harrington writes, are "like the fireproof safes of offshore finance: asset-holding structures designed for the sole purpose of insulating their contents from risk . . . [thereby providing] protect[ion] from bankruptcy, creditors, and litigants."[52] This explains why multinational firms like Coca-Cola and Microsoft have entered the market with business partners who have been linked to the jade trade or are mired in allegations of corruption and human rights abuses.[53]

Most of the research subjects I interviewed either managed money for these people or worked to procure money from wealthy elites who controlled offshore funds set up somewhere else. Highly compensated financial professionals do the grit work of setting up an artificial paper trail to make it appear that the capital flows from an offshore entity in the Cayman Islands, Bermuda, etc., into a special purpose vehicle or holding company in Singapore or Hong Kong before that money is invested onshore in Vietnam or Myanmar in a complex web. Jimmy, an investor

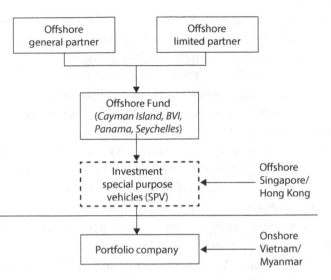

FIGURE 1.4. Artificial Flows of Capital (*Source:* Kimberly Kay Hoang)

based in Hong Kong, who has invested in a healthcare company in Vietnam, explained to me:

> In Southeast Asia, the idea that capital flows from nation "A" to nation "B" is not the reality. There aren't official statistics on this because that would require us to open up the books of all the sec[retary] offices. Their main business is privacy so why would they do that. I am Korean, educated in America, living in Hong Kong. My company is domiciled in Samoa and my investments are in Vietnam. I have this complex structure for more reasons beyond just trying to hide money. This is all *legal.* You should know this, the Pritzker family is the family famous for setting up these structures and they are one of your university's biggest donors.

What Jimmy described was a simplified structure that was very similar to those of the vast majority of my research subjects. The paper trail through shell companies shows an ownership structure that flows through multiple structures before arriving onshore. Jimmy's reference to J. B. Pritzker, an American venture capitalist, entrepreneur, co-founder of the Pritzker Group, and Governor of Illinois, was his way of legitimizing these activities abroad. If the governor of a state with over 12 million people in a country with some of the most stringent laws is famous for these practices, they must not only be legal but legitimate.[54]

Figure 1.4 provides a general outline for typical capital flows into risky markets like Vietnam and Myanmar in a simplified web.

A general partner and limited partner will come together to set up an offshore fund in the Cayman Islands, BVI, Panama, Seychelles, Samoa, or Liechtenstein. These are legal technologies that create a paper trail of ownership in a different sovereignty. From there they set up an investment or *special purpose vehicle* in Singapore or Hong Kong, and funds from there are directed to a portfolio company onshore in Vietnam or Myanmar. It is important to note that the offshore structure of every investment project was different. Among the 67 different investment projects I followed, not a single one of them described the same structure. In fact, after the Panama Papers story broke in 2016, many of my interviewees moved their investment vehicles to less-known offshore financial centers (OFCs) like Samoa and Seychelles, which were set up with less-stringent reporting requirements. Therefore, it should be noted that, in practice, the webs were never quite as simple as Jimmy laid it out in figure 1.4. The presence of super spiders and their subordinates in non-Western countries leads to different reasons for the use of OFCs.

Function of Offshore Financial Centers

The scholarly work on capital webs takes a critical approach by examining the ways that offshore vehicles serve as threats to democracy, inclusion, and transparency. However, when looking specifically at frontier markets with less-stable governments, I found that these webs served some pragmatic functions beyond secrecy and evasion. These include privacy, tax concerns, finessing weak local banking institutions, offshore arbitration, access to a wider pool of global investors, asset protection from lawsuits, easier offshore exits, and the ability to send and receive payment in private through designated nominees.

PRIVACY

OFCs' main commodity was privacy and secrecy for Westerners. These same structures now provide a layer of privacy and secrecy for a crop of new elites originating from non-Western markets, as Kevin, a Korean national who lives in Hong Kong, explained to me:

> In this world you have big fish and small fish. Big fish have more to hide and more money to work with, so they have to pay for more-complex administrative structures. The people who have funds set up in BVI and Cayman, you are talking to very rich people who have to create layers

between their investments to syndicate the risk. In BVI they are not even allowed to ask who the account owner is. It's all set up through a nominee structure, so if you're trying to hide your money, yeah, that's the greatest thing out there. If a lawyer comes down from the US and ask who owns it, they're legally not even allowed to say. That is their main business.

Kevin introduced me to Susie, a company secretary based in Singapore who describes herself as an outsourced version of a Chief Financial Officer. Most of her job is devoted to managing the setup of offshore structures as well as the taxes of her clients' businesses. She explained to me, "We offer our clients privacy . . . many clients in Asia are afraid that the government can turn on them and grab their assets at any time. It is like the Jews fleeing the Holocaust. In Myanmar the unfair seizure of their assets [by the government is a concern]."

Like Susie, Tan, another company secretary, noted, "You have to distinguish between privacy and secrecy. . . . Privacy is maintained within a regulatory framework which provides sharing of information with tax authorities and relevant parties. Secrecy is about hiding, extortion, fraud. Those can be major issues, but for most people they worry about falling victim to criminals who want to go after their money or governments that are strapped for cash." The distinction, as Tan notes here, is that privacy is legal or moral, while secrecy is illegal or immoral. While these are functional equivalents, a key difference has to do with the state apparatus and whether investors feel like their assets are safe in frontier markets. Ironically this is a group looking to take advantage of frontier markets with weak states by front-running the regulatory system, but they want to secure their investments offshore to finesse the risk.

When I asked the company secretaries about the new laws affecting US investors, Bonnie, who is based in Singapore, said to me, "Oh, no Americans. . . . Only Chinese and Asian clients. . . . Because I need to report all the clients' information to the US government and if I do that then I have to report all my clients." What Bonnie is referring to here is the fact that she no longer accepts clients who hold a US passport. However, she can afford to do that by securing enough business from elites from other countries. Secrecy may be less viable for US citizens. However, according to Susie and others, offshore structures still provide privacy for the elite of the Third World.

Susie explained to me that when she started to do her due diligence checks on her US clients, many of them refused to respond, forcing her to close their accounts altogether. Following the new regulations that require company secretaries to identify the ultimate beneficiary owner (UBO) of the different offshore structures, she worried about the financial penalties and that her accounting license would be revoked. However, as Susie later explained, "When you have high-level government officials [from smaller countries] in this shell game they are not going to regulate themselves." What she is pointing to is the ways that political and economic interests often overlap in these states, making it virtually impossible to dismantle this system in frontier markets. In order to avoid the new regulatory body governing US clients, she deals primarily with Chinese and Southeast Asian clients whom she can offer some degree of privacy because those countries do not have the same KYC requirements as the United States.

TAX EVASION VS. TAX AVOIDANCE

While US regulators often used the language of "tax evasion" to go after people who they say are not paying the taxes they owe, all of the legal and financial experts I interviewed framed these same practices as *tax avoidance*. The key difference between tax evasion and tax avoidance, they explained to me, is that one is illegal while the other is legal. However, the boundary between the two can be quite blurry. For example, Paul, the managing director of a private equity fund that was making investments in both Vietnam and Myanmar, explained to me:

> I think this whole Panama Papers and the whole Obama giving a speech at the White House [on April 5, 2016, to discuss the Panama Papers leak]—like, welcome to the real world. Most of the funds in the world are domiciled in one building where lawyers are and everyone else uses the same address . . . no one is breaking the law here. We are all paying our taxes, but there is a dual tax agreement between Singapore and Vietnam where you only pay 5 percent tax on all capital gains made offshore.

Jim echoed similar arguments:

> I usually run my investments through Singapore or BVI instead of running it directly from one country to another as a function of the advice I got to be more tax efficient. They have tax efficiency in BVI, obviously, and less corporate income taxes in Singapore and I can keep the money in Singapore. Foreign direct investment is foreign direct investment, but there is no real way to know where the money came from to start with. Isn't that just capitalism?

Paul and Jim both sought out expert advice from a cottage industry of professionals who operate in OFCs to help them set up legal structures which would enable them to avoid taxes across multiple jurisdictions. Chapter 4 takes a much deeper dive into the varying tax structures and strategies. However, what is important to note here is that spiders are able to capture significant profits compared to their competitors who do not have the funds or relationships, or don't know how to finesse these laws by employing a set of legal professionals whom they generously compensate to do this work for them. For US investors, these services can mean a profit increase of up to 30 percent as a result of the tax savings alone.[55]

WEAK LOCAL BANKING INSTITUTIONS

Local Vietnamese and Burmese entrepreneurs who have lived in politically unstable nations with weak financial institutions often see offshore banking as offering places where they can securely store their wealth without having to worry about insolvency.

Al explained:

Offshore just means it's not visible, that's how I see it. There are estimates when you talk to people who know better than me, when you talk to banks, they estimate less than 50 percent of the money is with the people in the banks in countries like Vietnam, Myanmar, or Laos. My family lived through so many banking crises that we don't have faith in our banks. We remember the days when banks just shut down and there were lines around the block of people trying to get their money out. Have you ever thought about what you might do if the bank went bankrupt? This is why we all call Singapore the laundromat of Southeast Asia. Many of us have to keep our money offshore in Singapore, the Cayman Islands, Hong Kong etc. And we don't want them to have our names in there because the government can turn on us at any minute. You do not want to have a target on your back like that. We use nominees to hold our money. I have this guy in the Cayman Islands who does this administrative work for me and all of the companies here. Ninety percent of Myanmar is banked in Singapore, everyone here knows it and so does the government. Their main job now is to think about how they can build more stable banks to encourage people to bring their money back to this country. But that is not an easy task.

Almost everyone I spoke with in Vietnam and Myanmar did not keep their liquid assets onshore. In fact, almost all reported only keeping enough cash onshore to cover operational costs. Profits, investments, or savings were all stored in bank accounts offshore. However, this was not just about secrecy and evasion. Financial crises and crony capitalism create a context where few have faith in banks or confidence in the state's regulatory structure to protect assets deposited in the banks. This weak infrastructure pushed the wealthy into banking offshore.

OFFSHORE ARBITRATION

For the financial elite, frontier markets are risky precisely because there is "no clear rule of law" or reliable judicial system to safeguard investments. Offshore legal agreements provide some assurances for investors, as the demands for transnational legal orders help to bring some sense of predictability offshore to circumvent the unpredictability onshore.[56] One hundred fifty-six signatory states are now part of the Convention on the Recognition and Enforcement of Foreign Arbitral Awards ("New York Convention"), which is a step forward for many who see this as a pillar of international arbitration. Individuals could in theory file a dispute with a state-owned enterprise or private enterprise with close state ties in hopes of winning a judgment offshore. This is important because most private investors who are managing investments with state-owned enterprises have concerns about how to settle disputes in a neutral territory. Still, national courts can refuse to recognize and/or enforce a judgment won offshore.

ACCESS TO A WIDER POOL OF POTENTIAL INVESTORS

Frontier markets with weak legal and financial institutions offer potentially large gains, but also correspondingly large risks, which make investors hesitant. One way to encourage their investments is to set up offshore entities where investors can buy shares of a parent company that has a stake in the subsidiary company onshore without making direct investments in the subsidiary company itself. At the same time, when an investor wants to sell their stake in that local firm, they can just sell the shares that they own offshore without having to do anything onshore to exit that fund in Vietnam or Myanmar. This enables them to invest in offshore companies in such a way that the money goes into a fund in the BVI, and they can exit their investment by selling their shares in BVI without having to exit a fund in Vietnam.

Ben, the head of operations of a smaller firm in Vietnam with investments from all around the world, explained:

> I am the operations guy for this investment, but my bosses are Rob and Terry and those guys. . . . Jewel is licensed to VP Bank by a British Virgin Islands company called SAOFS Southeast Asia Online Financial Services. That company has licensed it to Richlife Singapore, and Richlife Singapore has licensed it to Vietnam, VP Bank. LocalLife Vietnam was hired to consult on how to launch the product when it went to Vietnam. What is key here is that when a foreign investor wants to come in they go and buy SAOFS. This way they get exposure to Vietnam without having to do anything in Vietnam.

In other words, the special purpose vehicle enables investors to make investments in the shell company or parent company that owns the subsidiary company onshore in risky markets. This means that investors who want to play in frontier markets can do so with a view from up in the air, making it hard for them to see, touch, or feel the material consequences of their investments on the ground. They do not have to deal with the day-to-day operations or finesse complex government relations because the subsidiary onshore handles those details for a small management fee.

ASSET PROTECTION FROM LAWSUITS

Investments that are held in offshore accounts are held in fireproof safes that make it (1) difficult for a claimant to locate and (2) challenging to collect a judgment against the assets. For US citizens in particular, while the accounts must be on a tax return, by law the assets are not part of any public record. Foreign judgment holders often have a difficult time enforcing a judgment obtained in their own country in another country.

In an interview with Sam, an investor in a large manufacturing company in Vietnam, he explained to me:

> In the old days maybe, it was a lot simpler. You would open a factory in this country and then open one in another county and the two businesses were yours. But if something went wrong with your business in Vietnam, for example, all of your assets in India or Cyprus could be tied up with that asset. So, what you have to do is create legal walls between your investments. When you set up a shell corporation for one business

it acts as its own asset and if it goes bankrupt for whatever reason all of your other investments in other places are safer.

Gavin, another investor, explained the complex structures, saying:

> It does not make sense to pay all of the fees for these complex structures unless you have a sizable investment. The bigger the project or investment, the more complex the structure. Put it this way, I have an SPV in Samoa that owns another SPV in Seychelles . . . the structure in Seychelles owns the subsidiary company in Hong Kong and the entity in Hong Kong is invested in Vietnam. If someone wants to sue me they have to win and enforce a judgment now across four different jurisdictions. No one wants to pay for that so it's a way of staving off the people going after your money in lawsuits.

What both Gavin and Sam describe are *asset protection trusts* (APTs), which are legal mechanisms that shield their wealth from lawsuits, creditors, current or ex-spouses, and the government of one's home country. My interview subjects reported paying between $2,500 and $50,000 to set up these trusts, with some firms asking for a percentage of all assets transferred. The more complex the structure—with more beneficiaries—the higher the cost.

EASIER OFFSHORE EXITS

Special purpose vehicles allow the owner to dispose of the asset onshore by selling their shares in the special purpose vehicle offshore. In emerging markets with widespread corruption or inefficient bureaucracies, OFCs' main value-add is that they provide far more-efficient and legally binding agreements which make investors feel safer with their investments. When an investor wants to exit and sell their shares in frontier markets, they avoid the bureaucratic red tape as well as the taxes by selling their shares in the asset offshore in Singapore or Hong Kong. This sale of shares can occur without transferring or changing the ownership structure onshore in Vietnam or Myanmar. As such, new investors who enter a project at a much later stage do not have to deal with the reissue of licenses and permits. Not only do they avoid paying taxes in Vietnam, but this transfer of ownership never takes place in Vietnam, so that new owners do not have to deal with the onerous process of starting from scratch and having to bribe public officials for new licenses, permits, or to renegotiate new tax agreements.

Offshore structures enable spiders to expand their capital webs to nearly every corner of the world by front-running the legal and political systems onshore while taking advantage of investor protections set up offshore. The story here zooms in on one region, Southeast Asia, where so many countries are now vying for influence.

———

As we've seen in this chapter, social spiders cooperate to make webs not only possible but expansive. Spiderweb capitalism disrupts old binaries of First/Third World, developed/undeveloped, transparent/corrupt to show how these markets are in fact connected to one another in one large global ecosystem for the ultra-wealthy to seize. Like the tiny spider on the US one-dollar bill, dominant spiders hide in one corner of the world and use highly specialized agents to help build out massive webs that connect global markets around the world.

Still, it is not enough to map out this web or to outline the function of the varied structures in it. The purpose of this book is to explain *how* a community of spiders build out these very structures, by diving deeper into the practice of playing in the gray. To do so, the following chapters zoom in to scrutinize at the art of the deal, varieties of corruption, various structures of taxation, and the relationships between morals and markets that bind different people in spiderweb capitalism.

Spinning New Investment Deals

How does a spider's money make its way into remote corners around the world? What configuration of people and relationships is necessary to link offshore capital to deals onshore in frontier markets?

During the time of my research, Vietnam and Myanmar generated high levels of investor optimism. But these were countries with large *institutional voids*,[1] including but not limited to weak banking infrastructures, fuzzy and often corrupt government bureaucracies, insecure intellectual property rights, lack of local human capital, and problems with due diligence reports related to corporate governance.[2] Spinning deals in new frontiers is about how investors finesse these barriers by relying on a wide network of financial professionals to help them expand their capital webs.

I draw on the ethnographic data uncovered while trying to follow the people who move money quite literally all around the world. I wanted to figure out how global elites make investments in highly speculative, risky markets with large institutional voids. More specifically, I was interested in understanding how financial professionals raise money for frontier markets and then source deals to deploy that money. In Vietnam and Myanmar, I attended multiple investor conferences where I got to observe firsthand how investors confronted the harsh reality that the most promising deals were ones that involved tight government connections (in the case of Vietnam) or ties to old military crony–backed firms (in the case of Myanmar). As a result, in this local context, it was challenging for investors from places like the United States to finesse these markets without syndicating that risk by relying on someone else to do the work of *playing in the gray*.

This chapter underlines three central processes that make up the deal-brokering process in risky markets: raising capital, sourcing potential deals to deploy capital, and sealing deals. Importantly, the ability to weave small local webs into bigger global ones depended heavily on a form of relational capitalism between those with money offshore and the group of people managing the investments and government relations onshore.[3]

Raising Capital: Getting the Money from Offshore Funds to Onshore Investments

What makes spiderweb capitalism so complex is the fact that social webs do not have a clear beginning or end. Multiple spiders spin massive capital webs from different corners of the world. Investments in frontier markets do not simply involve interested investors going to scope out deals in those markets. Rather, there is a massive network of subordinate spiders weaving their own capital webs, which they hope to expand by seeking capital injections from bigger spiders with more money around the world.

Fund managers who were based in Vietnam and Myanmar employed strategies both onshore and offshore to encourage U/HNWIs to consider expanding their portfolios to include risky markets. Offshore *roadshows*—trips by investment managers for potential clients pitching opportunities to potential investors—provided investment managers who are usually based in Vietnam and Myanmar with a space to meet with those who managed U/HNWI individuals' money abroad to encourage investments in new, risky markets.

In an effort to follow the money and put a face on these deals, I flew with fund managers and their teams on roadshows to several cities in the United States (San Francisco, New York, Seattle, Chicago, Houston, Austin, Newport Beach, and even Lexington, Kentucky), Canada (Vancouver, Toronto, Montreal), Europe (UK, France, Germany, Switzerland, and Denmark), the Middle East (the United Arab Emirates), and regional countries within East and Southeast Asia (China, Japan, South Korea, Thailand, Singapore, Malaysia, Indonesia, and Hong Kong) to observe as they pitched investment opportunities to potential foreign investors. In the process, I interviewed 74 large and small-scale fund managers, CEOs of asset management firms, and brokers, all working in different capacities to raise capital for investment specifically in Vietnam and Myanmar.

I also spent time with the same group of fund managers as they hosted potential investors in Vietnam and Myanmar, where UHNWIs and the people who manage their money could participate in onshore investor conferences and experience highly curated tours, crucial to eliciting an emotional or gut feeling of Vietnam and Myanmar's market dynamism as places worth placing bets on.

THE ROADSHOW OFFSHORE

The roadshow is an important way to help potential investors get some exposure to the Vietnamese market without having to travel halfway around the world. Fund managers go to potential investors to sell Vietnam as a market, their capabilities as a team with respect to government connections, and access to insider deals.

Van is a general partner and Max is a limited partner of XVN Capital—a fund with a mandate to make investments in Southeast Asia. As part of their annual roadshow to court new investors, they had plans to travel to the United States, where they would present their deck of specific investment opportunities in Vietnam to potential investors based in Newport Beach, Houston, New York, Seattle, and San Francisco. They planned to give the same presentation to several different family offices in their referral network of limited partners who had made investments in an earlier fund that they managed. I sat in on many of these presentations but recused myself from the private meetings.

In an effort to connect their part of a smaller capital web in frontier markets to the people who control bigger webs in developed economies, the Vietnam-based team spent several weeks putting together an "investor deck": a 15–20-minute PowerPoint presentation that the deal team took with them on their US roadshow.

We flew together from Ho Chi Minh City to LAX and checked into the same hotel where we would be based for the first two nights in Newport Beach, California. They were scheduled to meet with Edward—a private wealth manager of a small family office whose clients were most interested in public equity and international markets. On the morning after our arrival, Edward's assistant Nathan met with Van and Max for breakfast at the hotel. That morning, I watched Van and Max work to try to get a general sense of the kinds of investment opportunities that the family office had interests in and to feel out the firm's risk appetite, in addition to its general investment strategies. This kind of in-person relational work was important for Max and Van to identify what to emphasize in their presentation to Edward.

After breakfast at the hotel, I accompanied them to the office—a large corporate building housing several other companies. A short elevator ride up to the 10th floor led us to an office space which had panoramic ocean and country club views. The furnishings were modern yet simple, with clean textured layers of white on white. Nearly hidden against this backdrop were two large white paintings with light outlines of women wearing rice hats standing on small rafts. The images were so delicate they just about vanished into the atmosphere of the space. And yet—the pieces spoke loud and clear: Edward's team had a clear interest in Southeast Asia and perhaps already had deals set up there.

Jenny, a young female assistant, greeted us before giving us a tour. Three offices in the back were adjacent to a meeting room with a view of the ocean in the distance. The office felt notably different from the high-rise offices in Ho Chi Minh City where Max and Van were both based, which had a view of a bustling city of motorbikes and cars zooming by outside. After the tour, Jenny offered us coffee and helped Van and Max set up their PowerPoint presentation before Edward entered the room. At the start of the presentation there were five people in the room: Van, Max, Edward, Nathan, and myself.

Van and Max started the conversation with compliments on the paintings in the hallway, noting how it reminded them of the Mekong Delta in Vietnam. They also talked about how the painting was so abstract that it was hard to locate it to an actual place. Edward then told them a story about how his grandmother had traveled all around the world in her twenties, and Burma was one of her favorite places. With this bridge back to Southeast Asia, Van fired up the PowerPoint presentation. The first slide of their deck was a map of Southeast Asia. There was a red dotted line outlining Vietnam, Laos, Cambodia, Thailand, Myanmar, Singapore, Malaysia, Indonesia, and the Philippines. Van began, "Your grandma was ahead of her time, because this is the best time to invest in Southeast Asia. Here are ten countries with a total population of 626 million people and a nominal GDP of 2.8 trillion US dollars." The purpose of this slide was to capture the sheer market potential based on population size alone.

The second slide zoomed in on Vietnam, with some key facts about Hanoi as the capital and central place for managing key government relations. Ho Chi Minh City, on the other hand, was the country's main economic hub. Van continued, "Vietnam is a hot market right now. It's growing 6 to 7 percent per annum, you have a population of over 95 million people that is young and growing, the GDP has gone from $200 per capita to $5,000 per capita over ten short years, demonstrating a growing middle class. And people are moving from the provinces to the city at 3 to 4 percent per annum." The work here is to sell a story about Vietnam's story of macroeconomic growth overall compared to developed markets like the US, which are only growing at a rate of 2–3 percent per year. The implicit selling point was that investments in a frontier market will generate a minimum of double the rate of return.

He paused and then turned to the next slide with several logos of the large-scale investments already in Vietnam. He continued, "The key reasons for this rapid growth have to do with the foreign direct investments of large firms like Samsung creating jobs and wealth for a growing middle class. This has increased the demand for better healthcare, educational opportunities, banks and access to credit, private property or bigger homes. These are all sectors [in which] we place our investments." Van provided a big-picture overview to demonstrate to the potential investors that since larger firms have already entered this market, it is likely much safer than it was in Vietnam's nascent market years. On this slide, Max also interjected that the returns on those investments were between 15 percent and 20 percent.

In the middle of the presentation, Edward interrupted and said, "You seem to be all over the map. Do you mean to tell me that you have investments in this wide and diverse group of sectors? What is your strategic know-how with respect to operations?"

Max smiled and said, "I'm glad that you asked. One of the key differences between a developed economy like the United States and emerging markets has to do with the way people tend to control the unknown and the unexpected in a manner which doesn't exist in the United States. We bring buyers and sellers together in the market and manage these unknowns by raising capital and providing seed funding or growth capital for companies looking to expand." This was Max's implicit way of trying to convey that they have the ability to capitalize on the unpredictability based on their relationships with key state officials.

However, Edward's confused facial expression led Van to interject in a far more explicit manner. "To be clear, this is not just about bridging the gap between capital and opportunities, it is also about navigating a complicated bureaucratic environment in these countries. We are also on the ground making investments in companies that are usually outside the comfort zone of most foreigners in terms of corporate governance." What Van was implying here is that by having the investment managers carry out the work on the deals onshore, Edward would not have to worry about playing in the gray himself, personally navigating a government without clear rules for investments. Instead, subordinate spiders would work on that part of the web for Edward; all they needed was his trust and his capital.

They paused, then Max moved to the next slide, titled "Investment Approach." "Our main approach is to identify investment opportunities that are not widely available through the general market's private equity structure." What was implied here was that they have an advantage in Vietnam because of their unique insider access and on-the-ground knowledge of deals in Vietnam that were not open to the general public. These deals were only open to U/HNWIs.

Max continued, "We conduct our own due diligence checks by hiring very good researchers to help with this. We also set up minority investment protections, which gives us the ability to participate on the board and make decisions alongside management. We generally hold our investments for three to four years and either take it public through an IPO or sell the investments to a trade investor, with an objective to develop a minimum IRR (internal rate of return) of 7 percent per annum, which is easy to achieve because the country is growing at that rate. Our actual rates of return have been between 10 and 15 percent in recent years."

Edward jumped in and said, "This is the allure of new markets . . . high risk, high return."

In agreement, Max responded, "When you want to make safe bets you can invest in developed markets; they have fewer institutional gaps, so there is a lot more you can control, but the IRR there as you know is only 2 to 3 percent per annum. In emerging markets, you can bank on the growth rate of the country, which is 6 to 7 percent alone."

Edward asked, "But how do you manage the risk? What kinds of risks do you have to zoom in on in this context?"

Van moved to the slide outlining the risks, titled "Investing in a Frontier/ Emerging Market." Pointing to the slide, he said, "There are macro risks, the biggest one being the local FX (foreign exchange) currency devaluing. The micro risks have to do with risks associated with corporate governance, which is not yet at the level that meets international standards." Going off script from the presentation, Van turned to them and said, "There is a lot of money to be captured in gray markets" where the law is open to interpretation. "That is our added value" he explained. Then Van went on to discuss how his team has been in the market for many years and "have spent a lot of time building relationships, particularly in government," that have given them exclusive access to the equitization of SOEs (state-owned enterprises) in Vietnam. Playing in the gray, he told them, means that you make an investment not based off calculated risk, but rather from a gut feeling garnered through trust in the people you hire to have the know-how to manage complex state relations. To do that, those raising money have to sell their deal team as part of the investment opportunity. Van then moved on to sell the story of their investment team and the important role they played in executing and managing the investments.

It is not just a story about how well their investments have done; it is a story about *who* they have as key people working on the deal and the unique configuration of experience they bring to the table. Key to expanding these capital webs is bringing in other spiders to carry out their unique roles to build out other parts of the web. Identifying subordinate spiders was the next part of the presentation.

Selling the Story of the Key Founders of the Fund

The next slide had photos of four people, their names, titles, and two or three sentences that described the kinds of investment experience they had.

Max Waugh—Chief Executive Officer

> Max is a founding partner of XVN Capital. He has lived in Vietnam for over 20 years and speaks fluent Vietnamese. Formerly country head of VNN, he co-founded VNN Asset Management, a Vietnam listed equity specialist, with peak AUM of over US$500mn, before exiting in 2010.

Van Nguyen—Chief Investment Officer

> Van is a Vietnamese citizen who has more than 20 years in finance and operational experience across Asia, with roles across various firms where he oversees venture capital investments, private equity, and listed equity investments.

Michael Burns—Head of Hong Kong Operations

> Michael has spent much of his career at HSBC in Asia. He led an Operations Department for Asian equity and derivative and convertible business lines prior to becoming head of JIA Convertible Bond Trading. He is certified by the Global Association of Risk Professionals as a Financial Risk Manager.

Son Nguyen—Managing Director

> Son is the managing director who oversees the investment portfolio for Southeast Asia. His former employers include HSBC Bank, HSBC

Asset Management (Hong Kong), and Credit Suisse (Switzerland). Before coming back to Vietnam, he was one of the Investment Directors for a Vietnamese holding that was a Swiss-based investment.

As the slide indicates, the team has nodes of their web in Vietnam, Hong Kong, and Switzerland, with years of experience offshore and onshore. Max stated, "Together our team has over fifty years of experience investing in Vietnam. Our fund allows investors to have access to the growth story in Vietnam's private equity market by tapping into our source of opportunities from a network of business leaders and government leaders. Our challenge today is not getting access to the market or sourcing deals. Our challenge is filtering the deals that come our way and identifying good companies to make investments in. In short, this market advantage that we have will allow investors to capitalize on Vietnam's medium- or long-term growth rate."

What was striking to me about this particular slide and their strategy to sell their deal team was that they talked not about their success rate, but rather about how much money they were entrusted to manage at various points in time. No one seemed to care whether that money generated returns, or whether there was any data to show that they were successful with the previous funds that they managed. The blind faith in *people* was crucial to getting a deal going. The turnover of investors in these markets is high, and as Max explained to me over drinks later that evening, people have a short memory when it comes to market losses. All they want to know is whether they will be the ones placing the next winning bet.

What makes for a winning bet? Well, the answer has to do with the key political connections to manage various investment projects. Van then flipped to the next slide, which included several images of them with leading government officials. These included members of Vietnam's Ministry of Finance; they also had photos of themselves with the current Prime Minister of Vietnam and with the Prime Minister of Canada. These photos are meant to illustrate their relational capital in a country where access to political ties is crucial to managing their investments.

Van explained, "Our team has spent many years working with government officials to manage some of the economic challenges facing the country. We have people on our team who are local and who understand how to navigate the complex regulatory environment. As you can see, both Van and Son both have extensive experience working overseas and in the region, and have a vision for how to capitalize on opportunities that are not widely available in the public market." Again, what Max and Van were emphasizing

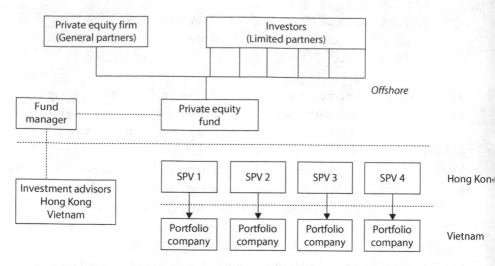

FIGURE 2.1. General Ownership Structure (*Source:* Kimberly Kay Hoang)

was a kind of access and insider knowledge that they had in the market, which was not open to just anyone who wanted to invest. They were selling their local know-how, connections, and insider access to a market without a clear set of rules because this afforded them access to some of the best deals.

Investor Protections

Selling the story of Vietnam's macroeconomic growth is not enough. As the key brokers between investors offshore and investment deals onshore, they work very hard to provide potential investors with assurances that they have the skill set necessary to protect both their investments and their investors. In this case the protections are more for Edward, the manager of a fund offshore whose name would be in all of the investment documents, and not for his boss, the chairman or super spider, who was notably absent in this entire exchange.

In order to encourage investors who might not know the Vietnamese market very well to make large investments there, Max and Van work hard to outline how they protect investors from both legal liability and financial loss. The key to protecting investors is extensive use of offshore structures.

On a new slide, they presented a diagram (see figure 2.1 above) of the holding structure that puts the family office interests at the top. This is their version of the capital web that they control and manage.

Max continued, "We manage a lot of the political and economic risks related to emerging markets by setting up structures to protect our investors. As Limited Partners, our investors invest in a private equity fund set up offshore. We sometimes use Delaware, which is not too far from here, and other times use the Cayman Islands or BVI, depending on the type of investments. But Delaware and now Florida work just as well. As you know, the recent press reports on offshore structures assume that this is all about tax evasion. What they are missing is that these structures are critical for investor protections in risky markets like Vietnam."

When Edward asked about the purpose of the Hong Kong structure, Max explained that that special purpose vehicle was specifically set up to protect Edward as the investor, because if anything were to go wrong with the investment, Edward could sue the Hong Kong company and thereby avoid having to deal with the complicated court system in Vietnam. In addition, Max explained that the structure safeguards the investments, as they only send money onshore to cover the cost of operations. Max added:

> The Hong Kong structure also allows us to take advantage of the dual tax agreements set up in Hong Kong because an offshore PE fund that does not carry out any business in Hong Kong qualifies for profits tax exemption. This also allows us to have set up a multi-currency corporate account, which is very simple these days with internet banking.

Edward said, "I'd like for you to zoom in a bit on the bottom part of the figure that outlines the relation between the SPV in Hong Kong and the portfolio companies in Vietnam. How is that structure actually set up?" Max states:

> Sometimes we make a decision to take on a minority stake in a company with provisions to take over if the firm does not meet the growth targets. If you become a limited partner, we will of course share all of the documents and details with you, but to simplify it for now, there are caps on foreign ownership in certain sectors. In general, it is 49 percent. This means that the local shareholder controls 51 percent of the shares. This is why we set up a two-tier structure. It allows us to do two things. Either we set up a provision of convertible debt for that 2 percent offshore, which gives us majority ownership offshore; or, we set up a structure where both parties sign shares transfer forms offshore, so that the Vietnamese shareholders only control an empty vehicle.

Essentially, what Max was working to convey here is something that was obvious to all of them but took me several meetings to comprehend. They had a strategy set up that would actually give them majority control over a company even though the documentation made it seem like they had a minority stake in the firm onshore. That is because the parent company set up offshore used a convertible debt structure—a form of short-term debt that converts into equity—which would make it very challenging for the local firm to achieve a set of goals within a limited time, so that they would lose their majority stake. This was a legally gray space because it meant that on paper, they had a majority stake in the company offshore while holding a minority stake in that same company onshore.

After walking Edward and Nathan through questions about *why* they should invest in Vietnam and *how* they could do this with a local team who had a great deal of experience, Max and Van moved on to describe some of the investment opportunities that Edward and Nathan might want to think about.

INVESTMENT OPPORTUNITIES

The first thing Van and Max did was work to contextualize the way that investment deals are carried out in Vietnam. Max explained, "The thing to remember about less-developed economies is that families have run these companies for a long time. Family-run conglomerates in places like Vietnam often cover diverse sectors of the economy. We have companies looking for capital injections that fall along a wide spectrum. One company is a family business that specializes only in logistics—they have been in this business since the 1990s and have expanded all across the country. Another family company has a combination of lumber processing plants, real estate investments, and imports in the healthcare sector." The main purpose of this slide, they later added, was to show that they are targeting services that would be highly sought-after by the rapidly growing middle class and new consumer class. These sectors include agriculture, tourism, healthcare, infrastructure and logistics, energy, and real estate. "We are also investing in fintech platforms that are filling in gaps related to local banking with new technologies to help bank the millions of people who operate in a cash-based economy."

Max continued, "Our firm sources deals through our own research team and local staff, who identify leads that come from accountants, law firms, deal brokers, and investment banks."

Edward asked, "How many opportunities do you look at a year, and how long does it take to get into a deal?"

Max replied, "We are constantly filtering deals. Sometimes we might identify a family company and will spend years working with them to get them up to meet our professional standards, and then we will make the investment. I would say that we probably go through 250 to 300 opportunities a year and successfully execute or close a deal on five of them in a given year. Due diligence is one of our biggest challenges, so we spend a great deal of time minimizing these risks by spending from six months to two years with a firm in order to get a full assessment or picture [by] doing background checks on management and evaluating the operations."

The presentation ended there, which was surprising to me because it did not include any information on firms or companies that Max and Van saw as ripe opportunities for investment, but nor did Edward seem to have any questions about what exact kinds of investment opportunities were available to him. Edward thanked both of them and told them that he and his clients were definitely interested in opportunities in the Vietnamese market. He told them both that his team would like to make a visit to Vietnam before making any firm commitments and asked for a tour of some of the deals that Max and Van were currently considering. We (myself, Max and Van) left the meeting together for a casual lunch, where Max and Van gave each other feedback on how they might alter the presentation for the rest of their roadshow over the next two weeks, when they would travel to four more cities.

The point here is that they can raise a great deal of money with very little information because investments in Southeast Asia are hugely speculative. Raising money for this market had much more to do with a history of relationships than with a record of success. The view from up in the air is very different from the view on the ground. The high-level view from the 10th floor of a beautiful Newport Beach office is removed from the grit involved in executing on the deal once the funds make their way through the various special purpose vehicles and onshore into Vietnam's market. Once again, this is about a connection between people. Someone knows someone who knows someone that is executing on the deal. Sometimes these presentations are not enough. Potential investors will want to either travel themselves or send someone to Vietnam or Myanmar for a look-see. Journeys into these new frontiers most often involve making decisions based less on hard data and more off a gut feeling or intuitive sense, after being able to touch and feel the dynamism of this frontier market. In other words, to raise money onshore fund managers must curate an experience that will make investors feel the potential.

RAISING MONEY ONSHORE: HIGHLY CURATED INVESTOR TRIPS TO VIETNAM AND MYANMAR

While fund managers often do roadshows all around the world to raise money, asset managers also host tours in Vietnam for financial advisors in family offices and their investors looking to travel to Vietnam to get a visceral sense of the market. As a result, a new kind of investment tourism has emerged as brokers, fund managers, and local advisors strategize to curate an experience that will persuade investors to expand their webs to this market.

During my time in Vietnam and Myanmar, I was able to interview several local fund managers who described the process of raising capital in Vietnam or Myanmar from investors touring from outside the country to complement the roadshow approach. They frequently entertained regional investors from East/Southeast Asia as well as a variety of investors from different corners of the world such as Russia, Ukraine, Kazakhstan, and of course Europe and the United States. This meant that local fund managers spent a great deal of time trying to match their investors' interests and needs.

All investors were invited to investor conferences which were used to introduce outsiders to the market. However, there were two different strategies local fund managers employed to try to raise money, and they varied with respect to the kind of investor they thought they were dealing with. For bullish investors willing to take more risks, local fund managers took the approach of selling exclusivity and inside access by curating the kind of tour that shows off their connections onshore, arranging experiences that connect offshore investors with key state officials and stakeholders onshore.

Investor Conferences Onshore

While moving between Vietnam, Myanmar, Hong Kong, and Singapore, I attended four different investor conferences. On one such occasion I was invited as a scholar at the University of Chicago interested in foreign investments to a private conference that was hosted in Myanmar in 2016. Invest in Myanmar, an event hosted by Tyler—an Asian American man in his early forties—included a small gathering of about 70 people who, in different capacities, all worked to encourage foreign investment in Myanmar. The various stakeholders included: government officials from Myanmar's ministry of commerce, representatives from the US and German Embassies, country representatives from the World Bank and IMF, country heads for local companies, fund managers and managing directors of various investment funds, bankers, and lawyers, all working in different capacities on FDI (foreign direct investment) in Myanmar. Hand-picked by Tyler himself, participation was by invitation only.

Tyler presented the conference as an opportunity for potential investors to listen to and interact with Myanmar's most promising entrepreneurs as they joined government officials, policymakers, investors, and corporate leaders to discuss Myanmar's development hurdles and opportunities. I was the only academic at the conference, mainly there to learn from the panelists and network with the people in the room. I sat down at one of the tables towards the back of the room where I could have my laptop computer out to take notes. Seated next to me was a man named Jake who appeared to be in his late thirties to early forties, dressed in a perfectly tailored blue suit with cufflinks engraved with his initials, striped socks, and brown shoes. As I vigorously typed away at my computer, trying to document everything the panelists said, Jake passed me a note that read: *Are you a reporter?* I returned the note with: *I am a professor.*

During the break Jake approached me and said, "You know the most important information at these conferences comes from the side conversations that people have during the breaks and not usually from what is said on stage." I later came to understand that the panels were just a formality that helped to get people in the same room. But the real business took place in the breaks, when people networked with one another. Seizing the opportunity, I asked Jake if we could chat after the conference about some of the topics on the panel.

We exchanged business cards—my one university card for his three. His first card was for a local business, of which he was the CEO, in the sanitation supply industry—basically he was in the business of importing luxury toilets, bidets, sinks, and water pipes into Myanmar. The second was from an office in Singapore where he also works as an associate for a fund that was raising capital to invest in Southeast Asia. And the third listed him as an investment strategist for a firm that specializes in real estate. After he finished handing me all of his cards, I jokingly asked him, "Geez, what don't you do?"

He laughed and said, "It's actually very typical in Southeast Asia. Most people have their hands in a lot of different projects."

Later that evening, Jake invited me to have drinks at the bar with him and Masao, a Japanese investor and a conference panelist speaking on the topic of identifying good local partners in Myanmar. We sat down on one of the sofas in the hotel bar, where I learned that Jake was a Burmese national who had been born in Singapore. He'd grown up mostly in Singapore, and had recently returned to seize some of the business opportunities in Myanmar as the country was opening up. Jake's father had been murdered in the 1980s during a time of political unrest and anti-government riots. Following his father's death, Jake's mother had moved the family to Singapore, but because Jake's father had always talked about returning, Jake felt an obligation to carry out his father's dreams.

Upon returning to Myanmar, Jake formed a joint venture with Masao for their sanitation business. Masao handles the purchase of sanitary products from Japan to import, while Jake deals with all issues related to customs, sales, and distribution in Myanmar. Like Jake, Masao has made investments in very diverse sectors of the economy, including used car imports, agriculture, and a factory in a new industrial zone to process food products for export.

Picking up from our earlier conversation, I asked Jake what he meant by all of the "side conversations" at these conferences. Jake went on to tell me that in countries like Myanmar business is murky, and getting access to information is key. Much of what the panelists talk about is macro and purposefully vague because they know that they are speaking to a room filled with different levels of stakeholders. Jake said:

> In many parts of Southeast Asia, the laws are very opaque so that govern-
> ment officials can abuse them. Myanmar is a country known for a history
> of crony capitalism and corruption under a military-controlled regime.
> For a long time, the country's economy was dominated by a small group
> of business tycoons who had good connections with powerful military
> generals . . . but under the new leader, Aung San Suu Kyi, everyone is
> waiting to see if that group will still maintain their dominance or if new
> players will be able to enter the market. The cronies are smart, they are
> rebranding themselves as potential local partners for foreign businesses.
> So, for now, most of the investment that is coming to Myanmar is from
> other emerging markets in Asia. Those people are fine dealing with cor-
> ruption and partners who are *ethically questionable* [his emphasis].

This conversation echoed very similar sentiments that Van and Max described to potential investors on their US roadshow in their attempts to raise money in Vietnam. As I began connecting the dots, parts of my research puzzle started clicking into place. The big black box in these markets is that they have the potential to yield nearly double the returns on investment just on the sheer dynamism of the country's growth, but to unlock that potential, foreigners must find a local partner. The trick onshore is figuring out how to either work with or work around hugely profitable but ethically questionable local firms that are controlled by cronies with deep ties to the military state.

In that conversation, Masao also emphasized the importance of finding a good local partner to help navigate the tricky terrain onshore. He told me that he didn't know many foreigners who were able to operate without a local partner, and that from his perspective you need a local partner because in Myanmar "it is about a personal relationship." In this way, a dominant spider must form a mutually beneficial relationship of trust with subordinate spiders working on other parts of this global capital web.

What Jake sharply pointed out was that the transition to democracy in 2016 did not automatically come with a complete transformation of the political and economic arrangements which allowed crony capitalists to amass enormous profits. Not only were they still in the market, but they were also the most profitable businesses, and as they were undergoing a process of rebranding and professionalizing, new investors would have to decide if their risk appetite included forming joint ventures with individuals who did not have a clean track record. As such, the art of the deal involves figuring out where along the spectrum investors were willing to play in the gray and who they could partner with to manage the complex relations in country. In doing so, they could create layers between themselves and the deal so as to soften the material and reputational risks involved with this kind of investment.

Bullish Investors: Speculative Imaginations of a new Frontier

To project confidence in Vietnam's booming market, some locally based fund managers work very hard to curate a First World experience for the investors who visit the country. In a conversation with Eric, a foreign citizen who runs a local asset management firm in Vietnam, he echoed something I had heard many times from other local fund managers and investors. He told me, "Saigon (HCMC District 1) is no different from New York or Hong Kong. You can get all of the same amenities here that you have there."

To curate this First World experience, locally based fund managers booked their guests into branded five-star hotels. These include the Park Hyatt, Intercontinental Hotel, Sheraton, and the Caravelle Hotel. On these visits they always give their guests interesting facts about the history of Vietnam that begin with the hotels where they are staying. All of this is part of a larger image branding for the country.

The Caravelle Hotel has famously been around since 1959, and for many represents an earlier time in history when the city was economically prosperous and often referred to as "the Pearl of the Orient." The Park Hyatt has a memorial at its entrance commemorating those injured or killed on

Christmas Eve of 1964, when a Viet Cong car bomb exploded near the lobby of the hotel, which was then the site of a US military accommodation. The city also boasts a new hotel called the Reverie Saigon, which is a 39-story building with 89 luxury serviced apartments, office space, and even a helicopter landing pad for VIP guests. In the evening, guests dine in Saigon's most expensive restaurants and bars, allowing them to indulge in both local Vietnamese cuisines and international foods from celebrity chefs in a plush, fine atmosphere akin to any Michelin-rated restaurant. The locally based fund managers and foreign investors often spend time getting to know each other at lounges that serve high-end whiskeys and cocktails on sky decks with spectacular views of the city. From up here one can easily forget the microscopic grime of a less-developed economy.

In an interview with Vincent, an overseas Vietnamese man who had returned to Vietnam in the early 1990s to conduct business before establishing his asset management fund in Vietnam in the early 2000s, he explained to me:

> When we host our investors, it is really important that we show them that Vietnam is not a Third World country. It is growing so fast and you can have everything that you would have in New York or Los Angeles here in Saigon. When they see how much the country has already developed it allows them to *feel* confident in the market [his emphasis].

He went on to describe how he maintained a fleet of company cars—a Mercedes, a Range Rover, and a BMW—with which to escort his guests around the city. Their offices are located on one of the top floors of a high-rise building at the center of the city and include a 360-degree view of the urban landscape. The meeting rooms look and feel like any other upscale international office abroad, with the exception of the modern Vietnamese artwork that hangs in the hallways. I realized how important this First World experience was on one of these tours as I watched a wealth manager take hundreds of photos to document the experience. By juxtaposing images of streets dominated by motorbikes and roads under constant construction, with the luxury inside the hotels and offices, Vincent pointed out to me that it was not hard to see this frontier market as on a fast track to becoming an emerging market. The dynamism reminded him of the early 2000s in Bangkok or Jakarta. This market had so much potential to generate wealth as a new frontier.

As part of the tours, investors also take meetings inside posh office buildings. At these meetings, deal teams pass out pamphlets and one- to two-page summaries of the current investments and recent profits. Investors also get a chance to ask questions. Afterward, someone in the office takes them on a tour to visit potential investment projects. In an interview with Christine, a woman who worked in Joseph's office in the real estate division, she told me that while Joseph sources deals and raises funds, her role is to figure out how to match investors to particular projects and then manage the execution of the investment. She described one of the tours around the city to me like this:

> The most popular question we get from our investors is, "What is the purchasing power of the Vietnamese dong?" For that, it is hard to explain in an office. We have to take them around the city and show them all of the new buildings and luxury condos that are sprawling all over the city. When we drive them around, we say to them, "How do you see that the per capita GDP of 5,000 dollars per year can support a lifestyle like that in Saigon? The normal office meal around our building is 6 dollars, that is the same as Australia six or seven years ago. This is not something we can answer in a statistical way. Everyone can talk about numbers, but you have to see and feel the future development in Vietnam. It is still a cash-based economy; there are no numbers or data that can explain how someone making $5,000 to $20,000 a year can afford to pay for a condo that is $100,000 to $300,000 in full cash, because there are not loans here. When people come here and see it they understand better.

The tours are intended to generate a feeling of optimism for investors who are looking to place bets on the country's rise in a rapidly developing market. But one cannot calculate this bet. Investments here are purely based on a *feeling* of market potential. This is important because of the lack of information or hard data on the Vietnamese market. By showing potential investors this interesting puzzle—an average citizen who can afford to support a middle-class lifestyle on an extremely low salary—they begin to stoke that gut feeling required to take the plunge into this opaque market. While global firms like Coldwell Banker (CBRE) help to fill some market gaps with data on real estate transactions, their data has a lot of holes in it because there is no public record that documents the sale price of the transactions. Additionally, similarly to more-advanced emerging markets like in China or India, oftentimes what is reported does not account for the cash that transferred hands to avoid taxes. In this way, this is still a market where buyers and sellers must bargain with each other at nearly every level.

At the same time, Christine worked hard to curate the kind of experience that projects confidence as these investors speculate about the potential returns on investment. She says, "When I first started work in the office we worked on much smaller projects, and in a fund we might have five to eight properties bundled into one. In that bundle some assets were really good, and we made huge profits, and others had a lot of complications dealing with the government or waiting for road construction to develop. Nowadays most investors want to go into a specific project. When you are trying to put together anything above $15 million it's a lot more work building trust and making them feel confident about this market."

Key to selling Vietnam's macro growth story is convincing investors that this market simultaneously has lower barriers to entry and higher rates of return; investors can get in with less capital and make more money in Vietnam than in developed economies. Robin, a banker for a large international bank that provides deal advisory services for new clients looking to enter the market, explained to me:

> I always tell investors, look in mature markets: the barrier to entry is capital. You need $100 million plus to even play in those markets, and everyone knows that the return on investment is 5 or 6 percent at best. Here in Vietnam, you only need 15 to 50 million dollars and you can see returns over double that. There are numbers, yes. As a banker we know the numbers very well. But this is not about statistics because the data cannot explain this kind of growth in a cash-based economy. I will take them to visit small real estate development projects, and they are shocked when they find out that the building is paid off even before construction is complete. People are paying double for their cars here because of the tax, and it's all cash. When we outsource some of our due diligence checks to a firm in Singapore, they come back to report money from a family business that's sitting in cash because they don't trust the banks. And why should they? These people have lived through so many bank runs.

Local fund managers engage in a performance meant to invoke this kind of visceral growth experience. They do this by driving through the streets of Saigon, visiting potential investment projects, meeting with fund managers, brokers, advisors, accountants, and family-run businesses in an effort to sell the same macro story of Vietnam's growth and shape this sense of investor confidence in the market. The First World experience in a developing economy creates a "feeling"—a word that came up over and over again in my conversations—that is provoked by the projected confidence in the market.

When I asked fund managers who approach investors with the First World experience how they manage investors' questions about high-profile cases of theft, fraud, or loss in the market, John, the CEO of a small fund, said to me:

There's a famous saying that investors have a short memory. If you lose money five to seven years ago and propose a deal now, they will have forgotten what happened. At the end of the day, the money market is so big they can invest anywhere. The point in time you make a decision, the people on the board probably won't be there in the next five to seven years, and they will have a different risk appetite.

Tony, a fund manager from a different fund, echoed similar sentiments:

People forget about market losses very quickly. No one is paying attention to what happened 3 or 4 years ago, let alone 5 to 7 or even 10 years ago. Ten years ago were the cowboy days of Vietnam. Money was pouring in everywhere and there was a lot of theft; it was like the Wild, Wild West. But investors have gotten smarter, firms professionalized, and we also raise money from new investors to the market. Nowadays Koreans are the fundamental players in Vietnam because they are willing to play the "Vietnamese game" that comes down to informality and grayness.

In several follow-up conversations, Tony kept insisting that I remember to pay attention to all of the money captured in these "gray" spaces. He said:

It's what they can't teach you in an MBA program: how to capitalize on the fuzziness and legal but sometimes morally gray areas. That's why Koreans like to drink together too much. It's all part of the trust building and bonding experience.

The art of the deal in spiderweb capitalism involves a strategy of raising money off of a sense of gut, intuition, and an overall feeling that this is the new frontier to reap significant returns. What makes this risky is that investors cannot calculate the risk in a rational way. To sell the market, subordinate spiders must convince dominant spiders to create new strands that will connect these capital webs. The way that they do this is by curating an experience that focuses on the country's dynamism and the political capital of the fund managers, and that generates investor optimism in this new frontier. Once investors express an interest, the next step involves matchmaking them to available deals or the sellers in the market.

Sourcing the Deal: Finding the New Frontier

Sourcing a deal involves finding a key site, identifying good local partners, and building a relationship whereby both buyers and sellers feel confident in their working relationship with one another.

My conversation with Jake and Masao at the Invest in Myanmar Conference led to an invitation to accompany Jake on a trip he had planned for a delegation of investors from Thailand. They were interested in taking a closer look at beachfront real estate opportunities that had not yet been developed because they had a long history of being military controlled zones or were once high-conflict areas.

Jake invited me to join the group, but dodged all of my questions related to the details for the trip. All he was willing to share with me was that the group was staying at the Shangri-La Hotel downtown and that a van would be picking them up to escort them to the airport. If I wanted to tag along, I would need to send him a photo of my passport so that he could arrange my travel, and show up to meet them at the hotel at 7:00 a.m.

For the next three days, I kept going back and forth about whether or not I should go on the trip at all, given how vague he'd been about the details. Although I did not feel unsafe around Jake, I worried about traveling to an unknown place as the only woman with a group of businessmen who were complete strangers to me. In this context, for me as an American seeking straight answers, the lack of details surrounding the trip was unnerving. In the ensuing three days Jake and I shared a few text messages in which he told me to pack towels and toilet paper, and to be aware that the conditions would be rough.

Nervously, I showed up to the hotel at 7:00 a.m. as instructed with a small duffel bag. As I waited, it occurred to me that I had never asked about how our sleeping arrangements would be set up, and I silently prayed that I would at least have separate sleeping quarters from the men on the trip—rookie mistake. That fifteen minutes in the hotel lobby stretched for an eternity as I considered my personal safety and ran through all of the worst-case scenarios in my head.

Some of my nerves were calmed when Jake walked into the hotel, dressed casually in jeans, and greeted me. He then walked me to the dining area, where he introduced me to Gamon and Prasong Chai, two brothers who ran a family business, and Harris, their director of strategic investments.

When Jake introduced us, he said, "Kimberly, meet the Chai brothers, two of Thailand's youngest up-and-coming property tycoons. Gamon is only thirty-eight and Prasong is forty-one." Jake then teased Gamon by asking me, "Did you know that Gamon was written up in a local magazine as one of Thailand's most eligible bachelors?" We all laughed. Jake then introduced Harris to me as an ex–Swiss banker who is now in Thailand working with the Chai brothers as their Chief Investment Officer. Jake introduced me to the group as a professor from the University of Chicago who was studying people who manage foreign investments. After I obtained permission to follow and observe them, the five of us piled into a van headed for the airport.

At the ticketing area, before we could even get in line, we were immediately greeted by an airline attendant who handed us our plane tickets. These were in paper form with our names and seat numbers handwritten on top. Here I learned we were headed to Dawei. We bypassed the security lines and were escorted straight to the gate, where a private car awaited us to transport us to the aircraft. The plane was an older commercial aircraft. We sat toward the front while the other passengers boarded. Jake sat with the Chai brothers in one row while I sat with Harris in the row across from them.

On the airplane Jake informed the group that we would be looking at some prime real estate located in a town slated to become one of the new special economic zones and a focal point with direct infrastructure links to Thailand. The plan was to visit the town's power plants, small port, and sites to build commercial and residential real estate. We would also meet the local group that owns and controls this land.

During the plane ride, I tried to initiate small talk with Harris by asking him what I thought were simple icebreaker questions: "So what made you come to Thailand? And what has been one of the greatest challenges moving from Switzerland to Southeast Asia?" Harris told me:

> You know, I think there's more fun in getting big than being big. . . . I made it as a Swiss banker, but I was locked away looking at numbers on a computer screen. From there you can't really see the engine that drives markets. Asia is hot right now, this is where there is a lot of money. The Chai brothers are under forty, and they have offices in Hong Kong, Singapore, Bangkok, Ho Chi Minh, and Yangon. Those are all really exciting cities. The biggest challenge is having to learn that Southeast Asia is just different from the West. Here, you have to deal a lot with people because it's a market controlled by family groups. It is very much a frontier.

> I do all kinds of due diligence work for the investments that I advise the Chai brothers on, everything from financial diligence, tax diligence, legal diligence, commercial diligence, and due diligence on *people* (his

emphasis). You have to adapt fast to your environment. You quickly learn that Asia is a different game. Of course, there are a few white horses who deal in clean money, but everyone is chasing them, so the deal is always in their favor and not good for us. So, then I have to weigh the risks of dealing with dirty money and a lot of times, dirty people.

This rogue trip to Myanmar's outer frontier gave investors a sense that they could go to a place that no one had access to. These were remote areas of pristine beachfront land where investors, together with their local partners, could build out prime real estate to cater to the needs of a growing local elite who now have the funds to buy these developments. There was a lot of local money and potential just waiting to be unlocked by those with outside money and local expertise to make it happen. The Chai brothers were comfortable navigating an Asian market with murky due diligence practices.

When the plane landed, we got our bags and were greeted by an entire caravan of cars. There were four different cars: a black unmarked car that looked like a government car, two Jeeps, and a Toyota 4Runner. All of our bags went into one car. Jake and the Chai brothers got into the 4Runner, and Harris and I were assigned to one of the Jeeps. We drove for about thirty minutes, then stopped and had lunch at a local restaurant. The restaurant seemed prepared for our arrival, because all of the dishes were set on the table and covered with plastic covering. We ate a quick lunch and then we made our way back into the cars for a two-hour drive, along barren dirt roads running through a rural community of modest homes, to our first site.

When I inquired about what part of the country we would end up in at the end of the two-hour ride, Jake told me that it was a region not yet on Google Maps, so there was no real address. Formerly a military-controlled zone, the area is transitioning from public land to private. The only information that he was willing to share was that the region is a key corridor that will soon connect Myanmar to Thailand. As the caravan charged forward, it occurred to me that none of the people in our entourage cared to know how they would get to this particular site because they were accustomed to being escorted to uncharted, off-the-grid locations.

This trip was part of a strategy to make the investors feel as though they were first to visit this new frontier. The Thai group had developers and the funds; what they needed was the right spot to place their bets. Like everything else, this was cultivated by a *feeling* of connection to the land, the place, and the people escorting them. For this trip in particular, that connection emerged in a way that felt organic to the Thai investors because of the land's close proximity to Thailand, and the potential of the area to attract tourists from Thailand and other parts of Southeast Asia. The market potential felt promising to them. Getting them out of the car, having them breathe in the fresh air and walk the untouched lands was all part of this effort, meant to generate an emotional connection to this new place.

On this tour, the Chai brothers expressed an interest not only in building luxury hotels and residences but also investing in key infrastructure. Among their priorities were constructing a hydropower plant, building out a road, and hiring a local team to provide them with a summary report on the local community living there, so that they could invest in schools and communities for new employees.

Over the course of two years, the Chai brothers would make three more visits to the location before assembling a team on the ground to execute the project. They planned to front-run the investment by breaking ground and starting construction without the local licenses to build and operate, hoping they would secure those during the process of construction. However, because they had set up a contract offshore in Thailand, which outlined the terms of their agreement, investors felt comfortable with their local partners' strategy of front-running. Curiously, their visits to the sites were always curated through similar tours. They never traveled to the sites on their own and did not want to be bothered with the local travel logistics. So their view was still through the tinted windows of a caravan of cars, always looking at the big picture, without an ability to connect with the lives of the locals.

The experience of getting on a plane and traveling to a remote region of the world that is only accessible to people with insider knowledge or access is enticing to investors, like the Chai brothers, looking for new frontiers. In a country closed off to the rest of the world for many years, the process of sourcing a deal feels "exhilarating," as Harris describes it, because you can physically touch and feel another part of the web that has so much market potential. This connection to the place in a very localized kind of way is precisely how new frontiers become part of a broader capital web.

Sealing the Deal

Once an investor is sold on the general market and demonstrates a keen interest in investing in Vietnam or Myanmar, the fund managers—often alone, but sometimes in coordination with the offshore investor—will work to close the deal. At this stage of the process, the relationship between buyers (investors/dominant spiders) and sellers (local family businesses) often requires a great deal of relational work on the part of a middle person (fund managers/local firms/subordinate spiders) to build personal relationships of trust not only with each other, but also with political elites crucial for sealing the deals.[4]

For the dominant spider, the risks of fraud, theft, or an unpredictable regulatory structure require the help and trust of local partners to seal a deal. From the local seller's perspective, there are often potential investors, commonly referred to as "tire kickers," who spend a lot of time going from fund manager to fund manager to get information without ever making an investment, thereby wasting a great deal of the time and resources of local fund managers and advisors.

As a result, dominant spiders must rely on the local professionals to help build out the part of the web that covers frontier markets. In this context, subordinate spiders do all the work of playing in the gray by building trust with those who wield state power, and this is done through male bonding rituals. There are two primary ways investors work to seal the deal: (1) by establishing personal relationships of trust or assurance through homoerotic bonding experiences with both local partners and government officials, or (2) by staying away from deals involving heavy state licensing and refusing to "pay to play."

Relational Capitalism and Homoerotic Bonding

Roadshows, investor conferences, and informal gatherings were places where the topic of insider access through key government relations emerged. While foreign investors knew that ties to political officials were key to sealing any deal, it took some probing on my part to dig deeper into *how* they established these relationships. It was through homoerotic bonding rituals. This is probably the most crucial area where dominant spiders syndicate the risk of playing in the gray out to smaller spiders in the web.

In an interview, Nhan, a local developer, bluntly stated, "Everything is about relationships and *who* you know in this country. . . . Here you have to pay to play (*ăn bánh trả tiền*). . . . You have to pay a bribe to get the land . . . then pay 'taxes' to keep it every time they come for an 'inspection.'" Daniel, an overseas Vietnamese man who oversees investments across different sectors of the economy, including power, construction, real estate, transformation and logistics—all of which involve high levels of government engagement—echoed similar sentiments, saying, "[H]ere the first thing you learn is that you need people who have [government] connections. . . . This is their playground." Both Nhan and Daniel were referring to the economic and political structures that enable massive capital accumulation. Nhan's and Daniel's investors relied heavily on the ability of their local partners in charge on the ground to establish close relationships with the necessary public officials.

In the interviews, I often probed by asking *how* they developed those relationships. Minh, an attorney and the right-hand man for the chairman of a property group, laughed and said, "A lot of beautiful women and whiskey!" What Minh alluded to is the practice of homosocial bonding rituals that involve using women as props to help lubricate business deals by brokering relationships of trust between the power elite.[5] But not just any men—it was about brokering relations between men with political power and those with economic capital. In *The Power Elite,* C. Wright Mills argues that "to understand the very rich we must first understand the economic and political structure . . . in which they become the very rich . . . [as] the state guaranteed the right of private property."[6] Women are a key component in these homosocial bonding rituals in what Eve Sedgwick refers to as an erotic triangle.[7] The presence of a woman mediates tensions between two men by serving as a common object of desire.[8] The woman is the glue that helps to seal the patriarchal homosocial bonds through intimacy.[9]

Homoerotic bonding fell along a spectrum, from mere drinking and dancing around models or escorts all the way to private sex or orgy parties in someone's home. At one end, men relied on bars and clubs to provide them with the space to entertain state bureaucrats. This featured late nights out at multiple bars that included a local version of Wall Street's "models and bottles," except that here it was not just about sharing inside information between two private parties; it was about gaining access to information from the state. I spent several late nights with these men, and observed many of these intimate interactions. Women spent a great deal of time working to break the ice among a group of men who hardly spoke with each other over a variety of drinking games, dance shows, and other forms of entertainment.

Roughly one-half of the men I spoke with in frontier markets described the even deeper ways that they relied on women to help lubricate business deals that, over the course of the evening, eventually led to someone's private home, where they suddenly found themselves in orgy parties where sex with the women was not clearly consensual. While only a small number were explicit about what happened in these parties, others would nod in acknowledgment when I pressed them, or they would allude to it after quickly trying to move on. In one example, Daniel spoke explicitly about male homosocial bonding experiences, particularly among state bureaucrats, private entrepreneurs, and foreign investors, which required women's bodies, stating:

> In Asia it is mostly dog-eat-dog. It's so fucked up. Last night we started with dinner, and then we went to four different bars and clubs before ending up at a private house party around three a.m. It turned into this orgy party. I am talking to, like this [making erotic gestures to a person sitting next to him] . . . and then back it's like, shit, [we are] banging three or four girls, having an orgy, and I have to keep a straight face.

The interview with Daniel turned into what felt like a therapy session the Sunday morning right after he was involved in this very intimate party. After describing the events, he began reflecting on how sexual encounters are framed differently in his experience in Asia compared to the United States. Daniel talked about the orgy parties with a sense of shame and even disgust in my presence, saying, "It is so dirty." He also compared the sexual relations with those with women in the West by telling me that at least in the United States there was a language around rape and consent, whereas in Vietnam there were no words to describe nonconsensual sex. He said, "Sometimes those girls are so drunk, you know . . . and we are just having sex with them . . . and the next morning, no one really says anything, but it's like, you know . . . it's dirty." This is the kind of dirty work that dominant spiders have the privilege of opting out of, because they can rely on their local partners to do the work of playing in the gray on their behalf to seal these deals.

While Daniel surely participated in the party the night before, the interview was raw; it felt like he was still processing what he was saying out loud to me. Among this group of men, many of them described how the heavy drinking, drugs, and late nights out wore on their bodies, but it seemed like a necessary evil that came to represent what Daniel's partner, Coy, referred to as "the ultimate family sacrifice." As Coy remarked:

> I don't know about you, but for me, I have an appreciation for what they go through. The girls, the guys, the government . . . they sacrifice their family. At the end of the day, it doesn't seem worth it, when you get to the deep end. They get sick [their livers give way from all the drinking], but they're all like, I made a million dollars for my family. . . . It's the ultimate sacrifice for your family. I'm willing to die, go to jail for my family.

Both men made it clear that this is just par for the course when it comes to doing business in Vietnam and building relationships with state bureaucrats.

When investors want access to prime real estate or to be able to complete a project and get the correct approvals through, this kind of entertaining is required to expedite excruciatingly slow processes. These relationships matter not only for raising capital, but also for executing on a deal and turning a profit.

Those who spoke bluntly about these intimate experiences shared among a group of men were also clear that they engaged in these activities in service of a much larger end goal: that of risk assurance by forming a relationship of mutual hostage. While trust was one dimension of these bonding experiences, no one fully trusted the people that they were around, and thus they worked to get insurance. As my interview with Daniel unfolded, for example, he began to talk more explicitly about this erotic triangle. In describing a profit-sharing scheme where investors pay bribes to state bureaucrats, he said:

> We have to literally get in bed [with each] other. If one goes down, we both go down.

> They [state bureaucrats] will say, "I thought we were brothers," and these guys want to go drinking, party, girls, you name it, A to Z, but at the end of the day, it's the trust. . . . Even at the highest levels, there is a certain level of mistrust, that's how it works. Everything you are doing is reading between the lines; drinking and all of that, it is the surface, but underneath you have to read people.

When I asked Daniel to reflect on the role that women played for government officials, he said, "It's simple . . . mutual hostage." He then told me a story that had been recently publicized in the media. While I cannot confirm whether his account of that story is true, his interpretation revealed what he saw as potentially threatening. As the story goes, a group of his friends were rising in the ranks of the property world. They got access to prime areas and, in exchange, they developed a profit-sharing scheme with a number of government officials. Over time, as the investment group grew, there were disagreements between themselves and the state officials over the profit-sharing ratios. State officials wanted more, while the investment group felt that they did not have enough to cover costs.

After a series of unsuccessful attempts at shaking down the investment group for more money, someone released graphic photos of one of the investment executives at an orgy party all over the internet, thereby publicly shaming him and his family. Since the state controls the media, Daniel interpreted the fact that no one censored those images as a state-sanctioned reputation smear.[10] The images stirred a media frenzy, as the general public had a debate about sex and business relations. For Daniel, that sequence of events served as a warning that if he did not put in a lot of effort to manage his own relations, photos of himself at those parties could be released as well. When I asked him if state officials worried about whether their photos were also at risk of being released, he told me that the photos assured mutual destruction on both sides and were used only as a last resort when one of the two parties felt that it was not being met somewhere in the middle.

Relational capitalism in this context depends on homoerotic bonding rituals. In the absence of clear rule of law or faith in the state to enforce contracts, personal relationships are crucial to sealing a deal. These personal relationships involve highly intimate encounters that rely on the gendered labors of women. However, subordinate spiders in this web shoulder much of the burden involved with these bonding rituals, while dominant spiders stay free of the moral issues of these practices *and* the legal liability/mutual hostage that arises from them. But not all investors were comfortable with this route. Bearish investors who refused to seal the deal with these norms approached the market with an entirely different set of strategies.

BEARISH INVESTORS: STEERING AWAY FROM STATE-BACKED DEALS

While the majority of my interviewees expressed a sentiment that the "sweetheart deals" all went to those who were willing to "pay to play," a small group of people refused to play by those local styles of deal brokering. Instead, they worked hard to steer away from sectors of the economy that involved heavy government ties and tried to establish alternative methods of bonding that did not involve heavy drinking, sex, or orgy parties. Rather than using tactics of sabotage and mutual hostage, this group of people employed strategies of coordination to set up cleaner deals onshore.

These investments were often concentrated in the service sector, which included retail, trade, manufacturing, transportation, information, the arts, and recreation. To appeal to a more careful group of investors, these fund managers adopted different strategies of cultural matching.[11]

In striking a tone of caution, they referenced highly publicized stories of fraud and theft in the market to incite fear in new investors and steer them away from shady competitors. In contrast to those who curated a First World experience in these frontier markets to pull in bullish investors, these managers worked to provide potential investors with a unique Vietnamese experience in country. Trust building for this group did not involve homo-erotic bonding rituals, but instead appealed to a different moral compass, taking investors to visit schools and orphanages while talking about their human capital investments in the country. This opened up discussions about philanthropy, charity, and impact investing. Together, these strategies appeal to a very different kind of investor looking to enter this market by partnering with local managers who set moral limits on how far they are willing to play in the gray.

Fund managers who adopt a more prudent approach worked to appeal to investors wary of financial loss or theft. Richard, the CEO of EMIA Capital, described their process of sealing the deal:

> It's about matching the right opportunities to the right investors or limited partners. Investors are a lot smarter now and they are looking for honest partners. A lot of the guys who came to Vietnam in the early days, like 2006, did not survive, and they had to shut down whole divisions because of theft and fraud. Let's not delude ourselves, you need relationships in America too, but relationships matter a lot, not just in Vietnam but in Asia in general. . . . We try to avoid deals that have a dependency on the government. . . . In general, anything involving government revolves around their incentives. . . . In general, my rule is that you should not *pay to play* (emphasis in his intonation). If the only way to do a deal is by paying, then you shouldn't do it. I think there are the costs of doing business like small licensing things, but you should never pay to play. These days, most of it comes down to *my reputation and how much skin I have in the game* [heavy emphasis in his intonation]. A lot of my own money is tied up in here. If you asked me ten years ago if I'd be here doing this I would have laughed, but, well, here I am. But the cowboy days of 2006 are over in Vietnam now. If they lose money, I also lose money. And I'm here to keep growing. If I steal from my limited partners, I may raise the first fund, but there will not be a second or third round of fund-raising. I am here for the long game, not the short game.

Unlike other fund managers—who market themselves to investors by talking about the exclusive access they have to the most profitable projects through their close government connections—Richard avoided many of those sectors and operated with a strict policy that he was not willing to pay to play.

When potential investors arrive in Vietnam, EMIA often recommends that investors stay in some of the unique local boutique hotels. The boutique hotels are brand-new serviced apartments, which come equipped with a full kitchen, washer and dryer, along with a health and wellness center that includes personalized yoga, meditation, and spa services. These hotels cost USD$70–$100 a night, a fraction of the cost of the branded luxury hotels. Neither Richard nor the firm owns a suite of luxury cars to chauffer themselves or investors around in. Instead, he told me that he prefers to take taxis everywhere. Richard explained:

> I was having this funny conversation with some of our investors who are billionaires—they drive themselves around. Of course, in Asia everyone has drivers, maids, nannies, and all the accoutrements. I was doing a deal with one of our LPs [limited partners] and I was running around carrying my backpack, wearing a suit because we were meeting government people and I took a taxi. One of the government people asked, "If you're the boss why are you running around with a backpack and taxi?" and I said, "Because it's more efficient." No one gives a shit about your fancy watch, your tie, or how much alcohol you can stupidly drink. It's about having the best product. . . .

In conversations with Richard's investment partners, they told me that Richard's approach has given him a reputation in Vietnam for being frugal, but that benefits him on two fronts. The investors he's trying to court feel that he is being prudent with the funds they entrust to him, while the local investee companies trust that he would be a competent board member and financial advisor.

Additionally, rather than treating investors to the fine dining experiences in the city, he takes them to local boutique-like restaurants that serve Vietnamese food. He assures them that they are not eating on the street and that the places are still very clean, but this offers the visitor a uniquely Vietnamese experience. In one open-air restaurant, visitors can watch local chefs preparing a large part of the meal within the open kitchen layout. Madeline, a British citizen who spent 20 years living and working in Hong Kong's private equity sector, and is one if Richard's limited partners, told me:

> There is a lot of rubbish you have to sort through in these markets. It is like finding a diamond in the rough. But every experience in the country with Richard feels uniquely Vietnamese, like you have a deeper understanding of the context you are investing in and a full picture of the process rather than just one narrow slice [of a project] when you're working in developed economies. He is the real deal because a lot of his own

money is invested here . . . and he's just someone with a strong sense of family values. His daughters are precious and his wife is just lovely. Those are the kinds of people to work with.

What Madeline felt was a sense of connection not only to Vietnam, but also to Richard, because he had made a great deal of money with a company he helped to found and later sold. Richard is not known as someone who circuits the nightlife scene, but instead talks a great deal about his wife and daughters with the investors he courts.

EMI's approach is also unique in that they target female-owned or -run businesses to invest in because they feel that is a large and untapped market that other investors overlook. Richard said:

I am not a smoker and bars don't do it for me. I have nothing against beer or whiskey, but I am more of a wine person, and I think a lot of the people that we work with are women. This is a very matriarchal society, and some of the best run businesses here are owned and oper-ated by women. When potential investors come to visit, I always tell them, "There is very reasonable, very smart capital in Asia. Asia is still dominated by families in the public sectors. Seventy five percent of our firm is women and about 35 to 40 percent of the companies we invest in are women run. I think that women are very reliable here in Vietnam, and that's a fact. They are more reliable than men in many ways. I also think it is kind of stupid if you alienate half the population, mathemati-cally speaking." I get along well with women not because of gender but because of the things that we share in common, and when I take investors to visit their companies, they are always impressed by how well-run and organized everything is. At the end of the day, if you want to put money in the market and you want to close gaps related to emerging markets, this is the way to go. It's frugal and careful and will generate slow, steady, and honest returns. When you deal with men you have to deal with their drinking, gambling, mistress drama, which all comes with mixing per-sonal and business expenditures on their books.

The approach of targeting female business owners seems very novel in an industry that has long been dominated by men. The gendered relations here are significant in cross-border transactions because female business owners make foreign investors "feel" that they can trust them more. At first, when Richard described the companies headed by women that he invests in with words like "organized," "careful," "frugal," and "honest," it led me to wonder if in fact investors thought that female business owners might be easier to control compared with male business partners. But this was far from the case. Instead, potential investors who met with these women held them up as incredibly smart and savvy. I listened to Steve, a potential investor for Connecticut, say to Cathy, one of Richard's investment team members:

> I was very impressed with Ms. Chi today. She turned the tables on us and really asked us tough questions about the investment terms and what our "add value" is. It makes me really respect her because you can see how invested she is in the business. She is not someone who will just take the capital injection and then kick her feet up. She will push to grow the business because it's her pride as a businesswoman. She seems like a straight shooter—no nonsense, no games, no time for BS, including from us.

Ms. Chi was the chairwoman of a large retail company that had brought several brands to Vietnam which would appeal to a growing middle-class population. She had an exclusive license for multiple franchises in Vietnam. Steve's impression of Ms. Chi was multilayered. In the process of investors (buyers) partnering with investment opportunities (sellers), Steve learned that simply having capital was not enough. Mrs. Chi wanted them to outline what strategic contributions they would make to help her grow the company if they took a board seat, and flipped the tables on them by asking them to come back with a proposal or vision for growth. Steve also told me that in the meeting with her she bluntly told them that she was wary of private equity investors who came to the table with unrealistic goals which, over time, would give them more control over the company than her as the current chairwoman.

I asked Steve to introduce me to Ms. Chi so that I could interview her separately. When she sat down, she greeted me with a warm smile. I was taken aback by how kind and gracious she was, because I was so used to dealing with men whose egos I always had to work around. I told her about my book project and asked her to briefly tell me a little bit about how she got into the fashion business. When I asked her what she thought of having Steve and Richard as potential partners, she said to me:

> I like Richard a lot. I am part of a group of friends, we are all female business owners. We are like a club that meets once a month for brunch to share business tips or go to each other for advice. Some are chairwomen of small businesses and some are big, but we are all in different

businesses, so we don't compete. He has partnered with one of the women in the group, and [she] said that he just works very well with women. He is about the business and the work. and when you ask to go line by line on the term sheet of a deal, he is happy to spend the time doing that without being condescending.

When I asked Ms. Chi how she carried out her business in a world where men were doing backdoor deals over orgy parties. She quickly pushed back, stating, "If you have a good business, people will come find you and want to invest."

Importantly, her bluntness garnered a sense of respect in the partnership that she would eventually form after a year of back-and-forth with Richard and Steve, because from the get-go, as Ms. Chi made very clear, she was not looking to be controlled by an investor who had absolutely no understanding of the business operations. This actually garnered more respect from Steve, as he said to me. "The best deals don't need your money. So the best companies in the world will always be able to raise money."

———

The art of the deal outlines three processes most critical to the expansion of capital webs: raising capital, sourcing deals, and sealing attractive deals. Each one of these stages involves different people who are ultimately responsible for connecting the dominant spider's money to deals in frontier markets. UHNWIs syndicate out the moral, reputational, and criminal risks of playing in the gray to a group of highly compensated financial professionals who work in coordination to integrate these capital webs. Subordinate spiders traveling around the world on roadshows sell Vietnam and Myanmar as sites with great promise, and their deal team as one with access to key government ties and the ability to execute on deals. The work of raising money involves a kind of whiplash travel on roadshows to pitch deals all around the world. In addition, asset managers put together teams responsible for hosting investor conferences and highly curated tours onshore to generate market excitement.

However, it is not enough to generate a general interest in the market. The art of the deal also involves careful coordination and matchmaking to source the most lucrative deals that are not open to the general public. Sweetheart deals, as insiders call them, often involve access to key investment projects controlled by state-owned enterprises or former cronies. As such, the decision to enter this market is not usually based on rational calculations of risk or potential returns. Instead, most of the decision making revolves around a gut feeling of the market potential as well as the ability to form important relationships with local interlocutors who help to source out the best investment opportunities. Subordinate spiders have a great deal of agency in building out their part of the web as they entice/lure UHNWIs to remote corners of the world by making dominant spiders feel like they are literally touching a new frontier, where they can turn dirt into gold.

While the matchmaking work of putting the right buyers and sellers into conversation with one another is important, perhaps the most important aspect of the art of the deal is actually sealing a deal. This work is the trickiest, as it involves coordination with political stakeholders in this market who also want a piece of the pie. On one extreme end of playing in the gray, local asset managers and fund managers assume the greatest risk, playing in the gray through homosocial bonding experiences that require heavy drinking, sex, and orgy parties to establish relationships of assurance and mutual hostage. When a deal takes a wrong turn, the dominant spider loses money while those carrying out the work on the ground stand to lose not only money but also their reputation, possibly incurring criminal consequences along the way. Those who play closer to the white of the gray instead adopt a strategy of refusing the pay to play, but that comes with the consequence of not getting inside access to sweetheart deals and having to create new markets that did not exist.

This chapter highlights the importance of looking at global capitalism as a webbed market rather than through binaries of developed and undeveloped economies. Economic models suggest that UHNWIs will not invest their money in places with large institutional voids, and yet here is a market where money is absolutely flooding into Vietnam and Myanmar. This is because spiderweb capitalism is not about simple flows between banks, but rather relies on webs of relationships, mediated through carefully curated trips and sales pitches by subordinate spiders, which give dominant spiders the gut feeling that they need to expand their capital webs into virgin territory. Once the capital of the dominant spider is injected as the result of a gut feeling, the final deals themselves are mediated even further through relationships of coordination and mutual hostage, which create a version of assurance "in the gray" where legal guarantees are lacking. This model allows for investment in areas with unclear or weak regulatory regimes, and accounts for the rapid movement of capital into frontier markets with large institutional voids.

By zooming in on the different types of people working on different parts of a deal cycle all around the world, it becomes clear how sabotage, coordination, and relational capitalism are different strategies employed based on the cultural fit between offshore investors looking to profit through insider access to new markets and their professional managers, onshore fund managers, and local businesses that need capital. But raising money and finding the right deal to invest that money in are just the beginning of a long-term partnership. What happens to these deals once they are all set up?

3

Varieties of Corruption and Bribery

What happens after investors decide to place bets on frontier markets? How do they and their partners finesse a context "in which corrupt practices are not only ubiquitous but more or less institutionalized as 'unwritten' rules of the game?"[1] Under what circumstances are foreign investors able to steer clear of corruption, and when do they cave under the pressure to pay to play? How do U/HNWIs pursue different strategies to obfuscate disreputable ties, and what are the advantages and disadvantages of each approach?

Investors who specialize in gray markets understand that they are tiptoe- ing up to the limits of the law. Yet much of the work on corruption focuses primarily on the motivations of public officials who abuse their position of power for private gain, and fails to consider how private actors carry out different kinds of bribes.[2] Few studies on corruption look at "both sides" of a corrupt act.[3] In fact, while there are numerous theories that account for the varieties of corruption, the only words to describe the person carrying out the act are bribers or legal co-conspirators. The scope of existing work does not account for the different kinds of people on the other side of the bargain and the varied strategies that they utilize to finesse corrupt markets.

This chapter looks closely at how private actors—in this case both firms and individuals—carry out bribes and the varied ways that they cover over their use of illegal or shady contacts to streamline inefficient bureaucra- cies or crack open doors that would otherwise be closed to them. In some cases, entrepreneurs and foreign investors carry out bribes directly, while in others they rely on third-party intermediaries commonly known as "fixers" to handle this business for them. Lastly, I illustrate how markets without clear rules of law leave investors vulnerable to fraud and theft—a risk many accept as part of the cost of doing business in these markets. The social webs of bribery include greasers, gift-givers, brokers, fixers, and thieves.

With respect to the intersection between legal and illegal activity, investors articulate the practice of "playing in the gray" along a continuum as they opt to be (1) *anti-corrupters* who steer clear of corruption, run very strict, clean operations, and accept that they will therefore grow more slowly than competitors; (2) *greasers* who agree to make small "facilitation payments" for licensing and permits; (3) *bribers* who engage in graft through multiple obfuscation strategies—gift-giving, bundling, and brokerage—to facilitate greater investment outcomes; or (4) *thieves* who work in coordination with public officials to engage in theft, principal-agent issues (competing priorities between agent and owner), money laundering, and embezzlement.

The vast majority of dominant spiders maintain that they are anti-corrupters or are comfortable as greasers. However, a closer look reveals that they adopt multiple approaches that involve syndicating that risk by generously compensating other professionals—often referred to as agents or fixers who act on behalf of a principal—to carry out the work of bribery on their behalf. One consequence of the reliance on sub-spiders to carry out these practices is that it leaves room for outright theft and principal-agent problems. In all these relationships, it is important to note that the illicit activity plays a critical role in facilitating investments in licit parts of the economy also, thereby illustrating how the boundaries between legal and illegal activities intersect in complex ways.

Anti-Corrupters: Steering Clear of Corruption

In every interview I conducted, corruption was a topic that occupied the mind of each investor, fund manager, accountant, or lawyer. The question of how to navigate government relations in a context of widespread corruption was one that people spent hours talking with each other about over drinks, meals, and even in first-time meetings. What makes frontier markets qualitatively different from developed markets is that investors from all around the world are looking to capitalize on them. And as a result, they come to the market with different ideals and strategies for navigating the complex reality on the ground. For most, steering completely clear of corruption was an ideal that was virtually impossible in practice. Nonetheless, among all of my interviewees, less then 10 percent spoke about how they worked diligently to steer clear of corruption. By far the minority, this ethically bound group spoke most about the great costs that came with refusing to pay to play.

Those who refused to follow the local expectations described how they often had to work on projects that were less attractive to others, drawing far less competition, while also having to invest larger sums of money, which resulted in slower returns on investment. In fact, those who spoke of being successful at this strategy were people whose investments in the country spanned fifteen to twenty years, a far cry from the typical seven-year exit strategy employed by most private equity firms. For other investors, steering clear of corruption meant developing land in faraway places without the infrastructure of roads, water, or electricity. Others described the approval process as taking longer. To overcome those common barriers, investors needed significantly more startup capital, so that the investment was large enough that they could leverage the size of their investments to gain direct access to government officials.

Among the 30 individuals who spoke about steering clear of corruption, more than two-thirds were working on investments in Myanmar, while only 8 were making investments in Vietnam. Notably, several investors skipped over Vietnam and went straight to Myanmar following the democratic elections of Aung San Suu Kyi in 2016, in the hope of working in an environment where the new political leaders spoke fiercely against crony capitalism. In an interview with Sam, a Burmese-born investment consultant who spent many years living in London before returning to Myanmar to start a business in the early 2000s, he remarked:

> FDI is something very close to my heart because my day job is working with foreign investors thinking about market assessment, market entry, and see[ing] who they can partner with in Myanmar. We also work a lot with Myanmar businesses to help think about growth strategies. With these two activities—our job is to bring them together . . . via strategic alliance, joint venture, et cetera. After living for years under the cronies, both the locals and foreigners want a fresh start to clean up the corruption. From the local side, not all FDI is automatically welcome. To be candid about it, there are benefits to the market, but the challenge is that these investments have to be responsible investments with a long-term vision. From the foreign investor side—they want to see the government pass clearer investment law that digitizes the thousands of applications, has clear tax breaks for new areas, and clears land use right

titles. For businesses, we are moving towards stronger corporate governance through a process of professionalization to allow management to take ownership to run the business and the increasing need to access finance for loans, equity investors, and joint ventures. This allows local businesses to open up to more financial stakeholders. So, to do all of this everyone needs to be on board in a push towards greater transparency and corporate governance.

My conversation with Sam highlighted a multi-pronged effort on the part of state officials, foreign investors, and local entrepreneurs who shared a vision for economic development that worked to steer clear of corruption. State officials under the new democratic government had an incentive beyond their own private gain to mitigate the corruption: to brand themselves as different from the former cronies and encourage a new wave of potential investments from the United States and Europe.

Sam's sentiments were echoed at a 2016 ribbon cutting ceremony that I was invited to attend for a new special industrial zone. This new development was a four-hour drive from the city of Yangon, Myanmar's main economic hub. At the event U Kyaw Win, the Minister of Planning and Finance, expressed in a speech to the crowd that this ground-breaking ceremony should help to kick-start the development of the country. He not only described his expectation that the chosen developers would steer clear of corruption, but also outlined a vision for an industrial park that would include housing, a school, a hospital, and an athletic center to provide workers with spaces for positive forms of leisure and entertainment. The list of approved businesses for the industrial park also included hotels and shopping malls, in addition to logistics, construction, back-office operations like call centers, and remote human resources. Prohibited businesses included production and processing of arms or weapons, production of narcotics, and production of any product hazardous to the environment. As Keith, an American who I met at this site, described it, "This is a project of turning dirt into gold. That's where you can do something the government needs and wants, to avoid corruption."

In the Minister's remarks he invoked Myanmar's relationship with other countries and the past in order to set the stage for the present and future. He said:

> This is a time where we create the destiny of our nation and rewrite the history of our generation. . . . The first step is to ensure that everyone can be part of the process. . . . We want to establish the new MIC [Myanmar Investment Commission] law for foreign investment to make it proper

and up to the international standards, to make it clearer and more transparent how to get a business license and operate in Myanmar.

Transparency here comes at a great cost. For investors, this means that the startup costs would be much higher, if the government demands that investors not only build out their factories but also invest in longer term infrastructure for the local community. The higher cost of entry compared with other industrial zones meant that investors would have to help shoulder the costs for social services normally provided by the state. In addition to money, there was the added cost in time. Investors would have to fly into Yangon and then make a four-hour drive by road to the industrial zone. But in exchange, investors got direct access to a government office stationed onsite who provided expedient investment approvals, company registration, business taxpayer ID numbers, foreign visas, fire safety certificates, building permits, and immediate inspections related to factory equipment systems, building work, and fire protection systems.

Unlike many of the government officials I tried to approach in Vietnam, U Kyaw Win surprised me by how approachable he was to all of the individuals at the event. He posed for pictures and handed out his business cards to several people, telling them to come meet him directly if they had any questions regarding the business registration and licensing process.

Following the event, I began to ask several of my interviewees how Myanmar, a country that for fifty years embraced isolationism and a socialist government, was suddenly going to make progress towards economic growth and transition to democracy and global financial integration. Off-the-record conversations with a handful of people who worked in the offices as assistants to state officials provided a more nuanced analysis of the situation. They told me that they have personally lived through years of political conflict between the military and civilians and in an economy controlled by the cronies. This was not going to suddenly disappear overnight. Rather, the most profitable businesses that are already embedded will themselves have to undergo a process of restructuring and professionalize to meet global standards for development. At the same time, public officials will have to take a firm stance to clean up corruption in the country by refusing to take bribes and forcing all businesses to wait their turn. This means accepting slower growth at the beginning to gain the trust not only of the local people but also of foreign investors.

These more measured comments made it clear that highly profitable crony businesses were not just going to disappear overnight. Economic development here would require a balanced approach between the trans-formation of crony enterprises and the state's encouragement of foreign investors in new sectors of the economy that did not have crony ties. At the same time, in a context like Myanmar where corruption was par for the course, these anti-corruption efforts also leave state officials vulnerable at any moment to sudden corruption charges in order to oust them from power. For example, following the 2021 military coup in Myanmar, sev-eral top National League for Democracy (NLD) government officials faced imprisonment on charges of corruption.[4]

This transition requires a balancing act between protecting and pro-moting the growth of local firms and at the same time encouraging foreign investment. For instance, another government official who asked not to be named said, "You cannot operate a mine or a hydropower plant with just local resources. We need foreign investment and expertise to make sure that it is executed correctly." She referenced industries like mining, jade, timber, and banking as areas that will need state protections so that they can grow locally before a complete takeover by foreign investors from offshore with larger pools of capital to compete with. She went on:

> We have lived through over fifty years of operating in the gray, and we tell people in our government circles that not everybody is completely corrupt or completely clean. We need to work together between busi-ness and government because even the people who made money during those years want clearer tax laws, laws that are fair and clear so that they feel protected too.

What she was referring to here was something I heard from a number of indi-viduals in firms that were hugely profitable under crony capitalism, which was the desire to have a clearer set of laws in order to *protect* the assets they have secured. To move away from playing in the gray and towards a cleaner operation, state officials saw their efforts to support businesses striving for greater transparency as a way of encouraging former crony capitalists to change their ways to thrive under the new democratic regime. Importantly, what this reveals is a story around development rather than morality, as those who are embedded in this market are hoping for development into a non-crony system, but they must balance that with managing FDI into a system that has operated as a crony system for so long.

There were a small number of business leaders who gained widespread reputations for steering clear of corruption. They often served on panels at investor conferences, and hosted monthly dinners and business networks established through various foreign chambers of commerce and set up locally. Once a month on Sunday Aung Lwin, a local business leader, hosts a meal at his house where local entrepreneurs and foreign investors come together for informal conversations to help each other solve the many challenges they face doing business in Myanmar. One of my interviewees invited me to attend and introduced me as an American Fulbright scholar studying the foreign investment climate in Myanmar. Right after I introduced myself to the host Aung Lwin and three of his friends over hors d'oeuvres, the topic of corruption immediately came up. Aung Lwin said to me:

> Many of us here think about the long-term vision for Myanmar and the importance of stability and transparency. We want to pay taxes and support a strong base because that means we will have better hospitals. We pay taxes, our employees pay taxes, we have zero tolerance about not paying taxes. As responsible business owners we want to encourage a broader tax base. We are all grown up, we can assess risk and taxes. But it's an ongoing conversation with government officials to provide us with clear, transparent, and predictable regimes of tax collection. Issues like stamp duties [tax on documents] are a huge problem for small SMEs [small and medium enterprises] like ours and we would like more help.

At the dinner table a local business leader, Aung Naing Oo, chimed in and said to me:

> Most of the foreign investors remain from China and Southeast Asia. Aung San [Suu Kyi]'s visit to the US and UK sends a strong signal that Myanmar is open for business and that the government is supportive of private sectors coming in. The lifting of US sanctions is the first step towards enabling large scale operations and allowing local businesses to have their choice among investors. The government is moving away from a model of protectionism that is not that popular anymore in order to promote the private sector and liberalize FDI to promote local SMEs. It's this push towards greater transparency that will enable Myanmar to leapfrog countries like Vietnam that you are studying because those countries are inhibited by systematic mismanagement that creates a lot of hardships for honest business owners and smart investors.

Implicit in Mr. Oo's comments was the way that the current government worked to pit the US and China against each other by pushing for an ideal of greater transparency long associated with Western democracies. However, to attract capital from Western countries, local governments must work with a group of businesses to provide clarity on how to obtain proper investment certificates and licensing. Additionally, firms working toward this ideal want to be rewarded for professionalizing and hiring internationally recognized law firms and accounting firms to handle their contracts and audit their books. But for everyone at the table, this meant managing the kinds of investments that require a subordinate spider to uproot their life and plan to live in Myanmar for the long term, making a commitment that could span nearly a lifetime.

As an example, when I asked the group how they were able to deal with the slow bureaucracy without engaging in corruption, Ajay, an UHNWI from San Francisco, told me that it is a slow process that will take a while for everyone to get on board.

"It's not something that is going to happen overnight." Aung Naing Oo, his local partner, echoed Ajay's point, saying:

> I came back in the early 1990s with the foreign investment act [the Foreign Investment Law of 1988]. The open-door policy actually started then, not just with the recent elections. It was a very different landscape then. At the time there were three groups in the government. One, a group of ministers that were nationalistic and patriotic and good—after so many years of socialist rule they wanted to improve [they would not take a bribe]. Two, those sitting on the fence; they would probably take a bribe if you offered it to them, but they wouldn't insist on it; and third, those who were totally corrupt, and you couldn't get anything unless you bribed them. So, then you had to pick who you wanted to deal with. It wasn't a question for me about morality. It was about pragmatism. I believed then and now that if you pay a big bribe it will catch up to you. I've seen many people go to jail for this. But because of the government at the time, we were attractive to the second group. If there was an important project that needed transparency they would come to us. Those projects were in the least desirable areas—we had to build something literally in the swamps because they gave their sweetheart deals to their "friends" [using his fingers to insinuate those who paid bribes]. The early 2000s were the dark ages of cronyism, et cetera. At that time, we were under immense pressure, and at the end of the day we had to decide about whether or not we'd lose out on an important opportunity, but when you lose you have to be at peace with the whole process. It is only when you want something so bad that you are willing to do anything to get the project, then you have to deal with corruption. My observation is that at the end of the day it's the results that will determine the viability of a project. We are hoping that this new government will have the political

will to eradicate corruption. To do that they have to criminalize it first, and then they have the capacity to offer higher salaries. But the rule of law has to be put into play, and we need mechanisms and institutions to do that. There can be no sustainability of peace without economic growth.

Aung Naing Oo paused for a second, holding the dinner table captive, and then he said, "We just believe that you have to steer clear of corruption at all costs. To do that you have to accept that at the beginning you will be slow to grow and will lose money, but if you can survive those initial stages, it will pay off hugely at the end." Aung Naing Oo's aspirations and ability to steer clear of corruption were only possible because he and his team of investors were not "greedy," as he put it, and they were willing to accept a much slower growth process. Another crucial factor was their ability to choose to work with some government officials who shared a similar vision about eradicating corruption. What is key here is that to build a part of the web that "steers clear of corruption," both state and market actors must share similar goals and visions for economic development. Still, his projects were all on the outskirts of the city center, in the "swamps," as he called them, because the sweetheart deals in prime locations went to those who were willing to play in the gray.

In an economy where the state does not have the capacity to pay bureaucrats higher salaries, it is very difficult to control its own entities and their engagement in corruption. Investors who want to steer clear of corruption have to work either on projects that are large enough to involve central government, or on projects that fulfill the agendas of state officials for their electorate. In effect, the high transaction costs coupled with the risk of being too slow to grow meant that most investors could not afford to steer completely clear of corruption. In this business environment, the question was rarely whether you would engage in corruption or not, but rather *how far* one would be willing to play in the gray. The following three sections outline a continuum for those who play to the lighter side of the gray along with those that graduate to the darker side of the gray.[5]

Greasers: "Speed Money" or Facilitation Payments for Licensing and Permits

Close to 90 percent of my research participants described a common practice in both Myanmar and Vietnam of paying "speed money," or small facilitation payments, to government officials. Sometimes referred to as "coffee money" or "lunch money," these payments ranged from USD$25 to $100 and aimed to expedite some of the bureaucratic processes for licensing, permits, and business registration. Facilitation payments are widely understood as payments to foreign officials and are not considered bribery according to the legislation of some states or by international anti-bribery conventions.

While paying bribes is officially illegal in both Vietnam and Myanmar, many of my research participants told me that it was impossible to get around the practice of paying facilitation payments, and that states do not criminalize small facilitation payments. In fact, the off-the-record conversations that I had with government officials all highlighted their low salaries, so the states' limited capacity to provide them with higher salaries meant that they relied on these payments to supplement their wages. One Vietnamese official said to me, "My official salary is 200 US dollars a month, the GDP [per capita] is $5,000. How can we live on [$200]?"

Unlike local entrepreneurs, who are beholden to the gray areas that exist between the law on the books and the law in practice, foreign investors making investments outside of their countries of citizenship must strike a delicate balance between local and international laws regarding facilitation payments. For example, investors who are US citizens must adhere to the Foreign Corrupt Practices Act [FCPA], a United States federal law established in 1977 that prohibits US citizens and entities from bribing foreign government officials and that outlines accounting transparency requirements under the Securities Exchange Act of 1934. Germany, England, and Japan also have similar anti-bribery legislation that has far-reaching consequences for investors abroad. These investors must worry about criminal prosecution in their home countries and are less likely to shoulder the risk of bribery through direct forms of payment.

At the same time, within the United States federal legislation, a "facilitation payment"—defined by the FCPA of 1977 and clarified in 1988 as "a payment to a foreign official, political party or political official for 'routine governmental action,' such as processing papers, issuing permits, and other actions of an official, in order to expedite performance of duties of non-discretionary nature, i.e., which they are already bound to perform . . . [and] not intended to influence the outcome of the official's action, only its timing"—is legal.[6] Countries that prohibit facilitation payments include Argentina, Belgium, Brazil, Bulgaria, Chile, Czech Republic, Denmark, Estonia, Finland, France, Germany, Hungary, Iceland, Ireland, Israel, Italy, Japan, Luxembourg, Mexico, Netherlands, Norway, Poland, Portugal, Russia, Slovenia, Sweden, Turkey, and the UK.[7] Investors who hold citizenship in any of these countries must be mindful of the international laws which enable or constrain their behavior.

However, when it came to facilitation payments, virtually none of my research participants felt that the threat of criminalization was substantive for the "small petty payments" they made to incentivize lower-level bureaucrats to do their jobs more efficiently. For example, in an interview with Jay, an investment advisor who split his time between Vietnam and Singapore and who helped to connect investors from family offices to opportunities in Vietnam and Myanmar, he said to me:

> Whenever investors who come from the United States meet with me, I always tell them that the FCPA has this loophole in the law, which states that it is not illegal to pay a government official to do their job properly. It is, however, illegal to get them to overlook something . . . but it is a very gray area, and sometimes tricky to navigate. At the operational level the local teams will handle all of that, and they are part of the costs of doing business, and you have to manage them around certain parameters. . . . So we are willing to pay the facilitation payments because we need the bureaucracy to move at a faster speed. We can't wait one or two years for a business license when most people expect an exit in five to six years.

For Jay, time was of the essence, and waiting for the paperwork to move forward on a project ultimately was not worth the small cost to expedite the process. The grease money helps to get a project off the ground so that investors can obtain a return on their investment in the timely manner set forth.

Andrew, an investor who holds UK citizenship but has spent the last twenty years living and working in Hong Kong, echoed Jay's sentiments. Responding to the question of facilitation payments, he said to me:

> So, at the end of the day there's going to be the formal and informal administrative barriers. Um, but that has to do with licensing, land use rights, environmental issues, and labor issues. You will find that everywhere in Asia. It is the same for our investments in China, Indonesia, Malaysia, so we're comfortable with that in Vietnam. I think that Vietnam has learned over the last eight years how important it is to raise money from overseas. They need it. . . . I am fine with paying people to do their job in these countries [where] the governments don't have the capacity to pay government employees so when you go to the office everything runs at a very slow pace . . . so they will get it done with just routine facilitation payments. . . . So, it's this song and dance in each country

where you know what you are willing to pay, and they know what their bottom line is. Once you get past that it's quite easy to get things done.

Like Jay, Andrew was fine with paying facilitation payments; in fact, Andrew spoke of it as part of the fun of being in a frontier or emerging market. Because he specializes in bringing new products to emerging markets, he is able to tap into a brand-new consumer base each time he makes a move. When I asked him how he figured out what the payments were, he said to me:

> There's nothing complicated about it. They will just tell you they need coffee or tea money, and you just give them 25 or 50 dollars. Smile. And then wait for them to react. Sometimes they will tell you that you filled out the form incorrectly, and when they are vague about how you need to fix it you know that you need to give a little bit more. It's a song and dance, and every transaction is different. I like to hold whiskey and cigar hours with other investors because we will exchange notes on the different payments. In China there are consulting firms that actually take care of the payments and keep a ledger for how much each transaction costs, but Vietnam is just not that sophisticated yet and Myanmar still does everything by hand.

Aside from the small minority of investors who worked hard to steer clear of corruption and facilitation payments to the extent that they could, the vast majority of my research participants followed the same protocols as Jay and Andrew. For those who were working on smaller investments without direct access to government authorities, who could put pressure on lower-ranked officials to handle the paperwork in a timely matter, it was nearly impossible to get anything done in both countries without the small payments that would effectively help to move paperwork through the proper channels.

I asked Andrew if he would be willing to arrange a meeting with some of the people in his whiskey and cigar group to talk about doing business in Southeast Asia and how investors navigate the bureaucratic structures. Three months later, he sent me a text message that read, "We're having cigars. Come join." I asked him for the time and location, and he told me they were already there and sent me an address. I dropped everything, quickly changed, and ran over to meet them. The address led me down an old French colonial alleyway, up four flights of stairs and into a dark, unmarked speakeasy. I was instructed to push a button to the left. The door opened, and I found myself in a room with Andrew plus four other men lounging around a bottle of Hibiki 21, an expensive Japanese whiskey.

Andrew introduced me to the men at the table. Malcolm was a UK citizen based in Singapore who was making investments in the retail sector of Vietnam. Cyrus was a Chinese national based in Hong Kong who had studied abroad in the UK and was making investments in a technology company that developed a phone application for banking access to rural businesses. Chau was a lawyer who worked for a local Vietnamese firm that had been operating since the 1990s. Andrew, Malcolm, Cyrus, and Chau were friends whose wives and children spent a great deal of time together. They celebrated the holidays together and often sought advice from one another about navigating the immediate challenges ahead. Chau in many ways served as a kind of cultural broker, a friend who provided them with local insider knowledge about such things as how much to pay to grease the wheels while still staying aboveboard.

Over the course of the evening, Chau described his work as a lawyer who not only set up contracts, but also served as a greaser for many of his clients:

> You know what makes markets like Vietnam and Myanmar both really interesting and really frustrating? It's a true market. . . . That means that no two transactions are ever the same. You can interview hundreds of businesspeople and each experience that they have with the government will be different. A lot of people come to me to handle these things for them because our firm has a lot of experience managing government relations. But even for us, every business is different and has different rules and regulations that they have to follow, as well as different kinds of licenses they need to operate. Every couple of years there is also turnover in government. You spend years building relationships with certain key people and then after a few years they step down and a new person steps in, and when that happens everyone in the business world scrambles to figure out who they need to suck up to next.

The revolving door of bureaucrats who move around within government institutions, coupled with the different kinds of licensing and permits required in every industry, meant that lawyers took on a great deal of work navigating murky terrain on behalf of their clients. As the lawyer representing multiple investors, Chau probably had the best first-hand knowledge about how investors navigated the bureaucracy. His added value for investors had far less to do with knowing the law, or how best to fill out the paperwork, than with knowing how much side money to pay each bureaucrat at every step in the process. When I asked the men if there was an informal pricing list for the various business license and permits, Malcolm told me:

In China and Russia there are firms that you can contract who keep data on how much each payment costs. It is a bit more standardized there. Here in Vietnam, it does not seem to be the case, so a lot of times you also have to trust that your lawyer is not skimming too much off the top. You pay the legal fee, and what they pay to get things done is their business. But at the end of the day, you still have to think about what you are comfortable with in terms of paying the legal fees. Before, there were so few lawyers who could do this work that they used to require [a] $50,000 retainer. But now there are so many competing law firms that you can shop around and negotiate all of that.

Chau then chimed in, adding:

We are a local law firm that has been operating since the 1990s, so we are used to dealing with a lot of different people. There is a big difference between big foreign firms and local law firms. In foreign firms you have these white guys who are the face of the firm, but they have to hire local lawyers to take care of a lot of things for them. For local firms we have a lot more room to take care of those relationships, so we have more data on how much each transaction will cost. Sometimes people will go to the big firms to handle things like mergers and acquisitions and come to us to handle the small things like permits and licenses.

My next question was, perhaps obviously, what was the range of the facilitation payments? Chau responded, "It all depends on how big the deal is and what is at stake. I've done everything from 25 dollars US to several thousand." When I pushed him for more specific details, he told me that it was impossible to calculate because some payments were monthly while others were every year. He was insistent that it would be impossible to collect real data on these kinds of numbers unless every law firm agreed to publicize the numbers and share them among each other. But this would never happen, because in doing so they would mitigate the need for themselves as the greasers of such deals.

As the lawyer at the table, Chau reminded me that nothing Andrew, Malcolm, Cyrus and he were doing was illegal. He told me that facilitation payments were completely legal even for those who come from the strictest legal contexts, like the United States. Cyrus, who was quietly observing for most of the evening, said to me toward the end of the night:

When you do business in Asia or anywhere in the world, you quickly learn that everyone is *playing in the gray*; these small facilitation payments you're asking us about is playing to the white of the gray, not the black of the gray. Just remember, all we are doing is paying people to do their job. We are not bribing them; that is something totally different.

The way in which all of these men drew a distinction between facilitation payments, which they viewed as lower forms of corruption, and outright bribes, which involved higher levels of corruption, raised a larger question about how to distinguish between different kinds of payments and the relational work necessary to facilitate them. That is what differentiates a greaser from a briber. So then, among bribers, what were the different strategies they used to obfuscate these risky relations?

Bribers: Obfuscation via Gift-giving, Bundling, and Brokerage

The art of paying a bribe varies a great deal with respect to how close the briber is to the political official, the legal structures that constrain or enable their behavior, and the stage of development at which investors enter the market. Sociologist Gabriel Rossman outlines three possible strategies that individuals might pursue to obfuscate bribes: *gift-giving, bundling,* or *brokerage.*[8] "All three strategies have alternative meanings and provide [actors with] plausible deniability."[9] Here I outline the conditions under which subordinate spiders might choose one obfuscation strategy over another. And in doing so, I explain when U/HNWIs might choose to assume the risk themselves, and when they would reduce their personal risk by utilizing third-party brokers to carry out this work on their behalf.

GIFT-GIVING

Very early on in my research I learned that bribes are not always carried out through simple cash payments. For example, during a tour of a new real estate development project I naively asked Khue, a 45-year-old local real estate developer, "Do you just hand them red envelopes? How do you know what the right amount is?" Khue laughed and explained how he obfuscated disreputable ties through highly personalized gifts:

> When you come from the West, you think it's bad to pay government officials, but that is the way in Vietnam. Think about it: they are only making 200 to 300 US dollars per month. How can they survive on that? They have to eat too! We pay them to do their job. . . . [But] we are never that direct, you have to be a lot more *khéo* (savvy) than that. Every person is different,

and they have different needs. Someone might have a small child, so we will offer to pay for the kid's tuition. Or we might buy their wife an expensive watch or handbag, something they can easily sell for cash in Hong Kong.

Local entrepreneurs who are tightly embedded in closed networks of key political elites obfuscate ignominious ties through deeply personalized strategies of gift-giving in which the kind of gift varies with every person and every relationship. Failure to figure out how to finesse these deeply personal exchanges could result in a massive loss to a competitor. For example, in an interview with Nhan, a local Vietnamese real estate developer, he explained the struggle that he faced against his competition for access to prime real estate locations in Ho Chi Minh City, and how those interactions drove investors to innovate new ways to cement personal ties. Nhan explained:

> The best developers for the project are not always the ones who win a tender. The winners are the ones who know how to play the *local* game. Even when you pay, then you have to deal with the turnover in government. Every couple of years the party moves around, and then you have to manage relationships with the new bureaucrat who can push you out in favor of his friends. Everyone knows those top developers had very close relationships at the top level, but that also means you have to pay them and everyone below them off with something.

Building close personal relationships required intense levels of relational work to assess not only the appropriate bribe, but the best means to deliver that bribe in a carefully crafted manner. Failing to pay the right bribe could mean the developers would not receive the necessary licensing or permits to operate their business or that a license already issued could be suddenly suspended.

When I asked how developers managed those relationships, Nhan explained, "In our firm, the [C-suite executives] spend most of their time on relationships, while everyone in the back office figures out how to execute." Using his phone, Nhan showed me photos of himself and his partners at a signing with local officials. The photo depicted six men from their private firm, as well as five state officials dressed in their green cadre outfits. Three of the top firm executives were pictured in the middle of the photo holding the hands of the state officials. Nhan pointed to the handholding as a sign of the embeddedness of their relationship. To get to that place they spent a great deal of time appealing to the tastes of state officials through luxury gifts.

Hermès handbags and Rolex watches were common gifts not only because they were highly coveted items that were difficult to obtain, but because they served as stores of value that could be quickly traded for cash in the secondary market. After an informant told me that his wife gifted his business partner's wife a $10,000 Hermès handbag to obtain an occupancy license for a condo building they recently completed, I probed for more details by commenting, "That seems like such a nominal amount of money for a major [USD$2 million] project."

Khue responded, "That is why you have a long-term relationship. You gift them in increments so that it does not look exactly like bribery. We had to think a lot about the gift. What color she would like and what style she would like [showing me photos of Hermès Birkin Bags versus Kelly Bags]." Investors go to great lengths to craft a personal story about how they had put thought into the gifts they gave to political officials. For example, one investor told a story of how he had to give his daughter a monthly allowance for over two years just to purchase smaller items in the Hermès store to build a relationship with a sales associate at Hermès. This is because, at Hermès, one cannot simply walk into a store to purchase a purse; the customer must first build a relationship with a sales associate and wait to be offered the opportunity to purchase one of their coveted handbags directly from the store. Another investor sent his assistant to France to stand in line for five consecutive days to purchase a handbag and personally carry it back to Vietnam. As such, buying luxury items is in itself a deal-making process.

Rolex watches were among the most coveted watches, but not just any Rolex will do. As with the Hermès handbags, investors sought coveted pieces like the Rolex Daytona watch, which is extremely difficult to obtain. Money alone does not guarantee access, as people spend years on waiting lists in multiple countries to get their hands on one. The suggested retail for a stainless steel Rolex Daytona watch starts at USD$13,000, but because of the demand, prices on the secondary market are usually twice that amount. The value here is not just that it is hard to get, but that one can narrate a story about the great pains they took to purchase it.

Tze, a Singaporean investor, worked to establish and maintain long-term ties to state officials by providing their local partners with the funds to provide subtle gifts. As Tze told me, "These 'gifts' include free trips to Europe to visit other 'project sites' [luxury hotels], tickets to shows, restaurant reservations, and a team of tour guides to provide them with the ultimate vacation abroad." These vacations often serve as memorable shared experiences filled with a sense of wonder and discovery. They create an emotional attachment between the gift giver and the recipient that helps to seal or sweeten a deal.

In addition to handbags, watches, and vacations, artwork began growing in popularity. I suspect that what helped to prop up local and regional artists was a new obsession with speculative art that was used to win favors. One afternoon I was invited to visit the studio and home of a famous Vietnamese American artist, Dinh Q. Lê. Mr. Lê's artwork is abstract, but draws inspiration from the Vietnam War by juxtaposing iconic images of North and South Vietnam, using a specific basket weaving technique. Each unique art piece sold for USD$10,000–$20,000, and they were purchased as speculative collector's items, expected to increase in value over time.

Irony aside, handbags, jewelry, vacations, and artwork were all examples of bribes facilitated through gift giving, as local business elites worked to obfuscate illegal, disreputable ties by masking outright bribes. Bribes were no doubt necessary, but figuring out the proper gift and the right moment to give it was part of the art of deal brokering. Across the interviews, research participants shared how crucial these gifts were, because they helped establish a personal sense of connection key to brokering deals.[10]

From the perspective of state officials, they needed to strike a delicate balance with their gift givers and only accept gifts that were properly obfuscated. Successfully negotiating this delicate dance, however, provided investors with a long-term strategy that ensured access to information and assistance with ongoing development projects. Importantly, by providing officials with smaller-size gifts more frequently, they were able to maintain ongoing relationships with key officials; for those without high-level government connections, it was the only way to gain access to land or key information linked to investment opportunities.

The work of establishing direct ties involves what sociologist Dan Lainer-Vos refers to as "blurring practices," whereby actors work to complete a transaction while blurring the lines between gift giving, bribery, and market exchange.[11] Gift giving enables local entrepreneurs to gain access to the market through state officials, who make less than USD$300 per month as government employees. By blurring these practices, HNWIs doing the groundwork of bribery protect themselves from potential jail time or reputational risks.

BUNDLING

Gift giving represents only the tip of the iceberg. As the stakes increase, so do the size of the bribes and the form through which they are distributed. In addition to gift giving, bribers managed to make payments through a variety of bundling strategies that cleverly locked state officials into a relationship of mutual hostage and sabotage. Bundling involves a series of exchanges that make a disreputable exchange appear reputable. Examples of this include, but are not limited to, compensation in the form of salaries to close family members of political elites, and/or providing shares of a company to a designated nominee through offshore vehicles.

Regional investors from Singapore, South Korea, Thailand, Malaysia, Taiwan, and China operated in Vietnam and Myanmar with far greater ease with respect to bundling practices when compared with Western and Japanese investors. Notably, many of the regional investors came from countries where they had to navigate similar murky relations with state officials. In addition, because Vietnam and Myanmar were such small countries, regional governments rarely investigated corruption abroad.

As an example, South Korean investors are limited by the Foreign Bribery Act (FBA); yet it is difficult to identify and fight cross-border corruption outside of Korea in countries like Vietnam and Myanmar. That said, in 2014 South Korea ranked 31st out of 100 (with zero being the most corrupt) on Transparency International's Corruption Index.[12] So despite the FBA, many of my interviews with investors revealed that they could not avoid operating in the "gray areas of the law." And to mitigate the risk, they established long-term personal relationships with key officials in the central government.

These investors also described the cultural similarities around patronage in state-market relations that they felt comfortable navigating. Joon, a 35-year-old from South Korea, explained to me:

> Vietnam reminds us a lot of Korea in the early stages, so when we come here, we see the same potential. There are 90 million people in this country and a growing middle class. In the last couple of years, the GDP per capita went from USD $700 in 2005 to $2200 by 2015. What does that tell you? The new middle class [will] want to improve their lives . . . better housing . . . shopping malls. We know how to do this because we saw the same growth in Korea. What we lack are the language skills and the connections. The Vietnamese [government officials] have their ways and they are tricky to work with.

When I asked Joon to clarify what he meant by "tricky to work with," he discussed at length the kind of corruption that his company had to manage. He explained, "When you come with foreign money, you have to remember you are on their land. They want to make sure that they get 'paid' [emphasizing the word 'paid' to imply bribe]. They will always want you to come and develop it and then push you out when you're done." When I asked how he navigates a market where there is a general lack of access to information, the law is open to interpretation, and corruption is widespread, he said:

> When you line their pockets, you make them beholden to you. Not only do they need the money, but if something goes wrong with the project you can always threaten to expose them. This is a dirty world filled with tricks and revenge. You hire the family members of party officials. The closer the relationship the better. . . . I will take the niece or nephew but even better would be the son or the daughter, because if they want to take us down [they] would be taking their own family down with us.

What Joon described is a relationship of "mutual hostage" and mutual destruction: by taking bribes from foreign investors in the form of offshore shareholding, state officials implicate themselves in criminal activity. The decision to hire close family members of party officials also provides investors with some assurance that the state will not arbitrarily expose their disreputable activities, because doing so would harm their close family members. To keep the money flowing into the pockets of state officials, they also assume the risk of potential exposure. East/Southeast Asian investors, however, worry less about the risk of exposure, because there is a general sentiment that their governments will not enforce anti-corruption laws outside their native countries.

When describing their office space dynamics, several respondents talked about being very strategic in their hiring. Rather than hiring law firms or brokers from third-party institutions, they spent time establishing personal relationships with third-party individuals who had ties to local Vietnamese business and political leaders. By hiring the close family members of party officials, they established arm's-length ties that enabled them to obfuscate bribes by bundling them through higher salaries, offering shares of the firm to a designated nominee (to maintain anonymity), and a carry-forward on the firm's return on investment that other employees within the firm would not receive. Jing, an investment broker from a Hong Kong firm based in Vietnam, explained:

> Everyone [local Vietnamese] who works in here has some kind of connection. They are somebody's son or daughter. We do not rely on their connections for personal favors; it's more about who has access to key information.

His partner, Kang, elaborated:

> In our office, we have people whose job it is to get us key information when we need it. That person advises us on how to manage government

relations, so obviously they have to have government connections. They advise us on the form of payment and the size at all levels, from top-level to low-level petty payments. We of course make the final decision, but they advise a lot on that.

These investors engaged in relational work by establishing close relationships of trust on the ground, garnering them access to inside information about the market, quick approvals processes, and successful closings on business deals. Jing further elaborated:

You can submit the paperwork for approval, and it will just sit on their desk. They will make up every excuse about why they cannot move something along. Like something on the form is not filled out correctly or you need five more signatures that are not listed on the actual form. To move something forward, someone needs to go there and manage that relationship. It is a relationship, and they need to be paid.

By acknowledging the variable legitimacy of the state and the importance of local "sons and daughters" as mediators, Asian investors can establish indirect relationships with top government officials at the state level simply by participating in the local styles of deal brokering.

Depending on how high a level the sons' and daughters' connections are, firms will also designate between 5 percent and 20 percent of the shares of investment deals to a nominee. Kang explained, "That nominee is essentially a paper owner who partially owns a part of the deal anonymously. [Family members of said government officials] put the names of their drivers and maids [laughs]. But we can trace the true owner if something goes wrong with the investment, and [if] there is any kind of investigation of the firm for wrongdoing, they go down with us." In other words, the sons and daughters risk exposure for getting a kickback on the deal, which would affect not only their reputation but also that of their parents.

Many of these firms also build relationships with high-net-worth local Vietnamese elites who later invest in the firms' projects. Celia, the 32-year-old Ivy League-educated daughter of a local Vietnamese family, works in the real estate division of a Korean asset management company that has subsidiary companies in Hong Kong, Vietnam, and Shanghai. Celia reflects on her position in the bundling process to me:

In America, my friends in the major banks call this "friends and family" or "sons and daughters." Firms compete to hire the best [politically] connected children who went to college, business school, and law school in the US. This is true in China, and it is even truer in Vietnam, just on a smaller scale. These relationships are important for maintaining influence in the country. But it goes both ways too.

What firms are paying for by hiring "friends and family" is not highly skilled employees, but their relationships. Celia's salary was a form of bundling because what she brought to the table was not a unique skill set for the firm, but rather a set of relationships and political connections that would help the foreign firm navigate the murky bureaucratic landscape. By developing personal relationships with the sons and daughters of local business leaders, Asian investors can raise capital from local banks. In this local context, East/Southeast Asian investors do not need to go as far as to engage in veiled threats or outright bribery.

While local Vietnamese elites often develop indirect relationships of trust with influential political leaders, East/Southeast Asian investors work to establish relationships with political elites through their children. The children—all educated at Ivy League institutions or at elite Korean or Singaporean universities—are an important asset in these firms, as Yang explained to me: "They cannot get things done as fast as their parents, but they usually know how to find a solution to a problem more quickly than we do because they have direct connections." When I probed further about the kinds of things younger Vietnamese employees assisted with, Yang said:

> It depends on the problem. In our case, we had a problem with a local construction company who tried to cut corners and did a poor job. They wanted more money to finish the job and we told them we could not pay them anymore. There, we have political advisors who know the local judge, and they usually advise us on whether we have a strong case or what we would need to build a case. A lot of times our employees help to connect us with local investment opportunities. The Vietnamese developers dominate the market, but we have the power of a brand, so sometimes they help us to land joint-venture projects. This is important, because a foreign-invested enterprise can only own a land use right if a Vietnamese partner contributed to its share capital in a joint venture.

By hiring local Vietnamese sons and daughters with strong political or business ties, East/Southeast Asian investment firms develop strong ties of trust with a younger generation of elites who bring key relationships to the table while also bridging language and cultural gaps for deal brokering in local settings, something that their parents could not do.

At the time when JPMorgan Chase and Goldman Sachs were under scrutiny by the US government for hiring employees with family connections to enhance their deal-brokering strategies on the ground, these Asian-based property developers with local subsidiaries were far more successful than their Western counterparts and faster at advancing deals, because they could get around many of the FCPA laws concerning bribery and corruption. Korean and Singaporean investors and Chinese investors from Hong Kong, Taiwan, and China had no problem adopting a similar model in Vietnam. Alex, a Vietnamese-born graduate of one of the top three business schools in the United States, explained, "This is how business is done in Vietnam and all over Asia; everything is about connections here. Asian firms will always get ahead, because they don't have to worry about being investigated for breaking a foreign law." Moreover, the structural conditions—economic rules and expectations governing foreign investment—shape the kinds of relationship-building strategies available to each kind of investor.

BROKERAGE

Western and Japanese investors struggle the most with establishing strong direct ties with local authorities because they are constrained by the formal global governance structures of their home countries. Western investors are the most physically distant and culturally dissimilar to local political officials. Western and Japanese investors often come into the market at a more advanced phase of development, where the project has sophisticated cross-border legal contracts and professional audits and has begun a process of professionalization (e.g., establishing a board and moving from two books to one book). Western and Japanese investors provide local Vietnamese and East/Southeast Asian developers with an exit strategy by purchasing their assets at a higher price point after East/Southeast Asian investors have cleaned up and professionalized operations. The investment size ranges from USD$50 million to $900 million. Conversely, Western and Japanese investors also face higher tax burdens imposed by local authorities, which result in lower profits. Therefore, in a country with widespread corruption, where information is "poorly distributed" (as markets or hierarchies are incompletely developed), opportunities for brokerage emerge.[13] Brokers shoulder the risk tied to facilitation payments to move projects forward by serving as third-party fixers or intermediaries.

In 2009, when I first began interviewing Westerners who were new to this market, most steered clear of the land acquisition phase (the phase that cost no more than USD$10 million), because it involved several bureaucratic layers of bribery to purchase the land, re-title it, and access the proper permits for licensing and construction. Almost all the Western investors in my project sought investments in the property market by raising capital they would then invest in a local asset management firm, who would develop land already acquired through a joint venture.

Kevin, an investor from the United States, explained:

> The property market in Vietnam is still very, very corrupt. Our firm generally comes in at a later stage of development. By the time we enter, the most corrupt phase should be cleared up already. Sometimes we advise on projects that we might later invest in by helping them to set up systems, like moving from two books to one, separating personal from professional finances, hiring professional auditors, and setting up a board.

When I asked how they compete with Korean and Taiwanese investors in the market, Kenji, a Japanese investor, explained, "We are their exit. We are in different markets. They sell their investments to us and Americans." Andrew, a US investor, further elaborated:

> It just costs us a lot more to enter this market. We do not even look at deals unless they are north of 100 million. By then the project would have developed, professionalized, and we would obviously yield a much lower return on investment, but we would still be profitable. I guess you can imagine developers from Hong Kong, Korea, or Taiwan would enter the market with us in mind as their exit.

Here Kevin is referring to investors who enter the market at an early stage to develop a real estate project before selling that project to an investor, who could pour more money into it with the hopes of a greater private equity exit—or the ultimate exit, which would be an initial public offering [IPO] on either a local or foreign stock exchange. In contrast, Japanese and Western investors prefer to wait until investment projects have reached a more mature phase with clear tax implications. Larger-size investments enable local managers to deal directly with central levels of government, which enables firms to push for a greater sense of transparency. Jiro, for example, explained:

> This country is very corrupted from the top to the bottom. But when you come in with USD $100 million you know you deal direct[ly] with the Prime Minister. Of course, we set up a joint venture with a local

firm. But when that local firm takes a deal that big, they have to get us meetings to push for development and transparency. No one will come to the market with this much money if the government does not change its ways from the top down.

Similarly, most Western investors from the United States I interviewed in 2009–2010 began their responses with similar statements about how they could not afford to engage in bribery or corruption, because they could face criminal sentences back home. Jonathan, an investor in his mid-40s from Seattle, stated, "I don't know how others describe it to you, but there are these laws, FCPA and the RICO [Racketeer Influenced and Corrupt Organizations] Act. I cannot get away with bribing a local official to do business here unless I want to risk going to jail." Ethan, an investor from Arizona, echoed, "I am all about pushing for greater transparency in this market. At the end of the day, they have the land, and we have the money. When you control the money, you also control some terms of the deal." And Rich, an investor from New York, insisted, "I don't believe in bribing people to do their jobs. Not only is this illegal, it's morally wrong. As long as I can squeeze out a small profit, so yeah, my profit margin is going to be smaller than my competitors, I would rather keep my business outside of that gray area."

This initial round of interviews led me to believe that bribery took place only in the first phase of land acquisition or in transactions between local Vietnamese entrepreneurs and political elites. At first, I put these interviewees in the group that "steers clear of corruption." As my research continued however, I found that Westerners also attempted to finesse the system; the only difference was they rationalized it differently. Jon, a foreign developer, talked about the importance of figuring out how to pay bribes without implicating himself directly in criminal activity. For example, after five years of a stalled development project, Jon articulated his new strategy for brokering real estate deals on the ground:

> The most important lesson that I have learned over the last five years is that everyone has to localize in some way. You cannot come in as this American who is just going to tell government officials what to do. That, I learned the hard way, will not work. If you talk to [our mutual friends who are also Western investors], you will see that they've adapted too. I cannot have direct personal relationships with local leaders. Not only is there a language and cultural barrier, but as an investor, it puts me too close to possible charges of corruption. I still have a life in the US and I never want to risk going to jail just because international laws conflict

with local practices. To get around this we have to build strong relationships with intermediaries or institutional partners. . . . We work
closely with a local Vietnamese financial firm, and we also hire a team
of lawyers. We have to work with people who can help build our government relations.

And there it was again, "build[ing] government relations." Westerner or
not, the practice was ubiquitous. My interview with Jon, along with subse-
quent interviews with several other Western investors, revealed how they
negotiated disreputable ties via brokerage strategies: they hired third-party
institutional mediators who could carry out the bribes for them to syndicate
the risk of criminal charges.

After several years of unsuccessfully navigating the local market on Western legal terms, almost 60 percent of the investors I met in 2009 had left
the Vietnamese market by 2016. Those who stayed outsourced the local
demands of bribery through brokers. Third-party brokers include local
asset management firms, law firms, and public relations agencies, which
connected the investors with local opportunities on the ground. Perhaps,
because Western investors could not engage in the groundwork of bribery
and veiled threats without risking criminalization in their home countries,
they created a buffer between themselves and local officials by hiring local
mediators referred to as "fixers" to do this work. Eric, a Canadian investor
from Vancouver, explained:

> If you look closely at the different law firms that we work with in Viet-
> nam, you will see that all of the firms have a mix of foreign and local
> lawyers. The foreign lawyers meet with us to assess our needs, draft or
> review contracts and sometimes project proposals. We do not usually
> meet the local lawyers in the firm. But any good firm must have local
> lawyers. They are the eyes and ears on the ground. . . . The local lawyers
> in the firm do not practice law. Their job is to establish a strong net-
> work. . . . I pay them a "legal fee." What they do with their payment is
> none of my business.

During that same interview, Eric clarified, "To be clear, they are not doing
anything 'illegal' [using his fingers to make scare quotes]. It is technically not
illegal to pay someone to do their job properly. It is illegal, [however], to pay
someone to overlook a glaring error." In Eric's case, local lawyers that they
hired through international law firms based in Vietnam were key to getting the
proper approvals, licensing, and permits with government officials. To trace

this business practice, I spoke with three different local lawyers about how they practice law in Vietnam. Thuan, a 35-year-old lawyer, explained to me:

> Practicing law in Vietnam is not the same as the United States. I spent all of these years in school studying the law, but at the end of the day the best lawyer does not win. You have to have a relationship with the judge. I spend most of my time building relationships with judges and key party officials. It doesn't matter how smart I . . . am or how well I argue the law. . . . Without those relationships we will lose a case. Most of the time we never go to court. Once we show the other side how strong our connections are, they back down and we mediate or come to an agreement.

When I asked the three lawyers what kinds of conflicts might lead to a potential lawsuit, they all cited some form of payment. These included returns on an investment following the completion of a project, or payment to a broker who connected a foreign investor to a local investment opportunity. Western investors must rely on third-party institutions—in this case, legal firms and their relational work—to facilitate real estate deals. Individuals in these third-party firms—the fixers—were people with close government ties who could use their influence through bribes and gift-giving in order to secure a business license or gain access to inside information.

One such fixer, Dong, a Chinese real estate investor, introduced me to a woman named Thuy. During my interview with Dong he kept insisting that I meet Thuy in order to also include "advisors" with political connections. Thuy agreed to meet me at the Park Hyatt in Ho Chi Minh City. I arrived fifteen minutes early and grabbed a seat in a quiet corner of the room. Thuy walked in adorned in designer labels from head to toe. We made small talk at first by talking about her interest in fashion. She told me about how she travels all around the world just to go shopping, and that she travels regularly to Paris where she purposely spends thousands of dollars at the Hermès flagship store in Paris so that she can stay at the top of their VIP list, which grants her exclusive access to their ultra-exclusive handbags. She pulled out her phone and showed me an image of her most recent score, a crocodile purse which was $45,000 but had a value on the secondary market of $120,000. After making small talk about fashion, I asked her about her family background and current work.

Thuy told me that she comes from a family with very high-level political connections. In fact, she said, "You cannot do anything in this country without government connections." As we eased into the interview, I asked her to tell me about her family history and their ties to government. She told me that her father started out as an electrical engineer and then transitioned into becoming a construction contractor. From there he moved from small real estate into larger and larger projects. At the time of the interview, he was running a construction business with large government contracts.

Thuy was educated in the UK, where she received her bachelor's degree in architecture and master's degree in interior design. When she first returned to Vietnam, she ran her own interior design company until her father invited her to come help him manage some of his projects. Together they started an advisory consulting firm, where she serves as a local advisor and broker to foreign investors looking for a well-connected local contact on the ground. While her father himself is no longer in government, his connections remain deep, as their family members rotate positions in the party. One of her uncles is a party official who assesses the land use rights fees, which she described as "a tax charge in order to just 'use' rather than purchase the land. This is the same as excise tax or sales tax." This is important because, as she explained to me, the land is constantly revalued and reassessed, and no one knows the real tax liability because the law is open to interpretation. In addition to figuring out the land use rights, investors must also acquire an investment certificate and the regulatory approvals to do business. As a result, foreigners depend on local advisors like Thuy to help them bypass these hurdles. Thuy then said:

> The investment certificate could take an entire year to get approved and generally you cannot get this without greasing the wheels . . . a lot of money is made here because of the close relationship between party leaders in the state and local entrepreneurs with foreign investors. The rules keep changing and no one can really seem to figure out what the actual percentage of the appraised value is.

When I asked her what her role was, she told me that she was an investment advisor with deep local connections. When I asked her how she articulated that to potential investors, she said:

> If you pay the right people enough money, you stay in the game. If someone can pay your connections more than you, you are out of the game. . . . No one believes in the rule of law. The issue is how high those connections are.

Thuy also described how her firm managed payments. She said:

> So they pay our firm a "consulting fee" to ensure that all of the paperwork has been handled properly and they are the ultimate owners of

the property. . . . On our end, we know that party officials change hands every five or six years, so we have a limited time to make money, so we set up legitimate ways to get our money out of the country by getting paid in offshore accounts in foreign currency.

While Thuy initially only agreed to meet with me for an hour, our conversation ended up lasting three as we talked a great deal about the stress of managing her family's current connections for only a finite time period while they held positions of political power. She did not seem to frame her actions as a fixer as being fraudulent within the market. As she saw it, she offered investors a service, and that service was access to information, accuracy in licenses, and so on. Rather than perceiving herself as a kleptocrat, she saw her work as filling some of the institutional voids to provide investors with the kinds of assurances they might need for their portfolios.

After my meeting with Thuy, Dong asked me to meet for a drink so that he could learn about what she had to say. I met him at a cocktail bar. The first thing he said to me after we ordered our drinks was, "She's very good at reminding you that it's not about what you know. It's about *who* you know. Right?" I laughed, nodded yes, and we drank to that. Dong then walked me through the lengthy steps he needed to take and how hiring a fixer like Thuy helped him:

> You want to get something done? You have to have permission. To have permission, you got to get a license. . . . Where do you get the license? You go to the ministry. The ministry won't do anything unless they get paid or they were told to do something by someone higher in command. Anyway, why would the minister favor one group over another? Well, usually money.

When I asked Dong how he bribed them, he told me:

> This is the same everywhere. People who are in political power are supposed to think about the welfare of their people and the future of economic development in the country. But greed gets people. The last deal we did with them, we offered them $10 million above their reservation price, but we structured it as a loan. So then they are in this bind: Do they pocket the $10 million now and split it among themselves, but the future generations will have to pay for it, or do they say no and that they want to clean this up so their kids' generation won't have to pay back these loans? What would you do?

Dong never directly answered my question about whether or not the fixers took the $10 million. I tried asking the question three different times, each time slightly differently. First, I asked directly, "Did it work?"

He replied, "You're not one of my LPs, so I don't have to disclose that to you."

I backed off and tried to act confused: "I'm sorry, I'm a bit confused. Did the strategy work?"

To which he replied, "What do you think? Just ask yourself, what would you do?"

I responded, "Well, I would probably take the money, knowing that it would secure my family's future."

He responded, "Well then, you have your answer, don't you?"

This back and forth was common in many of my interviews. Yet several weeks later, when I met Dong and his public relations agent at a bar, and I asked about their relationship with Thuy, he quietly said, "It is a very powerful tactic to say, 'I can neither confirm nor deny' the payments that were made in this deal."

In this way, the majority of Western investors who participated in my study kept a degree of distance between themselves and state officials. They gained access to information through formal channels of hiring institutional intermediaries to facilitate both the deal-brokering process and the development of projects they sought. Ironically, brokerage helped ease social interactions, enhance economic activity, and facilitate development, while also breeding corruption.[14] Two investors that I interviewed stood out for being much more explicit about their bribery practices to obtain informal access to the market. William, an investor from England, put it bluntly:

There are so many Westerners who come to Vietnam running their mouths about anti-corruption. But they will sit on a project for five to six years before they close a deal. We can't operate like that. Our investors can't wait five to six years to see a return. We would never raise capital with those stats. . . . As a researcher, people are not always going to be honest with you, because they could end up in jail for telling you how they really do things. But maybe we should be more open, because these laws are man-made, and they don't reflect the demands on the ground. Let me tell you . . . to get around [foreign corruption laws], we funnel money through public relations firms. Our latest deal involved a one million US dollar transfer through a public relations firm for a major project. We were not just paying off one person; we were paying off multiple people. I cannot go into the exact details, but you get the point.

A number of Western investors used public relations firms to help them broker relationships with key government officials. Public relations firms often work closely with government agencies to write press reports and to promote many government activities. As a result, these firms have crucial relationships with a number of important officials. Both local and Western firms alike will pay a public relations consultant to set up an informal meeting with a key leader and, once they move on a deal, they will pay the public relations firm a sum of money that is underwritten as advertising, but used to pay off a government official.

While the Vietnamese lawyers and public relations consultants were far more direct with me about the importance of relationship building, Western lawyers and consultants in those same firms were adamant that they did not believe in promoting bribery or corruption. All worked carefully to maintain a public image as advocates for stronger anti-corruption laws. The contradiction between their stated values and their practices, however, was a direct reflection of the economic climate in Vietnam. Under these circumstances, Western investors have very little choice but to hire mediators (asset management firms, lawyers, principal agents, and public relations specialists) to push projects along at a faster speed.[15] To be clear, these practices also occur in the United States.[16] By hiring third-party brokers on the ground, investors gain access to inside knowledge about the economy and are granted significant tax breaks that are crucial for their profit margin. My interviews with Western investors and local brokers (lawyers, consultants, principal agents, public relations specialists) in Southeast Asia revealed that bribery strategies via brokerage enabled the investors to move from closing two deals over five years to closing an average of one deal per year between 2014 and 2016.

Thieves

In the worst-case scenarios, information asymmetry, poorly managed funds, and bribery combined to create high levels of theft and principal-agent problems. It was challenging to assess the prevalence of this, because few people talked about it in real time. Most who revealed their involvement with theft talked about deals that were at least two years in the past.

In an interview with Tan, a local Vietnamese accountant who has spent much of his career in deal advisory, he talked a great deal about the amount of money lost in one of his poorly managed funds over 10 years ago. A foreign group, WhiteSilk Partners, joined with a local bank, NorthFour Bank, to create an investment management firm that would manage a fund of $80 million. WhiteSilk Partners asked that the Vietnamese partners raise the first $40 million, and after that WhiteSilk Partners would raise the second $40 million. In describing the relationship, Tan told me that there were three people in charge of the $80 million fund who lacked any kind of investment experience in Vietnam. They had all this money but nowhere to invest it, and so, in a frantic effort to make it appear that they were putting the money to work, they outright stole from the fund by investing in fake companies.

When I asked Tan if he could provide me with an example of how people stole, he said:

> They made investments in a shrimp farm in Dalat. How can you raise shrimp on a mountain? But investors are far away, how could they know Dalat is not Mekong? So they took the money and ran and when they could not raise funds a second time, they ran over to Thailand or Myanmar, or other countries. . . .

The interview with Tan lasted only two hours and was one of the most densely packed interviews I conducted. Unlike many others who insinuate rather than speak candidly regarding issues of theft and fraud, Tan was the most direct. This led me to believe that his scenario, or ones similar to it, probably occurred more frequently than was being openly acknowledged, and people obfuscated the money trail through the bundling and brokerage strategies outlined above. Nevertheless, Tan outlined all of the ways that the fund he worked for engaged in outright theft and fraud along a continuum.

What became quite clear to me after this conversation was this: the two kinds of theft that were most common involved (1) setting up illegal structures overseas that effectively allowed foreigners majority control over the company, and (2) selling off profitable assets first to make the fund appear profitable while holding onto bad assets in order to raise capital. Tan also discussed a due diligence process that was, in fact, lacking in due diligence without any serious cross-checking of the data they presented. In essence, they engaged in creative accounting that showed profits without losses, which they could do because they controlled the financial statements. As HNWIs grew emboldened, they began to steal money from the fund by setting up fake companies that the fund invested in, pocketing the money for themselves, and then leaving for other countries like Myanmar, where they could run a similar scheme without new investors knowing about their crooked past dealings.

It is important to note here that subordinate spiders who engage in theft are not only local nationals or even regional citizens. Theft knows no citizenship. In fact, there are cases of Americans who have made frontier markets their home base as they exploit dominant spiders. For instance, in 2016 the US Department of Justice extradited a man named Michael Wilson from Hamburg, New York on charges of wire fraud, money laundering, and conspiracy. Investors, here UHNWIs, accused Wilson of using fake companies that were supposed to invest clients' money to instead pay for a variety of personal items, including a down payment for a Boston State Road property and several automobiles, ultimately defrauding investors of more than $8,000,000.[17]

———

UHNWIs rely heavily on HNWIs and their associates to build and expand capital webs in frontier markets by playing in the gray along a continuum. On one end, a small group of people engage in a concerted effort to steer clear of corruption, while at the other end, others engage in practices of outright theft. Those who steer clear of corruption are among the minority who accept higher transaction costs for access to less-attractive deals. The choice to adopt corruption-free business practices is afforded only to those with access to capital for long-term business horizons. Those who engage in outright theft take on a short-term strategy of stealing from UHNWIs and SOEs (state-owned enterprises) before moving on to other frontier markets to play the same game.

Somewhere in between those who run clean operations and thieves is the largest group of people, who adopt pragmatic strategies for playing in the gray. In a context where there is a great deal of overlap between the interests of public officials and private businesspeople, bribery is almost impossible to avoid. But as I showed, bribery takes many forms. There are a number of different kinds of bribers and legal co-conspirators—here I identified greasers, gift givers, brokers, and fixers—who work to obfuscate bribes in these capital webs. The same people might adopt multiple strategies to move a project forward.

Through a lens of spiderweb capitalism, this case illustrates how U/HNWIs export sophisticated strategies—of front-running the legal systems in some cases and co-opting political officials in others—to frontier economies around the world. Vietnam and Myanmar are not the only two countries in

the world where different kinds of bribers and legal co-conspirators exist—
these strategies come to the market by way of those who found them useful
in other parts of the world.[18] Dominant spiders and subordinate spiders alike
felt that greasing the wheels was par for the course in frontier markets. Few
seemed to have a problem making small facilitation payments in the form
of cash to speed up bureaucratic processes. Greasers legitimized these payments by pointing to laws which effectively legalized and justified them.
Greasers who pay small facilitation payments do so because it is the most
pragmatic approach in a context where the government cannot afford to
offer higher salaries. However, as the stakes grow, so do the modes of bribery.
Rather than giving cash payments, sometimes known as tea money, bribers
on the ground developed a variety of different strategies to obfuscate these
transactions through gift-giving, bundling, and brokerage, inspired by East/
Southeast Asian and Western investment strategies.

The gift form is the most intimate and personal, while bundling and brokerage strategies provide even greater distance and therefore plausible deniability. From this perspective, the special edition Rolex watch, the highly
coveted Hermès handbag, the abstract artwork, or the fancy job in an asset
management firm come to serve as more-discreet functional equivalents to
bribery for private actors seeking access to inside information and preferential treatment by the state. At the same time, the push to professionalize is
not always smooth. Investors finessing this market with greater capital injections also adopt a pragmatic approach by hiring brokers, fixers, or handlers
to do this work for them. The path towards professionalizing is not always
motivated by morally upright individuals. There are plenty of former crony
capitalists who want standardization because it helps them secure their ill-
gotten gains against the constant turnover and upheaval inherent in crony
capitalism.

What makes the formation of these webs so risky is the fact that everyone knows that they are vulnerable to theft and principal-agent problems.
In some instances, subordinate spiders work in coordination with local state
officials to steal and launder money from dominant spiders, as was the case
with NorthFour Bank and the fake shrimp farm in Dalat. Remarkably, this
kind of theft does not seem to deter new investors from entering the market, because they have a short memory for financial losses. Their gut feeling
makes them feel that they will fare better than past losers in the market.

By focusing on the people playing in the gray and the variety of approaches
they employ, this chapter provides a more nuanced way to conceptualize

strategies of corruption and bribery. While dominant spiders are never on the front lines carrying out these bribes, subordinate spiders in this web obfuscate an illegal transaction with one that appears innocuous and is difficult to trace. Still, HNWIs in frontier markets also create further layers in the web by syndicating high-risk bribes out to other financial professionals—the brokers, fixers, or principal agents whose sole responsibility is to finesse these bribes. Each person is narrowly specialized in their unique role, making it difficult to implicate any one person in this broader system. However, the relationships between U/HNWIs, their associates, and state officials together illustrate the co-constitution of legal/illegal, licit/illicit, corrupt/clean strategies in webs that are extremely difficult to systematically trace.

Tax Strategies of Global Elites

A central facet of playing in the gray is the varied ways investors work to reduce their taxes.[1] At the heart of spiderweb capitalism are the different ways that offshore shell companies help investors shift what would be tax burdens into financial profits. Tax experts often distinguish between tax evasion, tax avoidance, and tax certainty. Tax evasion is illegal, while tax avoidance refers to legal practices to minimize income taxes. Tax avoidance in the context of frontier markets often involves the use of legal strategies through offshore structures that either have not been discovered by state regulators or have not been tested in local courts of law.[2] Tax certainty refers to the creation of a clear set of tax agreements onshore between state officials and private investors onshore. However, a closer look at these three structures of taxation reveals that the lines between them are blurry.[3] I argue that while the strategies of tax evasion, tax avoidance, and tax certainty may differ, they ultimately have similar outcomes as businesses work to reduce their tax burden to maximize profits.

The different strategies of dealing with taxation vary based on investors' time in the market, stage of development, proximity to state officials, and ability to afford the process of professionalization. I look at cross-border tax systems through a lens of capital webs and the kinds of cooperation necessary among investors, state actors, and financial professionals at different stages of investment who articulate varied tax concerns and strategies, producing heterogeneity onshore. Importantly, investors' relations with tax authorities and financial professionals such as lawyers and accountants shape how much investors play in the gray.

A temporal and relational dimension shapes the approach investors take toward their tax strategy. In the early stages of an investment project, entrepreneurs pursue a strategy of tax evasion because they cannot afford to hire the big four auditing firms and professional law firms. However, as their businesses grow, they begin to undergo a process of professionalization by hiring third-party financial professionals to protect their accumulated assets. Firms looking for larger capital injections contract professional lawyers, auditors, and company secretaries who advise them on how to set up offshore structures—thereby engaging in the practice of tax avoidance through processes known as "round-tripping" and "transfer pricing." Round-tripping is a financial hack that involves selling an asset while at the same time agreeing to buy it right back at about the same price.[4] Transfer pricing is an accounting practice whereby one division charges another division in the same company for goods and services to legally write off parts of the costs of the business.[5]

At yet a third stage, as governments begin to catch on to these transfer pricing strategies, financial professionals, and auditing firms in particular, shift their language and begin articulating an aspiration for tax certainty—promoting themselves to investors as best able to avoid potential audits, fines, and back taxes. By focusing on how people finesse the three structures of taxation, I highlight the kinds of cooperation necessary among a network of financial professionals within states as businesses undergo professionalization to grow and attract foreign investment.

Tax Evasion: Early-Stage Entrepreneurs

Early-stage entrepreneurs, entering the market at the earliest stage of development in any sector of the economy, often shoulder the greatest risk. As we've seen, early-stage investors are often divided into two groups: local investors who have close relations with state officials and insider access to participate in the privatization of state-owned enterprises, and their foreign partners or investors. In addition to foreign and local status, the size of the investment matters. Smaller-scale investors often cannot afford the cost of professional lawyers and accountants to help them set up legal structures of tax avoidance.

Across all sectors of the economy—from heavily regulated fields such as real estate and mining to less-regulated fields like manufacturing, the service sector, and technology—investors who enter the market at the earliest stages of development describe having to *front-run* their entrepreneurial activities.

As noted in previous chapters, front-running is a practice of operating without the proper licenses, permits, registration, or tax receipts. In the context of taxes, however, by breaking ground for construction or starting to operate a business without state approval, most are evading formal taxes. But this does not mean they are not paying anything. Rather, early-stage entrepreneurs follow an informal legal style of deal brokering by developing patronage relationships with crony state officials, bypassing many of the bureaucratic hoops by paying bribes so that no one will enforce legal tax policies.

Dinh, a Vietnamese real estate developer who owned a chain of mini hotels, described a practice of front-running: "The only way to stay competitive in this business is to front-run your competitor." When I asked him to elaborate, he explained, "That means that you have to buy land and start construction before you have all of the necessary licensing and permits in place. Sometimes you have to open and run your business without the proper paperwork." He continued, "The thing about this market is that it rewards people who can work without a lot of assurances. That is the Vietnamese way . . . you have to put out all of this money to start your business without the assurance that you get the government permissions in the end." Dinh's wife added, "It is very risky . . . but if you wait for all of the proper paperwork and approvals, two years will go by, and you would be sitting on a pile of cash that is not making you any money." With a few exceptions, most early-stage investors established their businesses and began operations prior to having the proper permissions.

The practice of front-running also meant that most investors effectively evaded municipal taxes by paying small bribes to local authorities. Hai, the owner of a small restaurant chain, explained, "When you want to invest here, you just start your business and then wait for the local authorities to come and inspect your business. We ran for two years without anyone bothering us. After a few years [the local authorities] started to notice us, and they would come by every month to collect their taxes." The "taxes" that he was referring to are the bribes—on the order of USD$200 per month—that they paid in order to avoid both formal taxation and potential fines for operating a business that was not tax compliant.

Kywe, the owner of a small furniture factory in Myanmar, echoed similar sentiments: "In this country no one registers their business until they have had a chance to test out their idea to see if it successful or not. We opened this furniture factory and just started to manufacture and sell our products. We felt that as long as we were small enough to stay off the government's radar, they would just leave us alone." For newer businesses or ones that were especially small, the main tactic involved working to dodge relationships with tax officials just to stay under the radar and effectively evade taxes.

However, it is nearly impossible for companies in other fields to hide from authorities because they need them for customs stamps. For example, Jason, the owner of a company that imports sanitary products from overseas, stated, "In the early days of the business you just have to bribe the customs authorities to get your products through. Even if you wanted to pay the customs tax and do everything by the book, you could not afford to do that, because it would just take too long and your products would get stuck sitting in the freeports." While tax evasion was cited as a common strategy, Jason also articulated the problems with having to navigate an inefficient bureaucracy where local bureaucrats (customs officials, in this case) could operate with a great deal of discretion. Therefore, trying to be tax compliant was not an option because it would slow down their day-to-day business operations.

Early-stage investors that did file annual tax statements often adopted creative accounting practices to evade taxes. One such practice involved operating with multiple "books" that fudged their accounting practices. Earl, an auditor for one of the big four auditing firms, highlighted this pattern:

> A lot of Vietnamese private companies do have two sets of account books. . . . Five is the most I've seen in one company. They have one set of books they share with the tax office, they have another they may show their own investors, they may have another they keep for themselves, one guy said he had one just for his wife, another said he had one for his partner, so it is common practice to have multiple sets. Everyone has two or three sets of books, but that doesn't mean that you have to continue having two or three sets of books.

Nhan, a local Vietnamese from a family-run firm that specialized in the food and beverage sector, was the person who introduced me to Earl. In an interview, Nhan explained to me why they have multiple sets of books. They had one book for their own internal accounting purposes, one for the tax authorities, and another for their investors. The reason for this was that private companies like theirs in their early days "mixed a lot of [their] personal expenses with the business." It was a family-run business. Nhan justified the multiple books by saying, "In Vietnam you cannot afford to stay competitive in the market if you are paying 15, 20, 30 percent taxes and your rival business is not."

Vu was the CEO of a local family-run business. During an interview he also described the process of advancing ahead of his competitors through strategies of tax evasion. He explained to me that "all accounting can be manipulated," and the person able to keep more of their money and reinvest it will be at a significant advantage over their business rivals. As a local family-run business, Vu recognized that "the first guy with cash was going to run fast. . . . Having the cash was important for our long-term growth and strategic plan. You won't have cash if you are buried in taxes."

Dinh, Kywe, Jason, Nhan, and Vu were all very forthcoming about their post-hoc rationalizations to explain how they engaged in strategies to evade taxes as they tried to get their businesses off the ground. In these markets, with weak regulatory structures, the social structure of taxation was shaped by people's perception that paying taxes would lead them to lose money when compared with their competitors in the market who were not paying the same amount in taxes. For them, this was about converting what would otherwise be taxes into returns on investment for the company. Those margins, as Nhan articulated, were somewhere between 15 percent and 30 percent.

When I asked investors who articulated a practice of tax evasion whether they considered hiring accountants who could help them "legally" avoid taxes, all of them stated that it was too costly for the business to contract financial professionals to do that work. Khoi, the CEO of a food products company in Vietnam, explained to me that small family-owned businesses could not "afford to hire the global auditing firms [to] legally avoid taxes." The cost of hiring them was higher than the cost of bribing the tax guys. Accounting firms that specialize in legal avoidance often want to "charge $50,000 to $100,000 for their services. Who has that kind of money?" Nhan went on to tell me that "local firms do the same job, have closer government connections because it's local Vietnamese dealing with local Vietnamese. They do things the Vietnamese way." Compared with other interviewees, Khoi was the most direct in expressing how his company adopted a practice of tax evasion over tax avoidance. While tax evasion exposed them to greater risks, they simply could not afford to pay for the services offered by large accounting firms to legally reduce their tax burdens. As he stated, it was more cost-effective to evade taxes than to pay to legally avoid taxes.

Small businesses that wanted to comply with tax laws, or to avoid developing and maintaining relations of bribery with local authorities, found it particularly cumbersome because local bureaucrats had the power to interpret the laws with a great deal of discretion. This practice was so commonplace that several people described how challenging it was for them be tax compliant. Nga, the CFO of a small factory that produced small hardware for assembling furniture, explained to me:

> Kim, this place is so corrupt, you know. I did not want to pay bribes from the beginning because I wanted to be responsible and pay taxes. I wanted to sleep at night. But then, you know, I go to the tax office and fill out the paperwork and they keep putting the paperwork back on the desk for me. They refuse to tell me what I did wrong because I won't pay the bribe. So, I [was] stubborn. I just sit there and wait and come back. But you know after a long time I lost a lot of weight and I just feel like it is not worth it because it's time away from the factory. I yelled at them and said, 'Fuck you . . . fucking stupid . . . this is why this country is always going to be poor . . . people try to pay their taxes and CANNOT!

While Nga was laughing as she articulated her concerns, I could also see the frustration in her facial expressions and hear the anger in her voice as she threw her hands up in a gesture saying that she just gave up. Despite a context in which there were not many incentives to pay taxes and seemingly fewer sanctions for not doing so, Nga wanted to be responsible so she could court investors with her clear tax strategy. But paying taxes and being a law-abiding citizen in this instance was far more time-consuming and cumbersome than simply paying the bribe and moving on. In this instance, tax evasion was not so much a strategy as the consequence of an ineffective state bureaucracy.

The informal state bureaucracy leads to a great deal of variation within the country with respect to how individual entrepreneurs navigate their taxes. Among many family companies in Vietnam, few described following a protocol or clear procedure through which they paid their taxes. In fact, all of them described a system where the rule of law on the books operated differently from the law in practice. Khue, a Vietnamese real estate developer, articulated this tax maze:

> You have to know that in Vietnam there is *luật* [the law] and *lệ* [precedent]. Everyone knows what the law is. That is clear and not very hard to look up. What matters here is precedent, [which] could be a difference of 10 to 15 percent in taxes and fees. This is why you have to bribe them sometimes to get that right figure.

The lack of transparency of state tax regulations in Vietnam created a situation in which early-stage entrepreneurs had to spend a great deal of time lobbying and socializing with government officials and those with political capital to ensure preferential tax breaks and prevent hidden surprises along the way. From the bureaucrats' perspective, forcing Nga to engage in bribery is effective because it helps them earn money in a state with little capacity to pay government workers a livable salary. But as Khue stated, no two payments are ever the same. To have greater clarity and effectively avoid tax evasion, firms must undergo a long process of professionalization, through which they move away from practices of tax evasion towards strategies of tax avoidance.

Tax Avoidance

As local family-owned businesses grow and become profitable, they often think about how to protect their assets while also expanding their businesses via joint ventures. For many, part of the appeal of forming a joint venture with a foreign investor is that the investor brings strategic expertise associated with professionalization. Once a firm has grown large enough through private equity placements by foreign investors, they are incentivized to hire a team of lawyers, auditors, and financial professionals to help set up legal tax avoidance structures across multiple jurisdictions. However, this path towards professionalization comes with the higher costs of retaining professional accountants from firms with global reputations.

In my efforts to figure out what *professionalization* means, LeAnn, a local Vietnamese woman who runs a family firm in the cosmetics and healthcare industry, explained to me that the stage of professionalization often goes hand in hand with a family's succession planning strategies—that is, when parents hand over the business to their children to take over. But there is often a generation gap between the younger generation, who want to professionalize, and their parents, who, she explained, "are generally untrusting of foreign investors and worry that professionalizing will bring up unnecessary costs." Her parents have a history of success that has a lot to do with understanding that the Vietnamese way is about relations with local authorities. Those relations are their advantage in the market. The parents' generation do not want to change.

But for LeAnn's generation, "change [is] key to our survival." She wants to be able to attract foreign capital that will enable them to expand their distribution points beyond Ho Chi Minh City and the south by opening more storefronts throughout the rest of the country. To do that, they need partners and capital to expand. Those partners want them to set up better tax structures so they can avail themselves of legal cross-border advantages.

The intergenerational tension that LeAnn describes gets at the heart of the tensions between tax evasion structures and tax avoidance structures.

LeAnn's parents were able to get their business off the ground by effectively managing their relationships with tax authorities on the ground and having a deep understanding of the local market. However, to grow their business in the way that LeAnn envisions, they need to court foreign investors. To attract the money of UHNWIs and expand their capital webs, the family business would need to undergo professionalization by setting up legal cross-border tax structures. This process, however, is often foreign to local parents, so it takes a great deal of trust and succession planning to let the next generation take the reins. On the issue of taxes, it took three follow-up interviews with LeAnn for her to articulate how they would strategize to grow the business and stay competitive in the market. She began to articulate how she thought about the differences between tax evasion and tax avoidance.

From her perspective, profitable firms with greater visibility in the public eye attract an increase in random visits from tax authorities, who will try to shake them down for larger bribes. At that phase, they must transition from the mindset of a small firm struggling to grow to that of an established business looking for innovative ways "to protect the money we've made, not just hustle to make more." She explains to her parents that "one way (tax evasion) is illegal . . . bribing the local officials with tea money every time they come to audit our books . . . but there is a legal way: it's called tax avoidance." The advisory group helps them set up structures with legal tax breaks. This is critical to attracting capital from foreign investors who would much prefer to know exactly how the taxes will affect their overall bottom line.

For LeAnn, the question was: With whom do we spend time developing relations? It is a choice between local tax authorities and professional accountants. While her parents are comfortable dealing with the tax authorities and operating with multiple books, LeAnn feels it is important to build relations with accountants whom they trust enough to show them their firm's books, and who can help them manipulate their tax structures in a way that will protect more of their assets. They do this by working with firms recommended by others in her network who overcame similar barriers. Firms like LeAnn's often describe the complexities of charting out a plan to be tax compliant that does not set off alarm bells for tax authorities. They must figure out a multi-year plan that establishes slow growth over time. By taking on a foreign partner and using legal structures offshore to protect their assets, local firms move from playing in the dark of the gray towards the light of the gray while syndicating out some of the associated risks. What LeAnn described was a strategy to legally avoid paying taxes by taking advantage of exemptions set in place to attract foreign investors to the country through round-trip investment models. In this instance, the method of tax avoidance is to exploit legal loopholes designed to attract foreign investment.

Tu, a local tax advisor, explained tax avoidance in both Vietnam and Myanmar to me in a more nuanced way:

> Myanmar is like Vietnam was fifteen years ago. In Myanmar there are no tax avoidance laws, and it wasn't until 2017 that Vietnam passed formal regulations against tax avoidance. The people who got to the market before this were two steps ahead of the laws and avoided taxes. But [in 2014] the [Vietnamese] government issued a nationwide investigation into tax evasion and ordered 720 firms to pay back taxes for tax evasion. So we tell our clients they have to professionalize if they want to avoid these kinds of setbacks. When you're small and no one notices you it's different, but when you are big with a lot of employees you cannot hide.

My conversations with Tu and many others revealed the gray areas associated with the pathway from tax evasion to tax avoidance. As he states, tax avoidance was not even on the Vietnamese government's radar until 2014, and subsequently in Myanmar, not until 2017. However, as family companies expand, they encounter the risks of random inspections and back taxes. Regardless of whether they purposefully evaded taxes or honestly misunderstood the complex legal terrain, what matters is the realization that they need to outsource some of that risk by undergoing professionalization.

Western investors wanted to steer as far away as possible from operating within areas of the gray that involved anything more than "speed money"— small payments made to local officials to process the paperwork showing they are tax compliant. Investors looking for projects that involve a lower level of legal and reputational risk often wait for someone else to help these local firms begin the process of professionalization before they feel ready to make their investments.

During my time in the field, I saw deals close more frequently with regional investors from South Korea, Taiwan, Malaysia, Thailand, Hong Kong, and Singapore. Regional investors had a far greater appetite for dealing with companies that play in gray areas and helping them transition into a professionalized firm. They operate with Western and Japanese investors in mind as their exit strategy. In an interview with Anurak, a Thai investor who was about to close a deal with a local family business in the food and beverage sector, he explained to me:

> Vietnam is like Thailand fifteen years ago. It's unpredictable and exciting. It's a different frontier. Every time the government changes hands, business leaders have to watch and wait to see how the new underlings will handle business licenses, inspections, tax . . . As the market opens up, international competition comes in and these local companies need to grow. If they really want to stay ahead of the curve or keep up with the curve of the market, they can't rely anymore only on internal sources of capital. There is where the opportunity is to come in and provide external capital, like, for example, private equity.

However, a pool of eager foreign investors looking to expand into new frontiers was only half the battle. Onshore, they needed to find ways to convince reluctant local firms to have honest conversations with foreign investors. This meant that local firms would have to get their businesses to a place where they were comfortable not only sharing their books, but also setting in place a clear set of strategies for paying income and commercial taxes.

In a context where internal financing is challenging for local firms with ambitions for large-scale growth, local companies must weigh the costs and benefits of adopting a new shareholder structure. Foreign partners bring with them a web of experts and relationships crucial for helping their local partners set up offshore structures that are critical to take advantage of tax laws across multiple sovereignties. In transitioning from prevailing tax evasion strategies to ones of avoidance, foreign investors and their local partners undergo an intimate process that involves a great deal of relational work to get on the same page.[6] Anurak explained the challenges at this stage: "We realize that you can't force a five-year-old child to become a mature eighteen-year-old. We are comfortable working in the gray and dealing with the complex family arrangements."

At the same time, Anurak explained, the added value that they bring is the specialized skills to set up proper [corporate] governance structures at an international level. This was important because it enabled their local partners to expand their networks and build important international relationships to optimize finance and manufacturing operations. They do this by putting a plan into place that increases revenues slowly over time, so that local firms are tax compliant. "You can't go from claiming losses every year to then showing profits of $1 million. That is just asking for an audit!" he explained.

What Anurak was describing was a certain level of cultural familiarity and comfort with investing the time to build relationships of trust with their local partners. It was much easier for him to understand a family-run business with a board structure that mixed family business with the professional sphere. Indeed, this phase involves the greatest growing pains. In the process of professionalization, the risk is syndicated between multiple parties: the local firm, the foreign investor, and the auditing firm that helps with deal advisory to be tax compliant. This is the riskiest stage of investment for any foreign investor, because it involves a great deal of uncertainty, between the ways different bureaucrats interpret the law and the relational work required to establish trust with the local partner.

For Clarence, an investor from Singapore, the goal was to form joint ventures with local firms and help them undergo the process of professionalization to exit to an investor with an even larger ticket size. In their contracts with their local partners, foreign partners often set up contracts with key targets, and if the local firm did not meet those key targets, they would progressively lose more and more control over the firm. Clarence explained:

> In our joint venture we have certain targets. There is a short grace period for us to get in and hire a COO (chief operations officer). We also put in place a board of directors, hire a professional accountant to bring in the technology necessary to manage our books, and ensure that we have all the proper licensing in place to operate. We also put in place a plan to grow and expand. The idea is to go from having 9 or 10 storefronts to roll out 50 throughout the country . . . increase our business volume and sales. You have to do all of this in order to attract big-time investors.

A lot of the work involved with professionalizing a local firm has to do with keeping up with the ever-changing regulatory environment. As the Vietnamese government works to improve its legal framework and institutions related to business and investment, foreign investors and their local partners must professionalize with it and make sure that they execute on that on the ground.

For investors like Clarence, Vietnam is just at the beginning of its horizon for possible growth. As the government works to attract "higher-quality" capital, he hopes to be in a position where he can ride that wave of eager investors with deeper pockets who want to have some exposure to new frontier markets. In effect, it is the foreign partners' job to help take small family-run operations and professionalize them for large-scale private equity acquisitions.

It is important to note here that while setting up legal structures of tax avoidance certainly reduces the risks associated with tax evasion, the transaction costs are much higher, so that investors coming in at the later stages miss some of the grayest activities along with the massive gains (or potential losses). As I ruminated on the data I was gathering about how people transitioned to strategies of avoidance, I could not help but probe deeper by going to financial professionals to ask what the actual methods of tax avoidance involved.

METHODS OF TAX AVOIDANCE

The two most common tax avoidance strategies were *round-trip investments* and *transfer pricing models.* Following similar structures set up by Chinese firms, local Vietnamese and Burmese firms engage in *round-tripping*, or what Wei Shen refers to as *piggybacking,* which involves setting up special purpose vehicles or holding companies offshore, enabling the same local firm to reinvest in the company onshore as a "foreign investor" to take advantage of the tax benefits in low-tax haven jurisdictions.[7] While local firms must pay a 20 percent corporate tax, if they set up an entity offshore that then reinvests onshore, the vehicle makes it appear that they are also a foreign investor. In addition, foreign firms and joint-venture partnerships engage in a practice they refer to as *transfer pricing*: they engage in intracompany transactions that allow them to book their liabilities in high-tax jurisdictions onshore and their assets in low-tax jurisdictions offshore. In short, what they are doing are claiming losses in high-tax jurisdictions and gains in low-tax jurisdictions for the same investee company, using offshore paper companies.

As LeAnn's case highlighted, countries like Vietnam and Myanmar often offer tax incentives for foreigners to attract FDI into the country. These tax incentives come at the cost of trying to protect the business interests of local firms. To get around this, local firms engage in round-tripping, allowing them to reap the same tax benefits as foreign investors. Following the example of Chinese investors who set up similar structures in Hong Kong or the British Virgin Islands, local Vietnamese and Burmese U/HNWIs set up offshore firms in Hong Kong, Singapore, and other tax havens such as BVI and Lichtenstein. Firms incorporated offshore are used to temporarily hold profits made in Vietnam and Myanmar before they are reinvested onshore in the two countries.[8]

Through the round-tripping model, the offshore holding company is a form of financial engineering that essentially takes an onshore company and repackages it as a company offshore to take advantage of the lower taxes in the offshore jurisdiction. In this setup local companies with offshore setups "would only be subject to a withholding tax on the distribution of dividends from the [locally based] operating company."[9] Importantly, "the 'round-trip investment' model reflects the local business community's preference to be 'packaged' as a foreign investment and concern that the government may impose exchange restrictions on residents. . . . More importantly, the 'round-trip' investment model . . . is mainly driven by the idea of tax avoidance and tax-differential treatment between local and foreign investors."[10] Like many Chinese investors in China, local Vietnamese and Burmese investors who adopted a round-trip investment model were able to capture a tax break and preferential tax treatment. This model provides local firms with a huge incentive to connect their local webs to bigger webs set up offshore.

In an interview with Liem, the CEO of a local asset management firm in Vietnam, he explained to me:

> The laws are set up in a way that gives foreigners advantages over local companies because they pay less taxes. The special purpose vehicle (SPV) is the most common structure used by foreign companies to hold direct investments in Vietnam overseas. In China [referring to a news article] *"an SPV is a holding company set up by a foreign investor outside of China—usually in Hong Kong or other locations that boast notable tax advantages and favorable tax treaties with China—for the special purpose of holding equity interest in an onshore foreign-invested enterprise (FIE)."* In the same way, there is a dual tax treaty between Vietnam and Hong Kong, so that Hong Kong's double tax agreement with Vietnam reduces the withholding rate from 20 percent to 5 percent. While Chinese tax authorities are starting to regulate their offshore equity transactions, countries like Vietnam, Cambodia and Myanmar have not caught up yet. We are just one or two steps ahead of the regulators.

What Liem was describing is the practice of tax avoidance through "round-tripping." In this case, money from a country (e.g., Vietnam) flows to a foreign country (Hong Kong or Singapore) and comes back as a foreign direct investment into Vietnam. This strategy allows local investors to capture some tax concessions, because by parking their money in Hong Kong or Singapore before reinvesting it, they can enjoy significantly lower taxes. Investors and financial professionals almost always cited China as the model they followed when they mentioned "round-trip investing." This was not a model invented by the investors, accountants, or lawyers locally, but one set up based on case studies and news reports from this model established in more-developed countries within the region.

When talking to many stakeholders about tax avoidance, nearly everyone highlighted the legality of this practice. Minh, a Vietnamese businessman with investments in both Vietnam and Myanmar, stated:

> Legally all of this is in the gray area of the law. These tax-structuring strategies are technically legal in this setting. Apple did this, booking their taxes (or capital gains) in Ireland. In that case it might be gray to US regulators but clean and very white in Ireland. The same is true here. There are no laws regulating this, so we are not breaking any laws. The key here is to know how to make laws work in your favor.

The fact that Apple and other corporations have used this strategy points to the fact that tax avoidance is an ordinary business practice all around the world. Lawyers echoed the same sentiments. For example, in an interview with Thanh, a lawyer who worked as in-house counsel for an asset management firm, he explained the process of tax avoidance to me: "You will see the same thing here as you saw in China–Hong Kong and India–Mauritius. We usually draw on those case studies to conduct risk assessments. The government in Vietnam knows this happens, but they are not cracking down on it, because they know that if they do, it will affect Vietnam's bottom line. If they want to attract foreign capital, they will have to let the country go through the same growing pains as India and China." From the perspective of the state, tax avoidance structures are a double-edged sword. On the one hand, clamping down on these structures will discourage foreign investors and negatively affect the flow of FDI, while on the other hand, turning a blind eye to these activities results in a loss of important state revenue captured through taxes.

When I asked Thanh to explain the SPV to me in legal terms, he told me that firms set up SPVs to fulfill a very specific purpose and limited use. The paper entity is separate from the sponsoring or parent company for legal and tax reasons and can legally be controlled by several companies working together. It serves multiple purposes. The first is that it syndicates risk by isolating the risk from the parent company, so that back taxes or bankruptcy don't affect other investments. These entities are used for risk sharing, so that companies can pool risky resources in an SPV and securitize them to raise funds or obtain financing.

I probed to ask him how exactly SPVs syndicate risks. He explained that SPVs enclose each investment into a separate vehicle, so that if there are back taxes on one investment, the state cannot collect them from revenues obtained in other investments. The SPV effectively protects their assets and other investments. He explained, "In a lawsuit, the claimant can only put a lien on everything in this entity; they cannot legally touch other assets." In new frontier markets where different forms of bribery are everyday facets of doing business, the SPVs create a layer in the web which makes it extremely challenging for both state officials and business partners to figure out where the dominant spiders' money or liquid assets are located.

The SPV also helps to syndicate risks for both local and foreign investors involved in a joint venture, because it creates a legal wall between the invested asset and all other assets, so that investors can confine the risks associated with one investment from other investments.

Foreign investors or foreign invested firms also avoid taxes through transfer pricing, in its simplest form: an accounting method by which one part of a multinational company charges another subsidiary of the same company for goods and services, to distribute profits between jurisdictions. Large multinational corporations like Apple, Starbucks, and Fiat are often cited as the leading examples of transfer pricing. Large corporations often use "loopholes and creative interpretations of transfer pricing rules to artificially shift profits to countries where there are lower taxes or better tax breaks."[11] For example, Howard Gleckman, a former contributor to *Forbes*, explains, "For a company like Apple, nearly all of the value of its products is in its patents and intellectual property." So what Apple did was set up two entities in Ireland—a low-tax jurisdiction—and funneled two-thirds of its pre-tax income worldwide to Ireland.[12] In other words, different divisions of a company transact with each other to transfer the cost within a company across international borders to avoid taxes. Companies book profits for goods and services in a jurisdiction with lower tax rates and effectively avoid tariffs on goods and services exchanged internationally.

Transfer pricing in a tax setting is a topic studied primarily by scholars in accounting, economics, and law as a simplified strategy for multinational firms to reduce global taxes.[13] Economists have found extensive evidence that "firms arrange financial flows and intra-firm sales between parent companies and subsidiaries within controlled groups in order to reallocate taxable income from affiliates in high-tax countries to affiliates in low-tax countries."[14]

Yet few scholars look at how these same practices are modified for smaller firms in frontier markets. Foreign investors entering frontier markets are fully aware that the government does not yet have the capacity to regulate these practices. As a result of the weak state regulatory structure, financial professionals and accountants spend a great deal of time advising investors on how to structure their taxes to take advantage of these loopholes. In an interview with Kyaw Oo, a local Burmese investor with a diverse portfolio, he explained that in Myanmar, because state officials lack a basic understanding of how transfer pricing works, they rely on the business community to both explain and inform their policies. "You sat right next to me at this conference," he said. "You have business leaders on the stage and government officials in the audience asking business leaders how the state should regulate them!"

Kyaw Oo was cognizant of the fact that as the country develops and as his local business grows they will have to professionalize by hiring global accounting specialists to advise them on their tax strategy. It is the global advisors who help to explain why "going offshore" will "save a lot of money." Mr. Oo emphasized, "We did not invent this." These practices are copied from larger firms in the US and China, which are beginning to regulate this in ways that frontier markets lack the capacity to do.

What Kyaw Oo was articulating was a process of professionalization in which highly specialized financial professionals help spin out new parts of the web, expanding it from the frontier to offshore centers. For him, it was important to take advantage of the same tax loopholes at a moment when the Burmese government does not yet have the capacity to regulate these investment activities. However, he predicts that there will be a day when the government will follow in the footsteps of other countries and begin to crack down on these practices. He said:

> It is only a matter of time before this government follows the US, China, and India in cracking down on the transfer pricing strategies. They will not do that until they have given firms a chance to grow large enough where that is an issue on the table. In my conversations with government officials, I always say that you have to let businesses grow before you can start to tax them. If you want the firm to go from a $1 million firm to $5 million to $50 million, then we need time and tax incentives to keep growing.

The basic premise here is that as long as local companies onshore can keep growing, they will be better positioned to court investments from Wall Street with a better set of terms—that is, from a place of strength rather than desperation. This example illustrates how some spiders based in new frontiers begin spinning smaller webs prior to connecting them to larger global ones. As such, U/HNWIs weave these complex webs from multiple ends in a nonlinear fashion.

These webs depend a great deal on the highly specialized subordinate spiders who carry out much of the work building unique parts of the web. For instance, Win, an accountant inside a large firm in Myanmar, explained to me how he advises a group of clients who have already made their money and are looking for ways to safeguard it offshore. He explains:

> We advise them in three ways. One protection strategy is tax-related. It's setting up the kinds of tax structures that allow you to keep more of your money through legal means. The second is advising them on how to store their assets in safer places. It makes them feel safer to have a Singapore company because they lived through a time when the government would arbitrarily seize their assets. The third thing we do is, we help to anticipate future changes. That means that we pay close attention to government changes in tax laws and policies.

The conversation with Win echoed much of Kyaw Oo's statements. Frontier and emerging markets like Myanmar do not yet have policies in place to manage cross-border tax structures. As we've seen, following examples of larger firms in different jurisdictions, local firms set up offshore structures to book their taxes in low-tax countries. However, this setup also allows them to park their funds in countries where they feel that their money is in a more politically stable and secure place. At the same time, these firms know that over time they will eventually have to grow and evolve to a place where they can afford to become tax compliant as the state develops laws to enforce transfer pricing regulations. What's key here is that these investors have hired a team of lawyers and tax accountants to ensure that they are up-to-date on the latest tax laws so that they are technically not breaking any laws.

These conversations reveal the extent to which transfer pricing strategies, in practice, are not very different from tax evasion, where smaller firms operate with one, two, three, or even five different sets of books. In a more legally sophisticated transfer pricing model, firms use internal bookkeeping to allocate expenses among their various affiliates by charging the foreign subsidiary for use of its "services" rendered. For large firms, this includes a practice of charging their own affiliate companies for patents and other forms of intellectual property, while these smaller firms charge their own subsidiaries for "consulting services, royalty, and service fee payments" for the investments abroad. Moreover, smaller countries have not yet adopted global arm's-length standards, which are internationally agreed-upon prices for transactions within multinational enterprises. As such, transfer pricing serves as a legal functional equivalent to different modes of tax evasion.

Aspirations to Tax Certainty

In 2017, the Vietnamese government began to implement decrees to curb legal tax avoidance strategies under Decree No. 20/2017/ND-CP.[15] Nearly all of the major accounting firms in Vietnam published updates on the impact of this new decree.[16] Following the new decree in Vietnam, taxpayers are required to record and maintain documentation to submit to tax authorities that includes general information on the business establishment and related parties, the business establishment's transactions, and the methods of calculation of arm's-length prices—or the true market value price for intracompany services.[17] This new decree effectively places the state in direct conversation with businesspeople as they negotiate how to properly calculate arm's-length prices onshore.

Following policy transformations to investigate transfer pricing practices, accounting firms capitalized on this moment by offering services that would strive for greater *tax certainty*. In an interview with Vietnam Internet Television (VITV), Joseph Vu, then at PricewaterhouseCoopers (PwC) (and now at KPMG), stated that "Decree 20 is a huge milestone in Vietnam's transfer pricing administration. It's also very timely in that it aligns with Vietnam's economic landscape, development, and investment trends."[18] The aim of tax certainty involves maintaining the legal structures of tax avoidance offshore while coming to a shared agreement onshore with state officials on acceptable transfer pricing. For example, Kevin, an Australian auditor who works for one of the big four firms in Vietnam, explained how his firm grew from 200 people across the country to over 1,200, in large part due to their ability to help local firms set up systems that come closer to aspirations to tax certainty by "paying the right amount in employee tax, following the labor code" and establishing anti-bribery and anti-corruption policies. However, while the country undergoes growing pains, tax certainty remains aspirational.

Those who come the closest to offering investors some degree of tax certainty will be able to court the best investors from abroad, because everyone is afraid of getting slammed with back taxes. As Kevin mentioned, professional accounting firms grew by capitalizing on the new decrees and taking on clients looking to avoid hefty fees and fines related to transfer pricing strategies. Accounting firms often advise their clients that taxpayers should pursue tax certainty by staying up to date with the decrees and policies as they unfold in real time.[19] At the same time, the line between tax avoidance and tax certainty in frontier markets is still very blurry. No professional accounting firm can offer complete tax certainty. However, as the government establishes new laws, they can help firms figure out how to set prices through arms'-length pricing mechanisms using similar tools developed in the West, China, and India.

I also followed up with several investors to see how the new decree affected their day-to-day investment strategies. Long, the CEO of a logistics company, stated:

> Ten years ago, during the cowboy days of 2006–2007, no one knew what transfer pricing was. Today, the country has developed so rapidly that you are starting to see deals with much bigger ticket prices. Thai investors, US investors there are coming in with tickets north of $100 million. One Thai conglomerate invested $1.1 billion into [a local] group. That's all over the news.

That kind of visibility, he explained, will surely put the deal on the radar of the tax regulators. For firms, highly visible deals must expect a more aggressive transfer pricing enforcement environment in Vietnam. It will take time for the smaller guys to catch up, and the government knows that it will take time for everyone to adapt to these new laws. But the government also realizes that they need to set clearer tax rules that are not just open to the interpretation of the local bureaucrat.

Long made two important points. The first is that smaller firms generally feel like they have more time to get their business affairs in order, because they are not transacting on deals that immediately catch the attention of the government. However, Long is also fully aware that his firm, as well as others, will have to transform to keep up with the shifting regulatory body in Vietnam. The second point is that he has been briefed on the new decree to avoid getting left behind in a country undergoing rapid economic transformation. Local businesses must evolve by hiring a team of accountants to help set up systems to document their transfer pricing practices, so that they are in line with the new decree in the pursuit of tax certainty. Ultimately, the move towards even greater levels of certainty is also what will enable the firm to grow and attract a larger number of investors. As Long stated, "Every private equity firm looking for an exit must have their taxes in order. It is difficult to obtain a high valuation if part of their risk assessment is a back tax that they could be issued following the transaction. That is everyone's nightmare. Those who can offer some degree of tax certainty will have the ability to exit to investors with higher bidding power."

CHALLENGES WITH ASPIRATIONS TO TAX CERTAINTY

The irony in the tension between local and foreign investors is that foreign investors and accountants alike often push family firms to undergo professionalization to move from tax evasion to tax avoidance. Tax certainty was held out as the aspirational golden ticket that would allow firms to have their pick among potential investors. However, some global and regional firms are still testing the limits of the Vietnamese tax law as they challenge aspirations to tax certainty.

In a widely publicized deal, the regional technology transportation company Grab Taxi bought out Uber Vietnam. However, the deal has left tax payments unresolved. Several Vietnamese news outlets reported that tax authorities in Ho Chi Minh City sent a request to Grab in Vietnam asking the company to provide details concerning its recent acquisition of the rival company Uber Southeast Asia. By taking advantage of global offshore structures and setting up a holding company in the Netherlands, as well as offshore bank accounts, Uber and Grab both made it impossible for the Vietnamese government to enforce local tax laws. Uber allegedly owes the Vietnamese government USD$2.3 million in back taxes but refuses to pay the firm's debt. Uber claims that the $2.3 million figure is inflated according to the double taxation avoidance agreement with the Netherlands.[20]

At the same time, Grab Taxi claims that the $2.3 million debt is Uber's responsibility and has refused to pay the firm's outstanding debt. Grab told a *VnExpress* journalist, "This matter is Uber's responsibility. Grab did not buy Uber's legal status in Vietnam, which is the unit bearing all legal responsibilities for settling tax-related issues with the tax department."[21] However, lawyer Doan Van Hau, chairman of the Vietnam Lawyers' Commercial Arbitration Center, claims that Grab is in violation of the Vietnamese law, which states that Grab Taxi is responsible for paying all of Uber's back taxes. The primary challenge that the Vietnamese government has in this case is that while Ho Chi Minh City's tax department asked five local commercial banks to help it collect the outstanding sum from Uber, it failed because the company did not have a bank account in Vietnam.[22]

It remains to be seen how this standoff between the government and the two technology firms will end as the two settle this dispute. What this very public case points to is that while many of the big accounting firms have been able to profit from the increase in regulations, as they help to promote the professionalization process onshore to court UHNWIs, the move towards tax certainty is never linear. As companies work to avoid as many taxes as possible, there is some degree of subversion at the local level of the government's efforts to regulate tax avoidance structures. This case illustrates how methods of tax avoidance following the government's new decree flirt with a boundary of tax evasion in this game of chicken between the state onshore and investors who use special purpose vehicles and hold funds in bank accounts offshore. It is too soon to know whether firms will aspire towards greater tax certainty or whether they will set up complex webs, as Uber and Grab did, to avoid onshore taxes altogether. This case also suggests a tension between bigger complex capital webs with dominant spiders who have more money to invest and state regulators looking to attract that capital, which is key to the countries' development, while also trying to capture the taxes onshore.

———

A look at the spectrum of tax strategies through a lens of spiderweb capitalism reveals how social spiders—here, local and foreign investors along with their lawyers, accountants, and company secretaries—employ varied tax strategies based on an investment project's stage of development.[23] In a cat-and-mouse game between local states and onshore enterprises, small firms adopt strategies of tax evasion to illegally shift tax burdens into profits because they cannot afford legal strategies of avoidance, while larger firms set up legal tax avoidance structures to protect their assets by professionalizing. However, no firm is static. All local firms working to attract regional and international capital metamorphose over time. Dynamic firms expand their capital webs to include professional firms who help them not only to reduce or avoid taxes legally but also to meet international professional standards. One consequence of growth because of new partnerships with foreign investors is greater media attention and heightened levels of scrutiny by local state tax authorities. To get around this scrutiny, tax webs grow far more complex to shift assets offshore and liabilities onshore. Local states respond to such legal avoidance strategies by developing policies that will expand their tax collecting capacities onshore. However, in frontier markets, states often do this in close consultation with business leaders to figure out how best to standardize their tax collecting capacities without limiting growth and foreign investment.

As this chapter highlights, tax is a primary area where the market and politics are intertwined. All along this continuum, state actors are generally aware of the different levels of tax evasion/avoidance/certainty, because this is how small enterprises grow large enough to attract bigger investments for the state to capture an even larger tax share. The data here provides several insights on the state, its incapacities, and variations in the ethics of government leaders across ministries and levels of government in frontier markets. Both state officials and business leaders in Vietnam and Myanmar compare these markets to those of China, India, Thailand, and others, thereby placing themselves in temporal frames for learning from each other and competing with one another.

For Gabriel Zucman, the hidden wealth of nations is a story about how U/HNWIs have found a way to keep large sums of money in tax-free countries, thereby undermining developing countries' ability to generate revenue. But missing from that framework is an account of the varied ways in which the state and market mutually benefit from these strategies all along the continuum in frontier markets. At the heart of these different tax strategies is a symbiotic relationship between state officials and private investors, who both profit off these obscure webs, making these tax webs challenging to unravel. In strategies of evasion, state actors benefit by personally lining their pockets, while private actors shave off their tax burden and shift that money into higher return on investments. As firms become profitable and undergo professionalization, they utilize tax avoidance strategies to legally shift their tax geographies. Massive spiderwebs are the product of local partnerships with foreign investors who hire highly specialized accounting professionals to engage in creative accounting practices that involve shifting losses to high-tax jurisdictions and booking profits to low-tax jurisdictions. Because these methods are so complex and hard to trace, state officials often rely on business experts to help inform tax policies. As a result, this web is a system where the businesses have a hand in developing the policies to regulate themselves.

In many ways tax evasion and tax avoidance serve as functional equivalents to one another, with the shared goal of transforming tax burdens into returns on investments. The key difference has to do with whether a local firm has grown large enough to be able to afford the suite of financial professionals to help them set up a legal barrier of protection. By setting up offshore holding companies and offshore bank accounts, investors make it far more challenging for local governments with low regulatory enforcement capacities to enforce transfer pricing decrees.

As governments began to develop a bigger regulatory body to enforce such decrees, entrepreneurs, accountants, and financial professionals alike shifted from a language of tax avoidance to one of aspirations to tax certainty. Aspirations to tax certainty involve direct engagement with local tax authorities to set agreed-upon transfer pricing, so the state can capture some taxes that would otherwise be lost to low-tax jurisdictions. However, the case of Uber and Grab Taxi illustrates how tax certainty is more of an aspirational ideal than a realistic outcome. While the data here focuses on capital webs in frontier markets, it is important to recognize that these strategies were imported from models established in the most developed economies around the world. These practices are no different from the massive capital webs set up by firms like Facebook and Apple, which operate in much more complex webs around the world. Legal and accounting professions are key to establishing the kinds of tax strategies that connect frontier markets to developed markets in one large global ecosystem, enabling the world's wealthiest individuals to get rich and stay rich in the most boring yet highly effective and respectable way, so that it draws little attention or scrutiny from the public.[24]

5

Impunity in Stealth Webs

This chapter focuses on how offshore structures allow dominant spiders and their associates to play in the gray with varying degrees of impunity, both onshore and offshore. Ultra-high-net-worth individuals (UHNWIs) almost always have multiple layers of people and institutions who not only shield them from criminal or reputational risks, but who also serve as the "fall person" in the event of a scandal. The "fall guy" is the scapegoat who usually takes the blame for work they carried out to help make UHNWIs even wealthier.

But, as I show, even the "fall people" are hard to catch. This is because, as financial journalists Wright and Hope put it in *Billion Dollar Whale*, money moves through "a byzantine labyrinth of bank accounts, offshore companies, and other complex financial structures" around the world that uses separate due diligence teams, lawyers, accountants, and company secretaries.[1] This labyrinth creates layers between the financial professionals working on different parts of the bigger deal, allowing the world's UHNWIs to operate with impunity. Legal webs create protective barriers, which allow UHNWIs to be far less visible and therefore better able to quarantine the criminal and reputational risks associated with illegal and morally reprehensible activity. Their professional associates, on the other hand, are highly compensated for shouldering most of the legal and criminal risks involved with putting the money to work in risky frontier markets. In effect, special purpose vehicles (SPVs) enable UHNWIs to syndicate the risks to their high-net-worth individuals (HNWIs) associates while moving and making money with great anonymity and impunity.

Unlike Jho Low, the Malaysian financier—whose involvement in a USD $12 billion heist of Malaysian public pension funds was detailed in the introduction—the majority of HNWIs that I interviewed described themselves as anonymous and low-key financiers who operated through a strategy of "satisficing," working hard to lie low and stay small so that they could operate with greater impunity and outside of the purview of government regulators. While the authors of *Billion Dollar Whale* use the analogy of big whales and small fish for Jho Low and his associates, I use the analytic of big spiders and small spiders to capture the group of people in this study who are smaller, less flashy, and who hide in plain sight. To be clear, compared with the $12 billion heist of 1MDB, this group of spiders is by and large involved in smaller transactions that are far more common, and perhaps much more consequential than the big splashy ones that get media attention.

The goal of this chapter is to parse out the subtle yet significant differences in these massive webs between UHNWIs and the HNWIs they generously compensate to serve as their fall people, who take on the criminal and reputational risks of playing in the gray.

The Dominant Spiders: Anonymity and Impunity of UHNWIs

Will is a 42-year-old Vietnamese German who spent many years working in private banking for Lehman Brothers in London before the firm's collapse in 2008. After the sudden closure of the bank, he cashed out all his savings and moved to Singapore in search of new investment opportunities. Losing his job brought such a great shock to his system that he decided it was time to become an UHNWI, or, in his words, "an owner of capital rather than a worker for capital." To him the whole financial industry was corrupt, and you were either going to emerge a winner or a loser; after coming out as a loser in 2008, he never wanted to feel that level of economic precarity again.

Will had been a "fat cat" on Wall Street and had made between $500K and $1 million a year, between salary and bonuses, during the heyday years at Lehman. He had made more than enough money to retire at that point. But still, there was something about losing his job that made him feel precarious. He moved to Singapore because he heard from friends that Asia was on the horizon as the next big place for investment opportunities.

At the time that I met him, Will had grown into a dominant spider. With his accumulated assets, he wanted to begin making direct investments by taking equity in companies. However, he did not want to operate as a one-man shop without office and staff support, so he joined a family office—a full-service private wealth management company that serves one or a small number of ultra-high-net-worth families, and in his case, provides an exclusive pipeline of direct investments across Southeast Asia. The family office set up a fund to make investments in Southeast Asia with over $100 million in assets under management. They make strategic minority investments in companies onshore by taking a board seat and providing the investee companies with an experienced team of investment professionals with expertise across finance, law, management consulting, and business development. The sectors of the economy that they invest in include banking, consumer products, education, healthcare, infrastructure, technology, and telecommunications. For smaller, less developed countries, the typical target investment size is $5–10 million, with a seven to ten-year time horizon using privately negotiated debt and mezzanine instruments that are not pure debt or equity, but anything in between. A mezzanine deal varies from deal to deal.

Will operates with a strategy of satisficing—that is, being content as a big, but quiet, spider who does not let greed push him too far into the gray, to avoid drawing the attention of local and foreign state officials in the way that led to Jho Low's demise.

In the middle of our interview, Will brought up Malaysia's 1MDB scandal, and the first thing he said was, the one thing to remember about finance is that "greed always trumps trust": when people think that banks will reap remuneration on a deal, they will trust the shadiest characters with their money. What he explained was that banks have to make calculated risks around whom they are willing to service, and that middle-tier banks are more likely to take on "politically exposed persons" (PEPs) with deposits so large they are worth the risk.

About 1MDB, he said to me, "Jho Low was a greedy narcissist. Can you imagine if he'd just laid low and stopped at $1 billion? If he did not indulge in this playboy lifestyle? He would have gotten away with it because [the governments of] Malaysia and Singapore would have written off the debt . . . to avoid a very public scandal that would tarnish their reputation." The interesting story, though, is not the sensationalized cases that are covered by journalists. It is about the kinds of transactions that are made in the most low-key and mundane ways by people like Will, who set up shell companies and operate outside the purview of journalists, state officials, and, for the most part, the general public.

Will told me that I should look at the bigger picture and the people like him, who operate without anyone noticing. Lying low, staying quiet, and controlling one's greed is key to staying in the game, because the bigger one gets the more one assumes the risk of getting caught. He is characterizing himself as a stealth spider rather than a big flashy whale like Jho Low, "the greedy narcissist" who got caught because he could not control his greed.

When I asked Will approximately how many offshore structures he controlled, he told me he has lost count of the number of offshore structures the firm has set up for each of their investments. The whole thing was a maze, and unless he himself sat down to map it all out, it was not very clear. Their main fund was domiciled in Guernsey, where there is no income, state, corporation, or capital gains tax. But the majority of the company's subsidiaries are domiciled in the Cayman Islands, where they have tax-exempt status.

At the same time, some of the subsidiaries are set up in Singapore and have onshore operations in Vietnam, Cambodia, and Myanmar. They are tax-exempt in Singapore but subject to the corporate income tax in Vietnam, Cambodia, and Myanmar. But those taxes are low because the money distributed from the offshore vehicles to Vietnam covers mainly operational expenses, and therefore does not return a profit. The profit instead is booked in Singapore when they sell shares of the firm based on a valuation in Singapore that is separate from the operations onshore in Vietnam.

In addition, they created a mutual fund in Luxembourg, but investors who might want to invest in that fund would have to wire transfer money to Luxembourg. Anyone except those from sanctioned countries like Iran can invest in that fund. However, because of SEC regulations, US investors cannot invest in the fund directly; instead, they must establish bank relations and get a nominee from that bank to make these investments on their behalf. When I asked how US investors have done that, Will said, "So for example, you have money in Charles Schwab in the US. Schwab in the US can wire funds to London, and in London the bank would have a 'nominee.' That nominee would invest in the fund in Luxembourg."

Will explained to me that each investment operated from a separate holding company. While they tried as best they could to uphold a clear set of ethics around fraud, theft, and bribery, it was often difficult to assess whether his local partners were fully ethical, which always lurked in the back of his mind. He was fully aware that his local partners in Vietnam and Myanmar had to pay out bribes in their joint ventures, but he turned a blind eye to that activity from where he sat in Singapore.

Most of the money that Will has been able to raise has come from elites whose money originated in Southeast Asia. He said to me:

> In Vietnam, of course, there are people who have close government connections and are the new success in Vietnam. But there are also the underground rich ones, and they are interesting ones and there are plenty of those. Most of them don't keep their money there. They go to Singapore to reinvest it in more-secure vehicles in Thailand, Myanmar, or they run away with their money. Many of [the local UHNWIs] do not even have their names in there; they have the names of their nominees. In the Cayman Islands, I have a friend who does this administrative work to facilitate all of this, and it is amazing how much paperwork he produces for these companies in these countries here. It used to be Indonesia, Malaysia, the Philippines, and now it is Vietnam, Laos, Cambodia and increasingly Myanmar.

These structures were legal, he told me, and an important mechanism for keeping the government out of their business affairs. Importantly, the money that Will has been able to raise for his family office does not only come from those in developed nations. He was also able to raise capital from the rise of the new money based in Southeast Asia. While the firm facilitates investments in Southeast Asia from abroad, they also help to facilitate many of the round-trip investments from Southeast Asia back into their home countries through offshore shell companies. None of these structures appeared anywhere in the Panama Papers; he checked himself, and I later tried to search and was unable to find any of it.

What did appear instead in that massive 2016 leak of papers published by the International Consortium of Investigative Journalists (ICIJ) was the "foundation" created by his local partners in Vietnam to bribe local government officials, which I elaborate on in greater detail later in this chapter. During our interview, Will revealed to me that he had recently discovered that one of the firms he invested in in Vietnam had been exposed in the 2017 leak known as the Paradise Papers. The entity, Golden Pig Group, was set up in the Cayman Islands as a management fund. They hired an attorney inside a corporate service provider's office in Hong Kong who helped register the fund in the Cayman Islands. The fund had two separate vehicles, *Golden Pig Management Ltd.* and *Golden Pig Impact Fund L.P.* The only shareholder of Golden Pig Management was Golden Pig Impact. Golden Pig CSR (Corporate Social Responsibility) was the foundation that was a ruse used to pay out bribes. While there was nothing damning in the leak, he was nevertheless concerned because of its links to local fixers. Under this guise, the three directors who managed it onshore both engaged in "impact investments" and "carried out bribes".

Will explained to me that the fund served two purposes. First, with an official mandate of "impact investing," investments were to be made in companies or organizations with the intention of generating measurable, beneficial social or environmental impact while also generating financial returns. Second, the fund was also used as a veil to make "donations" to foundations that were tied to "social impact issues" of the new political leaders. Whenever new government leaders were elected to positions of power, the fund managers on the ground worried about being pushed out of their businesses through unsubstantiated charges of money laundering. To circumvent these charges, the fund was used to pay "consultancy" fees to fixers and government officials to maintain close relations with them.

The whole thing was "gray," as Will called it, because while they were making investments in firms that were said to promote education, women's empowerment, and human capital development in the country, it was unclear just how much was siphoned off the top of the investments. As long as they could demonstrate impact and the government officials were not too greedy by taking too much from the foundation, it was a win-win for all parties involved. However, if greed took over and less went to the actual impact investments his local partners were purporting to support, Will's team might be in trouble. When I asked Will just how much money was raised for that fund, he said:

> Ten bucks [meaning $10 million] . . . small, so small no one would notice what is happening to the fund. So yeah, it appeared in the [Paradise] Papers, but the papers can't tell you anything about the content of the fund or the deal flow through it. It's such small potatoes I doubt anyone would care to do the digging. . . . Our model is lay low and stay small—when you're the small guy no one cares to pay attention to you.

For Will "ten bucks" was a small amount in relation to the other funds he set up to carry out their investments. After our interview I looked up the name of this fund, and with a little digging and triangulating, I was able to find it in the ICIJ database. (See Figure 5.1.)

Importantly, the complex structure above has absolutely no visible links to Will or any of his vehicles in Singapore. A search through the ICIJ database

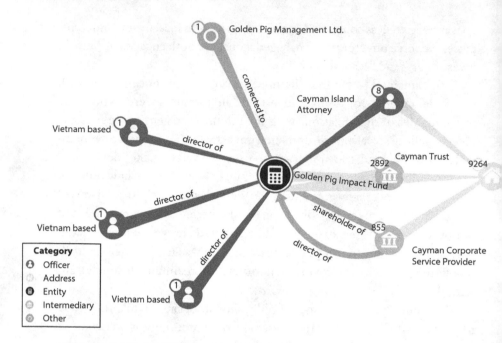

Golden Pig Management Ltd.

Cayman Island Attorney

Vietnam based

director of

Golden Pig Impact Fund

Cayman Trust

2892   9264

Vietnam based

director of

shareholder of   855

director of

Cayman Corporate Service Provider

Vietnam based

Category
- Officer
- Address
- Entity
- Intermediary
- Other

connected to

FIGURE 5.1. Golden Pig Offshore Impact Investment Structure (*Source:* Kimberly Kay Hoang)

also did not turn up anything under Will's name or that of the funds in Luxembourg or Guernsey. Moreover, neither Will's name nor his family office's name in Singapore was listed anywhere in the official documentation, meaning they were not listed as directors or shareholders of the fund. When I looked up the directors of this fund, Golden Pig Impact Fund had three directors and shareholders, all who were based in Vietnam, and whose names were publicly listed. They are all HNWIs—"relationship managers," as Will called them—who double as the local fall guys. However, aside from identifying the fund as an offshore entity, the database did not provide any substantive information related to what was behind the business.

A cursory look at this only tells us what the structure of the network looks like; it does not tell us anything about the material substance of the relations between the nodes. This structure also told us nothing about the relationships between outsiders of this immediate network and those inside of this network. In other words, these images show only one part of a web but do not show us how different webs are in fact connected to one another. As an "owner of capital" Will was nowhere to be seen. He was in fact hidden in a separate structure that does not even appear in the database. His primary risk was that his local partners could siphon off funds from Golden Pig and he would have no legal power over that. Giving up control of those funds used to pay bribes was ultimately just part of the cost of doing business. By ceding all his legal rights to highly compensated financial professionals (HNWIs), Will effectively syndicated the criminal and reputational risks associated with these vehicles set up to carry out bribes. What was astounding to me was that he could reveal all this stuff to me, knowing full well that it would end up in a book, and still be confident that his tracks would be covered because his involvement is hidden in a larger web of stealth capital.

As I came to interview and meet more people like Will, I often wondered how their highly compensated associates managed their own part of the capital webs. Did they understand the risks involved? How did they manage these relationships onshore? The time I spent in Hong Kong and Singapore motivated me to interview subordinate spiders in these webs between Hong Kong, Singapore, Vietnam, and Myanmar.

Subordinate Spiders: HNWIs as "The Fall Person"

Oliver Win is a 38-year-old private wealth manager from a multi-family office based in Hong Kong. His family was originally from Burma, but they left during the political upheavals of the late 1950s. While it was never quite clear to me what his family's source of wealth truly was, it seemed that his family had generated a significant amount of wealth as gemstone traders in Myanmar before transitioning to the manufacturing industry in Hong Kong, making plastics for export all around the world. At the age of 14 Oliver was sent to a private elite boarding school in California before getting a bachelor's degree in economics from New York University. He describes himself as a B-level student who was not quite cut out for the investment banking world on Wall Street. However, his father belonged to a secret society, an elite social group of millionaires in Hong Kong, and through that network he was able to secure a job in JPMorgan Chase in Hong Kong, working his way up over the years to eventually become head of investments for the Southeast Asian region of the bank.

He was a subordinate spider in relation to people like Will. Oliver's primary job was as a "relationship manager," a commonly used title for people like him who build and cultivate relationships with ultra-high-net-worth individuals—the "billionaires" as he calls them—who in his case are from Myanmar, Malaysia, Indonesia, Thailand, and Vietnam. He managed their money from the Hong Kong office. After the 2008 financial crisis, he played a crucial role in a number of mergers and acquisitions in which he and his partners made a combined $25 million. Around that same time, he felt a "calling" to do something in Myanmar, so he spent a year traveling around the country to reflect on what his next venture would be. At the end of his soul-searching adventure, he decided that $25 million was not nearly enough do the kinds of large-scale investment projects he was interested in, so he set out to raise more money. His goal was to one day become a dominant spider, so he could serve as a quiet chairman in the background and not have to do the hands-on work of putting the money to work onshore.

To raise capital, he set up an offshore fund where he could direct investment funds from folks all around the world. The first thing that he did was research on where best to set up an offshore company. He started by looking into the Cayman Islands, which, he knew from his years of experience in banking, had once been a popular jurisdiction for the incorporation of companies owned or operated by parties located in Asia. The popularity had to do with the fact that in the Cayman Islands there was no corporate tax, capital gains tax, or wealth tax on a company conducting business offshore. There were several Cayman Islands companies listed on the Hong Kong Stock Exchange, the world's tenth largest securities market.[2] However, through informal conversations with friends, he learned that there was growing concern surrounding anonymity in the Cayman Islands as it increased its information sharing with regulators in the United States due to its links to US banks and hedge funds. Instead, he set up VirginCapital in the British Virgin Islands, where several of his Chinese friends had set up funds due to its no-questions-asked approach.

After he established VirginCapital to house his new fund, he decided to set up another offshore company to build a labyrinth difficult to trace. A friend referred him to a corporate service provider in Hong Kong. By chance, I happened to be in Hong Kong when he was going to meet with the provider, and I asked if I could accompany him to the office. We met in the Central business district on the first floor of a 25-story office building. At the entrance to the lobby level, we showed the receptionist our passports before we were given access cards to the elevator, then made our way past security to the 10th floor.

Once inside the office building, I was surprised by the overall feel of the office. The office was one of 30 offices on that floor, and it was very small. The reception area was cramped, with a narrow reception desk manned by one person and just enough space for two chairs and a small coffee table in the waiting area. Oliver gave his name, and within five minutes we were greeted by a woman named Beatrice.

Beatrice invited us to walk with her to the meeting room in the back. Once we got past the reception area, I was shocked to see that there was nothing glamorous about the office. There were five or six open cubicles, but most were empty. Toward the back wall stood a row of file cabinets with thousands of paper stacks lined up and down the wall. There was clearly not enough room in the file cabinets: they had started stacking piles of paper on the floor that went all the way up to the ceiling, which was covered with a giant blue tarp, as if to protect the paperwork from potential water leaks in the ceiling. If there was an order or logic to the piles of papers it was not discernable at first glance. In addition, each desk had piles and piles of paper on it. There were two other employees in the building, who had boxed rice lunches on their desks that they were eating as they worked. The room was lit with fluorescent white lights, and there were no windows in the meeting room.

We made our way past all the papers and sat down in a glass meeting room that was tinted with frosted white window film, so that we would not be distracted by any of the activity going on outside of the office. Beatrice handed us each a folder of information on their office and the services they provided. Oliver introduced me as a professor from the University of Chicago who was studying foreign investment abroad, and himself as one of the people I was interested in studying. He told her that I was there to observe him going through the steps of setting up a company.

Beatrice asked Oliver to describe his company to her. He told her that he had set up a small family office incorporated in BVI, but that he was looking to set up subsidiary companies and wanted to incorporate in places that still granted anonymity. Without asking him any questions about *why* he needed a jurisdiction that granted anonymity, she told him that following some new regulations set forth by the United States under KYC (know your client) and DD (due diligence), all licensed registered agents are required by law to know who their client is and to provide certain documents that will prove his identity and address. As a result, a completely anonymous purchase of an offshore company is legally impossible. But the personal information of the client remains only with the registered agent and is not filed in any public records. As a result of these new regulations, this company no longer accepted American clients, because the US government was more likely than other governments to ask corporate service providers for that information. Since Oliver did not have a US. passport, this would not be much of a problem.

She then went on to describe the different packages they offered. The first was a "company pack" that offers worldwide offshore company incorporations and compares the pros and cons of one jurisdiction to another, such as the differences between what is offered in Samoa and in Seychelles. In addition to all incorporation documentation and government fees, they also offer a "privacy pack" that contains the appointment of a Professional Director and Shareholder, and an offshore bank account. Then she went on to describe Samoa as a new destination known for being one of the most versatile jurisdictions in the world in which to form an offshore company. Samoa was also cheaper. For USD$900, her firm would provide him with company secretary services based out of the Hong Kong office, where they could handle the paperwork involved with forming a company. This fee also included: registered office address, registered agent services, company secretarial maintenance, all government fees due on incorporation, certificate of incorporation, memorandum and articles of association, appointment of first directors, consent actions of the Board of Directors, Share Certificates, registration of directors and members, and a company seal. One person could set up this whole structure.

Oliver then asked Beatrice if she had a list of available company names. She got up to get the list, and as she walked out of the office, he said to me, "I already have a name that I want to use, but you should see the list of names—they are hilarious." When she brought back the list, he laughed, pointing to "Lucky Star 7," "Happymoon4," and the like. He asked if I could take the list of names home with me, and she obliged, putting the document into my folder. When he asked her how long the whole process would take, she told him a few weeks, and she would get in touch with him when it was done. That day he handed her the paperwork to set up Pinkleaf Investment Corporation as a subsidiary of VirginCapital. For Pinkleaf Investment he had a professional "nominee" director included in the Incorporation package, and appointed himself as a consultant. For less than USD$1,000, company secretaries help to set up a special purpose vehicle that separates the business activity of one entity from another. The weird names speak to the number of companies routinely set up in this small office.

After we wrapped up with Beatrice, I invited Oliver to lunch to debrief on the process of setting up an offshore company. What I thought would be a one-hour conversation evolved into an eight-hour conversation over lunch, drinks, and then dinner. During that time Oliver explained to me that he needed first to set up these companies in order to then open offshore bank accounts in Hong Kong. He has set up roughly five different offshore companies because, as he explained to me, he does not want the liabilities of one investment to affect the other investments.

From Oliver's perspective, Southeast Asia is managed by crony capitalists. If you want to make any kind of investments, you must pay off government officials and your business partners. In effect, the Samoa entity would be used to pay out bribes and kickbacks to get access to the sweetheart investment deals that he wanted in on. This was all a "shell game," as he called it, because by using different sets of company secretaries, lawyers, and financial professionals for each of the vehicles, he ensured that no one person could put them all together except for him. In essence, "corruption requires corruption": the fact that a government is corrupt requires a businessperson hoping to succeed there also to engage in corrupt practices. But, he told me, the lawyers working on the BVI entity have no idea what the Samoa entity is doing, and vice versa. This kind of layering provides him with some protection and assurance that it would be hard to "catch him."

The Samoa shell company would be used to conceal and disburse kickbacks to government officials to get access to investment deals. When I asked him if he ever worried about the risk of being exposed, he cited the Panama Papers, telling me that journalists had their hands full at the time because the Panama Papers included millions of documents. Journalists would mine that data for dirt on powerful politicians in countries much bigger than those of Southeast Asia. The United States, Russia, Iceland, and Brazil were getting far more coverage than small countries in a remote corner of the world that few can even place on a map.

He also told me that Myanmar was a unique case, one where the country had so much political and financial instability that the banking sector was very weak. It was a cash-based economy where few people had any faith in banking institutions. Consequently, offshoring was common practice. The fact that the rest of the world appeared not to care about Myanmar, and that offshoring was a common business practice for most everyone working in the country, made it so that Oliver was able to set up these shell companies with very little scrutiny and therefore greater anonymity.

As he said that, he paused and said, "Most people focus on the exception to the rule rather than the rule. They write about these sensationalized cases, but if you pay attention to the small guys, my guess is that it would add up to much greater volume of transactions offshore when you combine them." This strategy of satisficing allows even the smallest spiders like him to operate without the same fears of getting caught, because they are far less visible in comparison to the flashy whales like Jho Low.

In the case of 1MDB there was a fall person. That fall guy, Oliver said, was Timothy Leissner, an ex–Goldman Sachs Group, Inc., banker who carried

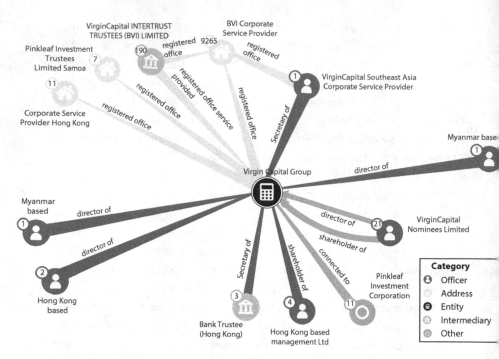

FIGURE 5.2. VirginCapital Offshore Investment Structure (*Source:* Kimberly Kay Hoang)

out bribes as part of the 1MDB scandal. As Oliver explained to me, every deal has its fall guy. He himself is the Timothy Leissner of the deals he works on and will be the person who shoulders the risk of going to jail if a deal gets exposed. The big spiders like the big executives at Goldman Sachs all got their bonus payouts, and none of them were charged with criminal activity, even though they reaped huge profits from those deals. As the known "fall guy," Oliver's name appears as the director of each these registered entities (see figure 5.2).

The BVI fund was the legitimate vehicle familiar to sophisticated investors and was used to draw capital from Oliver's network all around the world. It was less "gray" than the other offshore jurisdictions and made the people who would eventually become his limited partners feel more comfortable. Importantly, the vehicle used to "raise capital" would be different from the vehicle used to "disperse capital," and that vehicle was also separate from the vehicle used to pay kickbacks, making it such that no one person could trace the whole network of a single deal from beginning to end.

For VirginCapital, the BVI entity, some of the potential investors that he pitched had no idea where Myanmar was on a map. He joked with me that one of his potential investors spelled Myanmar "minmar" repeatedly in an email to him, but nonetheless they were interested in working with him and in dipping their feet in investments in Asia. The pitch to his investors abroad was that Myanmar was a newly developed country with cellular phone penetration of 98 percent within the last two years. It is a country that leapfrogged the internet, as people skipped computers and went straight to mobile phones. With this new cell phone penetration, he wanted to tap into this new market by targeting users with advertisements while also collecting data on the users. There was a telecom company in Myanmar where he had a relationship with the CEO (who remained unnamed in our interview) and was looking to form a joint venture.

He set up a subsidiary company in Hong Kong that he would use to form the joint venture in Myanmar. He was preparing to make a bid in the telecommunications sector and had a group of investors who were interested in putting together the bid for the deal. They wanted to partner with one of the local telecom companies to distribute "free phones" to subscribers who would agree to watch three minutes of advertising on the phone per day and allow them to collect user data through an application on the phone. Because they did not want to deal directly with government officials to secure a telecom license themselves, they wanted to form a joint venture with an existing company. However, to get access to the company, Oliver agreed to set up an offshore bank account that the CEO of the telecom could effectively use as a personal account to pay for his daughter's tuition and living expenses abroad. That shell company was the company he was setting up in Samoa. The issue was not just about money; the issue was that the CEO was having a hard time getting around the capital restrictions to get his money out of Myanmar, and needed a way to make this tuition payment without sending his daughter to school with suitcases of cash.

Oliver told me that after spending hours with the CEO, he learned that the CEO had a daughter who was in school abroad. He asked him point-blank how he was paying for the tuition. The CEO told him that they had no family in America or anyone they could rely on to help take care of his daughter. So every time his daughter traveled to the United States from Myanmar, she would fold hundred-dollar bills in between the pages of her books, put the books in her suitcase, and just check her bag. Every time she made that trip, he worried about her baggage being lost in transit by the airport baggage handlers, and worst, that she would get stopped and searched by US immigration authorities and have to declare the "source of funds." He much preferred bank transfers, but few banks were willing to direct his funds to the US, for reasons Oliver could not specify other than Myanmar being on a US sanctions list.

To help the CEO get around this, Oliver was setting up the SPV in Samoa, Pinkleaf Investment, which he would use to issue company shares to the CEO, but that vehicle was separate from the BVI company, and Oliver's limited partners in the BVI company did not know about the bribes that the CEO was paying on the ground in Myanmar. This separate vehicle would protect the limited partners from possible corruption charges in their countries of citizenship. The amount of money was so small in the grand scheme of things that he felt it was a small price to pay to build a relationship with the CEO. While he never had to justify this SPV to his limited partners (dominant spiders), he did justify the kickback to me during our interview by telling me that the amount of money was so small, and in his mind, it was being used to help a local Burmese national get a college education abroad. While it might be technically illegal, to him it was part of an investment in Myanmar's next generation. In a follow-up phone call he laughed and said, "Call it a scholarship to help build human capital in Southeast Asia."

When I asked Oliver if he planned to disclose this information to his company secretary in Hong Kong, he told me absolutely not. It was "none of her business" what kind of expertise a "consultant" brings to the project. When I asked Oliver what was considered "small," he laughed and said "everything under 100 bucks [meaning $100 million] but generally in the 10-buck [$10 million] range." While Oliver's job involves the work of "playing in the gray" on multiple fronts for many different people, he effectively was a highly compensated financial professional whom UHNWIs trusted not only with their money, but with some of their most personal and private affairs, to serve as their fall person and shoulder all of the risks.

Several weeks after our initial meeting, Oliver sent me a message asking me how my research was going. I told him that things were moving along. He said he was going to be in Hong Kong to pick up the Incorporation packet that included the company seal, and asked if I wanted to join him. I met him at the same office, where the exchange with Beatrice lasted no more than ten minutes: she had an envelope ready for him, went through the contents of it, and told him to reach out if he had any questions. He proudly showed me the new company seal, then told me he had an appointment at a bank and again asked if I wanted to join him. This time he had a roller briefcase with multiple binders of documentation.

On our way to the bank, he told me that he was going to a midsize bank because he knew that they would be more relaxed with their regulatory requirements. We walked into the bank, and he gave the name of a relationship manager with whom he had met once before. The person was out to lunch, and so Oliver asked the receptionist to call her and tell her that we were waiting for her. His tone and demeanor were completely different with the bankers than they had been with Beatrice. He was far more assertive and authoritative, almost as if he was the expert and they needed to service him.

Jessica, the banker, appeared. We were then escorted to the back office, where Oliver informed Jessica that he had all of the paperwork for the company, as well as the company seal, and that he wanted to open a bank account. He pulled out an inch-thick binder with information about the company, its directors, and the fact that this was a foreign fund that would be making investments in the telecom sector in Myanmar. The Samoan company was the holding company used for the Myanmar investment. In effect, Oliver used the real business and business activity to set up a bank account that would become the personal bank account for his Burmese business partner and the partner's daughter. The initial deposit would be USD$100,000 that he would send in two separate wires. When the banker asked him for documentation to show source of funds, he used the BVI entity and the money made through his previous work as a banker to demonstrate that it was legitimately sourced and not laundered from somewhere else.

In the end the telecom deal fell through, as a group of Korean investors won the bid. Over text message Oliver saved face to me by jokingly saying that his competitors probably had deeper pockets to bribe the CEO. I never learned what happened with all the companies he set up offshore or whether he was ever able to open a bank account. Even though his pitch failed, following him around to visit the company secretary offices and the banks revealed so much more about the structure and network of shell companies and offshore bank accounts in much smaller regions of the world where no one is paying much attention. It also revealed how routine, mundane transactions occur outside the purview of any regulatory body. Because each offshore vehicle was disconnected from the others, with a different set of lawyers, bankers, and company secretaries working on different parts of the whole puzzle, it was difficult for any one of them to piece it all together.

At the end of the day, the incentive structure was such that no one cared to trace the bigger picture, because what mattered to them was their service fees, not whether their clients were engaged in any kind of legally or morally compromising activities. This structure ultimately enabled elite spiders to operate with varying degrees of impunity and anonymity. As I complete the final draft of this book, five years after I started collecting the data for it, I am not aware of a single case of someone like Oliver who has been prosecuted for setting up such offshore entities for carrying out these kinds of bribes.

From London to Vietnam: Land Grabs from Poor Mothers and Grandmothers

Shell companies also enable foreign investors and state officials to place the blame on one another for dispossession of the local poor. Quang was a 32-year-old investment associate working inside of an asset management firm called Strata Capital in Vietnam. He was educated in Australia, where he got a bachelor's degree in architecture before switching gears and moving into finance upon his return. Inside the asset management firm his primary job is to carry out research on various investment projects. During our interview, he says to me, "You know, the world is very fucked up. . . . When you're rich you can get away with stealth crimes . . . and it's the small people that protest it who go to jail."

When I asked Quang for a more specific example, he told me about his experience traveling to London with his seniors for some meetings at the London Stock Exchange. On the trip the senior management flew business class. Everyone in the first and business class cabins was given a fast pass to move swiftly through the immigration control queue. The process took no more than ten minutes, and they were seamlessly escorted out of the border control area with no questions asked. The line was so fast that none of them thought of immigration in London as a complicated process. But on that same trip, Quang was booked in an economy class seat where no one handed him a fast pass. Instead, he had to queue up in a two-hour immigration line where the "riffraff" had to pass several warning signs showing the number of seizures of illegal goods—like cigarettes, alcohol, cannabis, other drugs—and signs warning about human-trafficking crimes into the UK. As his bosses impatiently waited for him at baggage claim, all he could focus on were the white-collar criminals like his bosses who got a fast pass to skip the queue. To him, that was a quick lesson on how wealth is related to impunity all around the world, because those who flew first class were not subjected to the same warning signs or personal scrutiny in their queue. The thing to remember about white-collar crime, he tells me, is that most of the time it's legal and outside the purview of any sovereign. He called it a "parallel economy" where no rules govern the money flow.

When I asked him to explain what he meant by a parallel economy where white-collar criminals operated with great impunity, he too referred to the offshore structuring that his firm had set up. He says, "Strata is licensed to XXBank by a British Virgin Islands company called DREAMS. That company has licensed it to Superstar Singapore, and Superstar Singapore has licensed it to Vietnam." So, if a Western investor makes an investment in it, he says:

> They buy into DREAMS. . . . So, the BVI is the main mother company, then there's Strata, I work for Strata in Vietnam, there's Superstar Vietnam, there's Superstar Singapore, they have been hired by DREAMS to basically license [the investment] to the Singapore company through a nominee structure. So, if you're an investor it goes directly to a BVI company with a Singaporean bank, but the money never goes to Vietnam because there is no need for it. ALL of the operating costs are a *loan* from DREAMS, there's no capital in Vietnam and we don't make any money. So you see, with this revenue model Singapore *loans* us the money to pay for the day-to-day operations. . . . Imagine it's not connected at all. Say I'm DREAMS. I have this awesome property, this awesome logo and tech platform.

When I asked him how they expatriated the money made in Vietnam into their own accounts, he said to me, "Everyone did a different thing. Dan and them, they put it into their own shell companies; they all have some weird company names. I opened a company in Hong Kong and one in Singapore and I split it between those two." He goes on to tell me, "Imagine if every person in the US had ten different bank accounts all around the world. They move the money around technically on paper by saying that they are giving loans or paying consulting fees. Well then, no one is paying tax on that money." But he says, "You have to have money, lawyers, and people to do this structuring for you. . . . I'm not a rich guy, I just piggyback off the richer guys who are my bosses, but your average Joe can't just do this." He says to me that with the new banking and tax transparency laws, it's no longer as easy to set up these accounts. But those who are set up in the system are only going to get richer, because it means that fewer people can even enter this parallel economy. Those guys, he says to me, are the ones who speed through the lines in London.

One consequence of these structures he told me about was how it played out in Vietnam. Quang offered to take me in his private car to drive past a group of women who were protesting. We drove in circles four times around the group so that I could snap several photos. He refused to let me get out of the car to take pictures, because public protest was illegal in Vietnam and as a Viet Kieu–looking woman, I could risk getting arrested or having my electronics confiscated.

Referring to a land development project that had not yet broken ground, he said, "They (his firm and government officials) just took the land. . . . Those women protesting look like they spent hours on a bus coming up from the village. They could be my mother or grandmother, and it is hard to drive past them when they are out there protesting like that. What is sad is that they lost their land, and for standing up for themselves like that they could go to jail, because what they are doing is illegal."

As he was driving the car and focusing on the road, I read some of the signs out loud. *"Strata Capital, with the support of the government, stole the homes of the people."* When I asked him to provide more context, he told me that for the last three years they have been working on a land development project to build out a new five-star resort. Strata Capital worked with government officials who had an appraiser assess the land, and they agreed to pay an amount that was a tiny bit above the market value as an inconvenience fee for the residents. But the government officials wanted Strata to pay one large sum to them, so that they could be in charge of distributing it to the current land leaseholders and take care of all the paperwork to transfer title. What happened, however, was that the government either did not pay the locals, or underpaid them. So a group of them bussed into Ho Chi Minh City, where they stood outside of Strata Capital's office buildings and outside of the courthouse with signs chanting that Strata had stolen their land. It was bad publicity for the firm, but at the same time, to its upper-level management, it was the government officials who had either siphoned off too much or never paid these women what they were owed.

Regardless, seeing women in their house clothing and rice hats outside of his office and having to walk past them as they stood in the blazing heat was something he could not just ignore. He told me that his position in the firm was too low to know exactly what had happened in the government dealings, but from what he gathered, some funds were paid out through an offshore entity, and then there was a separate set of funds that was supposed to be dispersed to the landowners. Either way, the government was placing blame on the firm and the firm was placing blame on the government, and meanwhile neither of them were going to jail or had to face the courts. Instead, it was the women protesting the injustice outside who were at risk of going to jail, because of the ban on public protests in Vietnam.

Then he said, behind the battle between the grandmothers in their rice hats, the CEO of Strata Capital, and the local government officials are the foreign investors who made investments in this project in the BVI. Their names will never appear in newspapers, tabloids, or any of the documentation regarding the conflict. In that way, Quang says, the CEO is still a white-collar slave, beholden to his chairman and ultimately to the people who are pulling the purse strings from offshore.

———

Unlike the Billion Dollar Whales, dominant spiders and subordinate spiders operate in a stealth economy, where they build massive capital webs that often go unnoticed by state officials, the general public, and even their specialized professional partners who build out parts of the web. By adopting a strategy of satisficing and working to lie low and control one's greed, they do not worry about running the risk of getting caught. The people in my study were dealing in such small markets and transactions that they were not generally targets for international investigations.

Nevertheless, the cases within this chapter highlight the importance of differentiating between UHNWIs and HNWIs embedded within these broader capital webs. Much of the work on global elites lumps these two groups into the same category, when there are extraordinary qualitative differences between them. In this space HNWIs see themselves as the white-collar slaves of the UHNWIs. Highly compensated financial professionals who make money by being the face of the deal or the "fall people" in gray transactions understand that they will shoulder the criminal, financial, and reputational risks of playing in the gray.

By setting up multilayered webs, UHNWIs and HNWIs create protective shields that enable them to operate in a parallel economy outside the purview of government regulators. Special purpose vehicles allow owners of capital and their financial professionals to play in the gray with varying degrees of anonymity and therefore, impunity. Before the chairman of any firm risks potential jail time, the "relationship managers" who serve as the public face of the deal would be the first "fall guys." This was their logic for the kinds of structures that they put in place to securitize themselves while also avoiding taxes and stealing the land from grandmothers.

In short, by setting up disconnected sets of corporations, trusts, and foundations, global elites operate with incredible degrees of impunity as they physically move their bodies and their money across borders with great ease in a parallel economy. At the end of the day, while 1MDB represents unprecedented levels of domestic corruption for Malaysia, there was widespread international complicity, as large amounts of funds were transferred across international borders with complete impunity.[3] As long as the investors I interviewed dispersed their deals through small stealth webs of capital, they would continue to amass millions with great impunity and anonymity across multiple jurisdictions.

6

Moral Dilemmas and Regimes of Justification

I was scheduled to travel with Gary—a retired technology expert turned entrepreneur and angel investor in technology and mobile telecommunications companies—from Ho Chi Minh City, Vietnam, to Shanghai, China. The flight time was approximately four hours and five minutes right in the middle of the day, and Gary offered to answer any questions I had about my ongoing research at the time. I was about a year into my ethnography and interviews at that point. He wanted to hear how my research was unfolding, what I had learned so far, and what questions I still did not have answers to. I talked with him about some broad overarching themes as they related to the different varieties of corruption, strategies of taxation, and my views of how the ultra-wealthy can exploit frontier markets with near impunity. As he nodded to most everything I was saying, he asked what was holding me back from writing the book at this point. I could not articulate it very well at the time, but I blurted out, "I feel like this book has no soul."

He laughed and said, "Capital has no soul."

But then I responded that something about that just did not sit right. For one, I was so focused on how people made markets and the ways that they finessed these complex terrains that I never bothered to ask any of them how they felt about having to do things that involved playing in the gray to make money in these markets. But also, as I got to know these individuals on our travels together, I came to understand that they were complex, multi-dimensional people. Caricatures of them that I had read both in books and in the public media did not quite resonate with my experience spending hours talking to people. To dig, I sometimes spent hours listening to people detail different strategies they used depending on the context, without probing deeper about how they thought about or rationalized it. I wanted to understand their own sense of self. As sociologist Al Young modeled it, "rather than privileging [subjects'] actions and behaviors . . . [I seek] to place their minds at center stage."[1] Put another way, cultural sociologist Michelle Lamont stresses that people often situate their moral dilemmas within the social, cultural, and economic environments that they are embedded in.[2] What might be immoral or illegal in one setting might not be in another, and as people traversed the globe, I wanted to know more about how their moral sensibilities transformed.

During that plane ride, Gary justified his desire to continue working as an angel investor in new frontier markets in two ways. First, he told me that because he had grown up as the son of a single mother, he had a unique understanding of the hardships associated with being poor. Now the father of three daughters, he wants to make sure that his daughters have a sense of financial security so that they "always know their worth." He wanted them to have enough money to feel empowered to walk away from toxic work environments, be financially secure in a divorce, and know that they were deserving of the kind of life his own mother was robbed of. Second, referring to my first book, *Dealing in Desire*, a study of sex workers in Vietnam, he told me he never wanted his daughters ever to reach a point of desperation where they had to put their bodies on the line in a world where men seem to rule the top of every sector, including technology, where he came from, and finance, where he is situated now.

That conversation with Gary reminded me that behind these deals and transactions of spiderweb capitalism are a set of real people, reflective people who, when pressed, have a great deal to say about their personal dilemmas and the process of having to adjust their moral compass in this environment. As Harris, the director of strategic investors for the Chai brothers, characterizes frontier markets: "It is a *moral maze* with a lot of *moral hazards*. . . . Well, as people, we have to think about our moral selves in a dark world." Pointing to his watch, he explained, "Understand that my *compass* is focused there, right? [pointing to 12 o'clock on his watch] Well, if I'm flying somewhere that looks like that [pointing to 9 o'clock] and there's a little bit of this [pointing to 6 o'clock], therefore, my compass is not there [at 12 o'clock]."

The question of what was moral or immoral for many of these people varied a great deal depending on the social and cultural context, as well as the kinds of partners they had to deal with. Here I focus on how people describe the process of having to *adjust* their moral compass as they engage in behaviors that they conceive as morally corrosive. This approach is important because in examining morals and markets, the focus is primarily on the dual relationship between the sacred and profane and the ways that money pollutes or corrupts society.[3] But, as sociologists Marion Fourcade and Kieran Healy point out, the view of markets and morality is necessarily reflective. That is, people will reflect on their actions as they participate in these spaces. Therefore, this chapter highlights people's *moral regimes of justification*—that is, how these people justified not only their actions, but the very personal process of having to adjust one's own moral compass to "play in the gray."[4] I illustrate the ways that people reflect on these moral dilemmas—in relation to their partners and family members, and geographically, across different cultural and social contexts.

Relational Moral Dilemmas

GENTLEMAN VERSUS CAVEMAN: GENDERED RELATIONS

There is a difference between gentlemen and cavemen here in Southeast Asia. If you're a gentleman, the caveman will rip you apart. If you are a caveman with a gentleman, you will never win their investment.

—CHRISTOPHER, 38-YEAR-OLD AMERICAN-EDUCATED SON OF HONG KONG TYCOON; EXECUTIVE DIRECTOR OF ROYAL CAPITAL.

Christopher describes himself as a global citizen. He was born in Hong Kong, went to an elite boarding school in the Northeast of the United States, and attended a small liberal arts college before "cutting his teeth" as an investment banker in New York for four years. After those years of working in the United States, he started to miss the close customer relationships that he grew up with in his family business in the retail sector. He also missed the ability to jump on any plane and be in a totally different city in just two hours.

While his family had made their fortune in retail in Hong Kong's food, furniture, and fashion sectors with several major franchises from around the world, Christopher's goal was to bring the game of translating global brands into local retail to less-developed countries in Southeast Asia. Their family office operates in six different countries in the region, with his older siblings controlling the markets in Hong Kong, Singapore, Indonesia, and Malaysia, while he is in the process of expanding their business to even less-developed economies in Southeast Asia. His three target countries were Vietnam,

Cambodia, and Myanmar, where he has spent the last years developing local partnerships as a minority investor with hopes of going much bigger.

To Christopher, Vietnam and Myanmar both offered high growth-potential due to low startup costs. These were also places where he sought to prove to his parents that he could take the lead on one area of their family business. The family group has several franchises which they negotiated to have exclusive rights for all over Southeast Asia. This meant that they would not have to worry about a local partner pushing them out of the deal. At the same time, they also bring capital to the market, and so the greatest challenge was dealing with partners in each of the different local contexts.

Christopher told me that when he meets potential partners, he first assesses whether they are what he refers to as a "gentleman" or a "caveman." Morality for him is constructed in relation to the different kinds of people he deals with. He carefully vets his partners by observing how those partners treat other people, especially women, to calibrate how he should treat them. What he prides himself on is his ability to be both a gentleman and a caveman as he modifies those dual sides of himself in his different business relationships. When I pressed him harder for concrete examples of what that meant, he told me that so much of his success depends on figuring out the moral psychology of the people he deals with.

To Christopher, there were both cavemen and gentlemen in every country, but they bring different things to the table. It was morally acceptable to him to behave like a caveman around cavemen, but he needed to treat gentlemen like gentlemen. When I asked him for more specific examples of dealing with gentlemen and cavemen, he explained that he is currently working with two different partners in Vietnam—Mau and Dzung. Mau was a gentleman and an Ivy League graduate. The two of them met through an alumni network event in Hong Kong. Christopher saw Mau as a total nerd who is extremely earnest and family-oriented, and he described Mau as the kind of local Vietnamese guy who is very reliable with money, and on the level of operations, very detail-oriented. However, because Mau was unwilling to spend late nights out drinking and building relationships with key brokers to government officials, it took an incredibly long time for him to get access to any kind of important information or permits to operate. The downside of being a gentleman was that Christopher did not feel like Mau had much of a hustle, so the business might be too slow to take off.

Dzung, on the other hand, was a caveman. Dzung was the nephew of an important political power elite who had the ability to make things move much more quickly. The problem with having Dzung as a partner was that he was one of Saigon's biggest playboys. Every time Christopher came into town, he felt compelled to drink with Dzung. Christopher told me that while he fully expected to have to "pay" Dzung in the form of bribes in offshore accounts to obtain construction permits and get his goods through customs, it was never a one-time payment. The relationship was ongoing because of a lack of transparency in the government's customs process. He revealed to me that on many of the late nights out he felt that Dzung's behavior really tested his moral compass.

Christopher told me about how they were out late one night when Dzung invited a customs officer out to join them. As their business grew more profitable, the customs official had started to imply that he wanted larger cut of the profits. Dzung tried to assure Christopher that he would manage the government relations and that Christopher had nothing to worry about. Over the course of the night, the group started to cozy up to a group of women dancing in front of them. Christopher could not tell whether the group of women were just female friends out for a good night, or if they were high-end escorts looking for clients for the evening. Regardless of what Christopher thought, Dzung invited them to three different bars as the night progressed.

At each new bar, the customs official and the women became more and more intoxicated. As the night wore on, the group ended up in one of Dzung's penthouse apartments, and it became clear that a sex party of sorts was about to take place. Christopher was not attracted to any of the women and didn't feel comfortable in the new private space. When he told Dzung that he was going to head out, Dzung grew irritable and told him that he couldn't leave until the customs official was ready to leave. They went back and forth until Christopher decided to leave.

The next morning Christopher met with Dzung for a late breakfast, and Dzung tried to make fun of him by calling him boyish for refusing to participate in the previous night's sex party. When Christopher brushed that off, Dzung tried to explain to him how important it was to manage the relationship with the customs official. Dzung explained, that "doing the dirty" would help to cement a personal relationship so that they could at least *negotiate* the customs bribes down. Christopher pushed back and told Dzung that he'd rather "fucking pay the customs official than be in an orgy party with him." Dzung pushed back, saying that the sky was the limit on the bribes and that cementing a more personal relationship might help them get a lower payment.

Christopher then said to me, "The customs official is a fucking caveman and Dzung is somewhere between a caveman and a gentleman. What do they need? Sex and fucking food! They need to 'eat.'" I could feel Christopher's blood pressure rising as he raised his voice. But I was also admittedly a bit embarrassed, as he was cursing with people around us in a relatively quiet café. I tried to ask him calmly how he felt about the whole interaction. His response was surprising to me. He told me that this was the price one had to pay to cut down on costs. The caveman rituals of sex and parties had both an upside and a downside. On the upside, it allowed them to front-run the market and manage both the costs and inefficiencies at the customs ports. The downside with dealing with a caveman is that you accept always having to be on alert because, as Christopher stated multiple times, *"If you're a gentleman the caveman will rip you apart."*

When I asked Christopher what it meant to get ripped apart by the caveman, he told me that cavemen, have no problem with stealing from you, diluting your shares, or pushing you out of a deal. He then said to me:

> The question I always ask myself is, how far am I willing to go? . . . It's my *moral compass* because it takes a very special individual—I call them "cleaner"—but it takes a very special man not to partake in extracurricular activities that are in front of you while traveling. In my travels all around Asia over the past several years, I have only met two men, myself not included, but two other men who said no to playing the game, and that is substantial. . . . It's not just about cheating. . . . You need the top folks like Dzung, and you go out with them a few times. You can see how they are. [It's] the small things—like if you're with a girl, and you don't tip her, and you're a multi-millionaire—what does that mean? When it's time . . . are you going to screw me over [if] you find some way?

What Christopher was referring to were some of the rules and rituals around drinking. Gentlemen, Christopher explained to me, were the kind of men who treated the women in hostess bars with respect and were not cheap tippers at the end of an evening. Cavemen were the kind of men who were cheap tippers. Men who treated women poorly in those spaces were the kind of cavemen willing to screw over their partner for a few extra bucks.

In my conversations with Christopher, he talked a great deal about how nights like that often left him in a haze the next morning as he overanalyzed the interactions from the previous night. These moments pushed him to reflect on his own willingness to engage in a world of sex and drugs as he gambled with these business partnerships. But beyond his reflectiveness about his personal moral sense of self, this triadic relationship between the men and women was an important tool that men like Christopher used to evaluate how far they were each willing to adjust their own moral compass for the sake of bonding with their local counterparts.

Interestingly, many of the men I interviewed most often assumed that other people's moral compasses were stable, while theirs was constantly in negotiation. The men's actions in these spaces revealed something about the moral character of their partnerships with other businessmen and government officials. Christopher used his observations of how Dzung and the customs officer treated the women to assess whether he was dealing with cavemen or gentlemen. For example, he paid attention to things like: Did they tip well? Were they respectful? Did they show small gestures of chivalry? The homoerotic subplots described in chapter 2 were all ways of assessing the moral character of business partners.[5] Knowing whether they were "gentleman" or "caveman" helped in developing a schema for how to interact with them in business affairs.

FAMILIAL RELATIONS: THE ULTIMATE FAMILY SACRIFICE

Chu Hy was the chairman and CEO of a joint stock company that has a diverse portfolio of investments across multiple sectors of the Vietnamese economy. One project he had was a residential real estate development in Ho Chi Minh City, Vietnam. He was a local Vietnamese man whom I approached on LinkedIn. As luck would have it, he responded and agreed to meet with me at his office inside the real estate development project. He sent me the address and instructed me to have the taxi driver call him if the driver could not locate the street from the main road.

The building was difficult to find because it was located along a newly paved road, past a lot of vacant land and hidden in a corner that wrapped around the river. As we pulled up, we saw security guards flanking large gates who checked every car entering. At the front of the building was a valet parking service and a red carpet with velvet ropes leading to the reception. One of Chu Hy's assistants, Vu, came down to meet me. He informed me that Chu Hy had asked him to give me a tour of the grounds.

While on the tour, Vu told me that the new development featured a resort-style ambience, complete with a private waterfront promenade along the river, a water park with multiple swimming pools and spa, a complete gym, and luxury condos with top-of-the-line appliances. Vu talked a great

deal about how this was one of the most sought-after luxury residential com-
plexes in Vietnam's new real estate market. The building had been developed
by an international group of architects from Japan, Thailand, Vietnam, and
the US who'd consulted on the project and worked with the developers at
multiple stages. The complex contained a diverse variety of trees and grass
meadows to give it a resort-like feel.

After the tour of the property, Vu dropped me off in Chu Hy's office. He
handed me several pamphlets about the property while I complimented
him on how much I loved the attention to detail and the green space that
was included there, because that is so hard to find in a jungle city. Chu Hy
told me that he had read several articles about me and my first book online
and proceeded to ask me questions about that experience. Once we got
past the small talk about me and my objectives, I began to ask him about
his background and relationship to this property. He had studied in Russia
for several years and had run a business there, which was how he had met
his business partners before inviting them to Vietnam, where they created
a joint venture in this real estate project.

According to Chu Hy, the project is estimated at $500 million, with over
98 percent of units sold before construction was complete. While these
numbers felt inflated, there was no way for me to double-check them, as
I did not have access to his books. The development project that we were
touring was just one of many in emerging markets around the world. Their
limited partner was part of a larger group that has a private holding company
headquartered in Singapore and has made similar kinds of investments in
Vietnam, Thailand, Russia, and Ukraine. They invest in diverse sectors of the
economy, including real estate, manufacturing, construction, and logistics.
The joint stock company specializes in mid-end to high-end projects in less-
developed, emerging markets.

The first formal question I asked him was what it was like doing a joint
venture with a foreign partner from the perspective of a local entrepreneur.
He told me that it was much like a balancing act, in which the local person
is trying to deal with the government and the foreign investor brings in
the capital to develop. Following the joint venture, however, several disagreements emerged between him and the partner, so he decided to sell the
majority of his shares to the partner. He said that the investors wanted to
have a more active role in the project—to become not just the investor, but
also the developer and operator. While Chu Hy has a minority stake now
(less than 10 percent), he continues to do much of the work as the middleman between the government and the foreign investor to ensure that the

investor gets the land lease, and that the investors and local partners agree on the valuation or capital injection into the property.

He also told me that in a country like Vietnam, where the regulatory body is not so strong, it is easier to "park dirty money" from offshore funds in real estate because no one cares where the money came from. For less than $1,000, he set up a joint venture in Singapore, that he suspects is used to move laundered money through offshore accounts in the British Virgin Islands to pay bribes to officials in Vietnam. He jokingly said to me that the country has a hard enough time regulating money laundered out of the country, and that it would be even harder for them to follow the money trail coming from cronies of other countries who need someplace to park their investments.

While he never disclosed the amount of money that he had made from the joint venture, or the ownership structure of the deal set up in Singapore, he did tell me that they had set up perfectly legal bank accounts in Singapore to manage the investments. During our interview, he never openly admitted to paying bribes himself in exchange for business favors, but he did say that it was virtually impossible to get anything done without paying them. When I asked him how he felt about operating within this structure, he said to me:

> So, the stock market here is not transparent. Scary, so a lot of people don't want to hold that. Gold is very heavy to carry, especially if you have a lot of it. There is a lot of money in Vietnam, right? So, every time you have money, what do you do? Every time you wake up, you get the money, what do you do? My uncle, he used to be the ward police—that is dirty money. He signs a paper and in the morning the money falls from the sky. All cash. You have to remember, going back to the very basic principle—most of them don't work for their money. So, in this building a lot of people are parking their money, I am just the middleman between the foreign developer who is parking laundered money in the whole project and the locals that are parking smaller money in each unit.

When I asked him if he had any moral concerns dealing with what he himself called "dirty money," he cut me off and asked me if I thought my father made sacrifices for my family. I nodded and said of course. He cut me off again and said to me, "That is the Vietnamese way." He rationalizes these actions as a moral sacrifice that he and many other men take on for their families.

He then began to lecture me about how I fundamentally was too American and did not understand Vietnamese culture. Referring to corruption in Vietnam, he told me that he had had offers to form a joint venture with two different American firms. However, their due diligence checks were so high that he decided it was not worth it and moved forward with the Eastern European firm. To a northerner like himself, it was less appealing to do business with Americans than with the Soviets, who had provided many of the northern Vietnamese with education and training when the country was closed off to the rest of the world. He said to me:

> Are you going to teach democracy when you are in Vietnam? They do business here and want to teach equality? Do business here, pay price. You're here to do a social program? Sorry, don't tell me that I'm here to make money but I play by my rules, I don't play [by] Vietnamese rules. So, how do you like it? When they say to me: "How do you like a guy from Vietnam that goes to the US, and say[s] I don't play by US rules I play by Vietnam rules?" You wanna do business, you do it the Vietnamese way. . . . They try to say that there are rules and international standard. I say "Yeah, great, is Vietnam the international standard? It is not. So, what's the point?

For Chu Hy, the idea of bribing local officials or getting a kickback on a deal was not morally compromising. Those were Western ideals that did not fit in this local environment. This was the Vietnamese way of doing business. He went on to emphasize that outsiders who want access to this market need to understand that this is not their country and that they would need to pay for access to a deal.

As we delved deeper into the moral questions, he told me that in all of business, regardless of the country, "It is all the sea of devils—because you can BS when you're in a crowd, but when we're together, in the finance-devils' circle, when we get together . . . you don't like it, don't come." He then told me to reflect on the sacrifices my father has made for my family. As I sat in silence, he told me that putting himself in the devils' circle was a sacrifice he felt he had to make to ensure the future of his parents, in-laws, wife, children, and multiple generations to come. He pointed to Korean businessmen who built massive chaebol empires (large Korean family conglomerates) for their families and, when charges of corruption became unbearable, either went to jail or committed suicide.[6] There is a saying among very successful businessmen in Korea that if they have not served jail time, they were never really in the game. Jail time is a sign that they indeed were rich and powerful.

That kind of wealth was only possible through close relationships between governments and businesses. This, Chu Hy explained to me, was par for the course in Vietnam and the way to drive economic growth in the country. He told me that this was the case in Korea, China, and a lot of the other Southeast Asian countries. It was not unique to Vietnam. The issue was not so much of a moral issue, because getting put in jail had more to do with the change in political structures and new people moving into positions of power. Morally, going to jail or even committing suicide was, to him, the sign of the ultimate sacrifice a man could make for his family to provide them with financial security for generations to come.

For men like Chu Huy, the way to resolve the moral dilemma is to ask how engaging in corrupt behavior serves a higher moral purpose. By justifying the risks involved with dirty money as "the ultimate family sacrifice"—one that men in other emerging nations like Korea and China also engage in— he draws on a breadwinning masculinity tied to family that helps to justify his actions at work. This is the way he makes meaning and finds a sense of purpose in the "dirty work" involved in his daily work life.

Geographically Bound Moral Dilemmas: Two Worlds Apart—"Separate Spheres"

Niccolo is a 57-year-old dual citizen of Italy and Canada. He currently lives in Vancouver, where he has been based for the last fifteen years, but he travels all around the world as a private equity professional. While living in Canada, he was working in a private equity firm before founding a boutique investment group that is headquartered in Vancouver. Most of their investments are in middle-market companies headquartered in Southeast Asia. Niccolo has been a limited partner in an investment group that has made investments in Vietnam for about ten years and has launched an independent investment group to explore opportunities in Myanmar.

In the last year alone, he flew over 200,000 miles; he prides himself on being someone who is always around for the important events in his children's lives while also managing the group's investments in Southeast Asia. His interest in Southeast Asia came from reading George Orwell's *Burmese Days* and *1984* when he was a teenager. During our interview he told me multiple times that he was a humble jet setter who flies mostly economy class. In fact, he told me that he only flies business class if the fare is either free or upgradable using air miles, so that he can justify the more frequent back-and-forth. His wife and children have no interest in travel or in Southeast Asia, so they rarely travel with him on business trips.

When I asked him to describe what it was like to have a life in two different regions of the world, he told me that this lifestyle worked for him because it allows him to reset his moral compass across the different cultural and geographical contexts where he lives and does business. He said to me:

> Me personally, I just cannot afford to give myself a bad name, because I have to live with it. That's me personally because I have people to feed. But I have realized that one of the things . . . I have created is a strong team that understands my *moral compass.*

> I'll be direct with you . . . I don't do karaoke; I don't do a lot of dinners. I am here to work. You pick me up and I will spend a whole day touring a factory or visiting a retail store, but I am not here to party, I am here to work.

> When you come here it is easy to get sucked into this world and way of doing things. You adjust your moral compass and bend your rules because at the end of the day it comes down to price and how to get the price down. . . . Let me ask you this, if someone offered you $100,000 under the table are you going to take it or not? In my time—and I am fifty-seven—at one point I thought some of the people I was traveling with were unbelievably honest, but as time went by, I came to realize how ignorant I was and what a bad judge of character I was. So, it is not all that it is cracked up to be, it's a lot of smoke and mirrors. Being blunt—I don't know too many ethical people. I just don't. So, you have to adjust, but that's why it's good I have a life in Vancouver to recalibrate.

What Niccolo was getting at here are the critical junctures where people have to reassess their moral compass. As a foreign investor, moving to the region is a juncture when people start to question or become reflective about morality, but then as they move through deals they must also situationally assess and respond. For example, when I asked Niccolo to be more specific about the kinds of situations that pushed him to adjust his moral compass, like Christopher and Harris, he brought up karaoke and bribery and the process of accepting the smoke and mirrors behind how people present themselves. For him, having the change of headspace between Vancouver and Southeast Asia helps keep him from free falling into the amoral world (previously) described by Harris. When I asked him how he managed to work with people who challenged his moral compass, he said:

> It is really a question, how to do business and what you are willing to give up for money, right? That's what it comes down to, right? Can you be bought, and can you be sold? Do you want to sleep at night? How many people do you know that are truly ethical, truly? Think about that one.

I stayed silent, sitting for a moment with his questions, unsure how to answer. After a short pause Niccolo told me that in every relationship both parties need to feel that they have something to gain. The key in this region is to find that sweet spot where everybody is making money and the country feels that progress. Bribery becomes the unpredictable variable in the equation, and that comes down to people.

Niccolo reflected a great deal on how he navigated moral dilemmas by maintaining separate spheres: his jet-set foreign investment lifestyle in Asia and his family life back in Vancouver. He said to me:

> My wife, my kids, they keep me grounded. They really do. When I first ventured out East, I was disappointed that my family couldn't be bothered. . . . Travel is lonely, your brain does weird things when you're out here . . . there is so much temptation and you see so many families fall apart. . . . Mental breakdowns, paranoia, is real. But for me now, it's important to have these worlds be apart. Some kids should never know the kinds of things parents do to support them . . . you know?

For Niccolo, "playing in the gray" in Asia was about maintaining geographic boundaries between the place where he makes money and the sacredness of family life. In our interview, he insisted that in this new geographic context everyone else is corrupt or immoral. At the same time, he did not want the hard reality of dealing in gray zones to affect his children's world view, so he was happy to keep them in Canada. His family's lack of interest in Southeast Asia helped him to maintain those two separate spheres. His ability to leave Southeast Asia on a regular basis also helped recalibrate his moral compass and avoid becoming a "caveman," as Christopher termed it.

When There is No Moral Compass—Theft Is the Name of the Game

Paul was an Australian-trained lawyer in his early 30s who recently left a boutique law firm that has set up representative offices in Singapore, Bangkok, Vietnam, and Cambodia. Before my interview with Paul, I did some background research on him and found that he spent three years working at a law firm in Vietnam before the two partners in the firm asked him to move to Myanmar to take the lead in setting up a representative office there. After two years of trying to set up the new office in Myanmar, Paul quit working for the firm and opened a local boutique firm.

He was at the first firm in Myanmar for less than one year before changing his status on LinkedIn to managing partner of Kingston-Swe Law Offices, with a local partner in Myanmar. Paul does not have a formal office. Instead, he set up an office in his living room, in a condo building located in Yangon, and all his business was generated on a referral basis. We met downstairs at a café in his building where he usually held his business meetings. During the interview, I asked him why he had left his previous firm. He bluntly told me that his former boss, Mark, has a long trail of convictions related to tax evasion and bribery. The guy, he explained, "[is] a sociopath. . . . There are documents on his history, but he pays search engine optimization experts to keep his negative stories far down in the search results. They also send letters to websites asking them to remove these stories about him." Paul told me that he spent more time cleaning up Mark's messes than working on legal issues. His former boss had studied law in the Netherlands, but it seems that he'd never had a practice there. He went straight into tax consultancy and was running a tax evasion scheme in Poland and Belgium. He made millions of dollars on that and then came down to Thailand . . . "spent it on cocaine and hookers and then spent some time in jail in Thailand."

When Paul started working for Mark, "he claimed that the scheme he was running was legal at the time, but retrospective [he probably meant "retro-active"] legislation made it illegal." While the authorities in Europe were looking for Mark regarding the scheme, Mark moved to Cambodia, where he started a new law firm doing tax consultancy. The firm then moved to Vietnam, where they got into very dodgy deals. Paul told me a story about how an American investor offered Mark a concession in Cambodia that came with a facilitation fee of $3.5 million. The American contacted Mark because he had a reputation as a guy who would make illegal payments for you. Paul did not know how Mark was doing it, but he did it. But when Mark went to Cambodia to receive his compensation, upon landing he got a phone call saying that he should get back to the airport in half an hour and get back on the plane, or else he's going to end up in jail. The government guy that he'd been paying had set him up.

After describing the situation, Paul then moved to describe how it shook his moral compass so much that he had to leave the firm and start a new one on his own. There were too many red flags. The guy he was working for was engaged in all sorts of criminal theft. He said to me:

It was toxic. You don't normally get asked to do anything illegal yourself. You know Mark was very childish, immature, and rude. But it's pretty, in retrospect, it's pretty toxic . . . I kept thinking he's not stupid enough to actually involve two lawyers in corrupt activities, because how are you going to keep your activities secret that way?

A lot of frontier markets attract a lot of bad foreigners like Mark. If you're really good at what you did, and I say this with a degree of [self]-consciousness, for me to say this might be mean, but if you're really good at what you do, and you earn really good money doing it in Singapore or Bangkok, why would he come to Myanmar? It's probably criminal.

So, in my experience, *Theft is the name of the game!*

Without my even probing Paul said, "Let me describe . . . I'm deeply cynical. There are a lot of white-collar folks running around the US and Australia." This is when he started to explain to me that while the Westerners laud themselves as coming from developed countries that are clean and honest, corruption often occurs "at a higher level there . . . where people really know how it works." On the surface the transactions "*seem* cleaner. . . . Powerful rich people in the West do these things." His point: "Don't think that the developed world is clean. Those guys bring those schemes and run them here where they are just two steps ahead of the regulator." In that way, he explained to me, "there is a lawyer for everyone." And the law firm he worked for had the reputation for doing that; if you wanted to play in the gray, you would go to them.

Paul told me, "This is not a *legal* thing. I'm talking about a *moral* thing. It is about moral culpability and how far you are willing to go to play in the gray. It can start with small facilitation payments and grow into theft." I did not even have to ask Paul what theft looked like, as he had so much to say. He told me the common Western-style corruption is on a bigger scale: "You hire consultants to facilitate the payments and the consulting fees get passed through to someone, but on your books, it's consulting fees." For Paul, working for a boss like Mark was a lesson that "most of the time these guys get away with the crimes they commit." Of course, he said, "there is always the risk of getting caught, but most of the time they don't." But Paul just could not look himself in the mirror every day and also shake someone's hand and turn around and steal from them. It was just not the kind of person he was. He believes in karma and was sure that all of this would come back to him somehow.

Here, what Paul was outlining was a legal-moral boundary, and the construction around behavior that might not be illegal per se, but was definitely immoral or unethical. As the conversation continued, Paul told me that this kind of work challenged his moral sense of self so much that he eventually had to quit, because Mark's actions grew more and more blatant. When I asked Paul to tell me what the final straw was, he told me that it was when Mark acted as a middleman in a bribery and fraud scheme. Mark pretended to have ties to someone in the Middle East who had government ties to a sovereign wealth fund. The fund was going to make investments in two large hydropower plants in Myanmar. The bribes were intended to pay the foreign official for making the investments, but instead Mark pocketed the money for himself, left the country, and set up a new office in Myanmar.

As the story unfolded, and the true reasons behind Mark's decision to open an office in Myanmar emerged, Paul decided that it was time to leave, because in a world where "theft is the name of the game, you are constantly on the run from one country to the next. . . ." For Paul, this just was not the way he wanted to live his life. He did not want to win by stealing so much from others that he would effectively be robbing potential investors, not of their profits, but of their investment capital. For Paul, skimming off the top—i.e., profits—in order to pay bribes or keep the firm afloat was fine, as long as investors saw some measure of return on investment. However, he drew a line when it came to spending investment capital to support a lavish lifestyle. To Paul, Mark was a criminal and someone who had no problem spending stolen money on luxuries for himself. "There is no honor among thieves, there is no moral compass, there is no soul!" he passionately proclaimed. Paul was worried and wanted to swing his moral compass north again because he had burned out watching Mark live a life of continually burning his bridges. Not only did Paul not want to go to jail; he felt horrible for the victims of Mark's crimes. This decision was not just for law-and-order considerations, but because of a sense of moral culpability that he increasingly confronted.

But for Paul, leaving that job also came with enormous financial costs. He no longer had a full-time salary or a list of clients who brought regular business. Starting over meant digging into his personal savings to open an office from his living room, where he tried to build the kind of law office that aligned with his moral compass. It was clear that the decision was a challenging one for him, because it meant stepping into a world where honesty did not have the most immediate payoffs. But as Paul's working relationship with Mark grew more and more fraught, Mark's lack of any moral compass ultimately forced Paul to leave for a more start-up type of law firm. During our interview, I could feel Paul's sense of internal conflict over this decision to cut off "the golden handcuffs" that could not only potentially put him behind bars, but also caused great anxiety around his moral sense of self. Leaving the firm and starting over on his own was the only pathway he could see to get himself out of a situation fraught with so much moral culpability. In many ways, Paul represented someone who was pushed to a limit. The moral boundaries became clearer over time as he watched his former boss lie, steal, and cheat—and get away with most of it. The threat of jail time was not what ultimately pushed Paul to quit; rather, it was this sense that his moral compass had been pushed too far into the dark of the gray.

———

When I asked different people to reflect on how they felt about playing in the gray, many articulated not only the moral and social dilemmas they had to navigate, but the ways they felt they had to adjust their moral compass. Research carried out by scholars looking at morality through the state, such as Bruce Carruthers and Terence Halliday, demonstrates how political officials in mature markets worked to make markets moral as a way of increasing investments from ordinary citizens.[7]

However, different moral regimes of justification occupied a significant amount of headspace among the people I was able to talk with about how they made sense of playing in the gray. They spent a great deal of time reflecting not just on how they maximized profits, but on how these business transactions pushed them to conduct a moral assessment of their partners—and of their own moral sense of self. During our interviews, people scrutinized every interaction they had, evaluating how much they had to adjust their own personal moral compass to finesse this market. At the same time, they assessed whether their business partners were gentlemen or cavemen.

In their reflections on how they had to play in the gray, people drew moral distinctions relationally, geographically, and through a narrative of legal morality. In looking for partners, they drew moral and social boundaries delimiting the kinds of people they would affiliate themselves with, given the pressure to implicate each other in activities that were morally reprehensible but *justifiable* as (1) part of the everyday course of doing business in Southeast Asia, and (2) the ultimate sacrifice for their families' financial health.

Still others drew moral boundaries through geography and physical space. As global citizens whose capital webs span several different social, cultural, and historical contexts, their subjective roles and positions morph with the different environments they are embedded in. Their sense of self provides a deeper, more personal view of how people finessing frontier markets shift their moral compass based on their ever-changing position in these webs. Niccolo illustrates how in a global world, it is possible for people to operate in two different moral orders, acting one way in one place and another way in another place. For those who operate with no moral compass, theft is the name of the game. But people like Paul provide a rare glimpse of the limits around theft, as he was thrust into a work environment where he felt so pushed to his limits that he had to quit. Paul exemplifies that there are limits to a person's sense of moral integrity regardless of the context or geographic space.

Together, these cases highlight the moral regimes of justification individuals establish in these webs. Each person makes judgments about themselves and who they are as gentlemen or cavemen; who their partners are and whom they will work with; and how they will deal with the different kinds of partners as they confront moral dilemmas along multiple dimensions. Nonetheless these very personal experiences pushed them to reflect on their own moral culpability and how far they would be willing to go in pursuit of their own wealth.

7

The Exit

FEAST AND FAMINE

> In a frontier it's feast or famine. It is risky because you can go up today
> and down the next day. When you experience famine and hit the
> bottom, things can get very dangerous. When you see your investment
> plummet [into] famine you will see the worst side of yourself.
>
> —DANIEL, A CANADIAN INVESTOR IN HIS MID-FIFTIES

For men like Daniel who are deeply invested in frontier markets like Vietnam
and Myanmar, "the exit," as they all refer to it, is the process by which investors sell their stake in a company. Exits involve one of two extremes—feast
or famine. "Feast" refers to the experience of exiting the market with large
profits. "Famine," on the other hand, is an exit from the market in which
investors experience devastating losses. I was able to interview 14 people
who were in the process of liquidating their assets and exiting from their
investments in these frontier markets. Of the small group of 14, only two
investors related an experience of feast, or winning and making out with
extraordinary profits. The remaining 12 were in a space of famine as they
suffered from colossal losses.

At the core, feast and famine are the product of relationships of coordination and sabotage. The ability to exit this market successfully hinges
on efforts of coordination, whereby every spider in the web gains in a relationship of mutual profit. However, when greed takes over, relationships of
sabotage lead to two possible outcomes: (1) one person walks away with

more profit by swindling their partners, or (2) the relationship devolves into one of mutual destruction that destroys the very silk that holds the capital web together. This chapter focuses not only on the relationships that result in feast and famine, but, in an effort to give capital a human face, I shed light on the intimate, personal, and embodied experiences of feast and famine in this market and examine how people made sense of these successful or failed relationships in the market.

In my experience as a researcher, interviews with elite investors who were successful were shorter, sometimes lasting roughly an hour. I could feel the respondents impatiently wanting to get the interview over with because so many people were clamoring for their time given their new-found success. However, my interviews with those who lost a lot on the market were extremely long. One interview lasted seven hours. The narrative around famine humanizes the spiders in these webs and illustrates a kind of economic precariousness in risky frontier markets that those who study elites rarely examine. The experience of famine takes a human toll on these individuals as they negotiate experiences of sabotage in their relationships with local partners, state officials, and investment partners, leading to unsuccessful exits. While I did not have the power to affect their positions in the market, many of these individuals spent hours talking with me because they believed that I had the power to share cautionary tales for those looking to enter these markets after them. This chapter examines the stories of individual people, going deep into Larry's and Evan's experiences of feast, along with George's and Damien's evocation of famine. I highlight the socio-emotional experience of feast and famine.

The experiences of feast and famine together highlight a particular kind of economic precarity that subordinate spiders feel in relations to global dominant spiders. In their aspirations to become dominant spiders, HNWIs who experience successful exits may take some time off, but lingering in the back of their minds is the question of how to stay relevant in the market and how to turn their massive returns on investments into even greater returns. Those who lost everything have reported taking time to figure out how to build out new webs in different corners of the world. Together these stories show that for some global elites looking to exploit frontier markets, profit is never straightforward, as they confront different modes of resistance from their business partners and smaller spiders looking to double-cross bigger spiders, in their own efforts to build out new webs.

Feast: Winning

Larry and Evan had just completed successful exits. Both described their experience as a journey that took many more years than they initially anticipated. Private equity investors often enter these markets with a goal of exiting from their investments within five to seven years. However, both Larry and Evan spent over ten years in the market as founders, general partners, and key stakeholders in new firms before a successful exit to new investors, only after undergoing a process of professionalization. An experience of feasting reveals embodied, personal anxieties about becoming irrelevant in retirement, or a fear of missing out on the next opportunity in a new frontier. Ironically, it is in the stories of feasting that I began to understand the economic precarity that HNWIs feel in relation to UHNWIs, such that even when they have made significant amounts of money, they may obsess over how to double or triple their net worth.

LARRY

Larry is a Canadian national who has spent over twenty years in the Southeast Asia region with an established private equity track record in the energy and natural resources sector. He first entered Vietnam in the mid-1990s, and spent much of his early career taking state-owned enterprises [SOEs] private, working with what he calls a "flawed system" to acquire the different kinds of licenses to explore, mine, and invest. He co-founded a minerals-based company with USD$150,000, raised a lot of money, and ten years later he sold the company to an Asian-based investment fund for over $250 million. He was also the founder and director of another natural resource company that was acquired for $50 million.

Following those successful exits, Larry could have easily retired and lived quite a comfortable life with his wife in Vietnam. However, the publicity he received around the successful exit drew other investors—and even bigger spiders—looking to capture new frontier markets. As a result of these new connections, he decided that he wanted to chase even newer frontiers, so he started to explore the natural resources sector in Myanmar and Cambodia, which included renewable and green energy. He also serves as an independent director for several other publicly traded resource-based companies.

When I asked Larry to describe the moment of feast back in the early 2000s, when he established his first successful exit, he paused, took a deep breath, looked up and said, "Relief. . . . I felt a sense of relief." For many years, he had worked obsessively over the project, trying to navigate an unpredictable licensing and relationship terrain across shifting stakeholders. There were times of great doubt. But then suddenly everything came to a stop in the exit, particularly after the distribution of profits to all the people involved.

He was "rich on paper," he tells me, with an elevated baseline that allowed him to explore new opportunities without feeling the same levels of anxiety or precariousness. While the successful exit made him feel financially secure in that moment, he was not ready to quit working altogether. It was hard for him to imagine a life of simple leisure in retirement, because he worried that he would be lonely. Working helped him to feel connected to people; it allowed him to explore and build new relationships, and now, as someone who has grown into a dominant spider with significant capital to his name, he wanted to find new ways to grow and reinvent himself on new frontiers.

Of all the people I met, Larry was probably one of the most low-key. He was not flashy, did not spend time in expensive bars or restaurants, and he did not care to be "seen" in any of the socialite groups or glitzy events he was invited to. Rather than constantly comparing himself to those with more money, he enjoyed being in the company of academics and artists, who he could spend hours talking with about history or the ways they perfected their own craft. But even when I accompanied him out to those social gatherings, he spent more time inquiring about his companions, and rarely talked about himself or his work. In his work, he was drawn to the geologists who he could travel with to remote corners of the world to visit, explore, and excavate various mines. At these sites he could nerd out and spend hours talking about the different properties of minerals. Those people who were far more into the science than the finance were the most fun for him to be around.

Wanting to stay relationally connected to a wide range of people, he decided to expand his role and his web to other parts of Southeast Asia, like Myanmar and Cambodia. In this capacity, he worked as an independent director of different exploration efforts while also managing his own money by exploring potential investment opportunities in renewable energy. Larry also joined an asset management firm, where he actively manages his own private equity placements alongside others' by establishing companies, executing growth, and structuring exits in the areas of mining, natural resources, and renewable energy.

While Larry took an active role in managing his capital gains, Evan's story of feasting took an entirely different turn. Evan's story reveals the active role that HNWIs and financial service providers play in building out parts of the spiderweb, thereby obfuscating not only the structure of spiderweb capitalism but also the agents behind its architecture.

EVAN

Evan is an American who worked on Wall Street in the world of financial services, where he lived a comfortable life, earning over USD$300,000 a year by the age of 29. While he was making more money than his parents had ever made, he felt that his life lacked a sense of purpose and adventure. His foray to Vietnam began with a vacation; he was drawn in by the dynamism and entrepreneurial hustle that felt palpable to him in all of his interactions with local street vendors. This market had so much potential, he exclaimed. After connecting with a friend who was already living and working there, he decided that he would take his cash savings of $150,000 and move to Vietnam, where he would first get a job working for a company that created websites for businesses in Vietnam. This would allow him to familiarize himself with the country and the market before eventually launching a job search company.

In the early days, his company operated much like a tech startup. They set up a company in the British Virgin Islands (BVI) as a vehicle to get a representative office license. In the early days of the company, they operated through the common practice of front-running: they created a platform and started operating while waiting on the slow bureaucratic process to get the proper business license, set up a representative office, and establish themselves as a local company. Looking back, this setup was incredibly risky, because Vietnam did not have a clear set of laws around foreign ownership. They hired a local Vietnamese woman named Lan who agreed to "own the company on paper" if Evan paid her a salary as a designated nominee. The salary they paid her improved her life so substantially that she trusted them fully and signed off on anything Evan asked her to without reading it. Within the company he hired an office manager who doubled as a lawyer and accountant and managed all of the relationships with the local ward leader, who demanded "tea money" in exchange for inside information about how and when to tip other "inspectors," like the local fire department.

Fast forward to twelve years later. Evan and his associates tried to exit and sell the business multiple times, but failed, so they eventually hired an investment bank, Morgan Stanley, to help them manage the process of selling this business. The investment bank helped to pitch and eventually sell the company to a Japanese firm that gave the company a valuation of $24 million. With that valuation, they sold an 89 percent stake in the company for $22 million. After taxes and payments to the other shareholders, Evan took home $12 million.

With that initial transaction, he had to go to Singapore to sign all the documents. After the paperwork was complete, he stayed in Singapore to wait for the money to come in. It arrived around 8:00 p.m. Singapore time the same day that the deal closed. To celebrate, he recalls going down to the hotel bar to have a couple of drinks by himself to savor the fact that the money was finally paid. Then he went up to his room to sleep. Around 1:00 a.m. his phone rang. It was a US phone number that appeared on his cell phone.

Describing the phone call, he says, "The whole thing was exciting because it was Chase. They were like, welcome to Chase Private Client. It took a couple of hours to realize that I had graduated from the normal citizen level to the *private client*." When I asked Evan to describe that moment of feast— of winning—he said, "All financial uncertainty was suddenly removed. . . . Although it is just money, and the cliché of 'money doesn't buy happiness' is so true. . . . But once I got the money, I felt a new kind of stress to *preserve my wealth and develop a new ambition. . . .* If I can do this once, I can make a lot more."

Chase had his money in a cash account rather than an investment account. Evan's experience of working on Wall Street made him cautious of private bankers, so he took a year and a half to sit on the money and do some soul searching. At the time of our interview, Evan had decided that, like Larry, he wanted to manage his own money, invest in other startups, and support young entrepreneurs. The investments have gone fairly well and have been intellectually interesting. But a new waiting period was beginning as he invested his new money and waited to see if he could double his $12 million into $24 million. That was his new target. Feasting for him was not just about winning and exiting. In fact, it's quite the opposite: it's about finding a new way to stay relevant, stay in the game, expand his network and make even more money.

Nearly four years after this initial interview I reached out to Evan to have a follow-up chat to see where he was with this new target. As the world was in crisis during the COVID-19 pandemic, Evan began to feel a sense of precarity on his journey up the HNWI-to-UHNWI ladder that he was hoping to climb. Over the course of three years, several financial advisors reached out to him, offering their services to professionally manage his money. It was through this process that he quickly learned about the capital flight from Wall Street investment banks into private family offices. These family offices were connected with a whole suite of regional financial service providers who had the technical know-how to build and establish investment vehicles, structures that would allow him to take advantage of tax holidays set up for new tech investments in the region.

They also helped him pivot to new sectors of the economy that involved moving out of tech and into manufacturing and logistics. He made extraordinary gains by investing in businesses that were improving efficiency and diversifying supply chains to take advantage of the global shortage of personal protective gear at the height of the Covid-19 pandemic—thereby strengthening Vietnam's position as the PPE supplier to Western nations.

The pivot to new markets and sectors of the economy meant that Evan had to rely on these financial and corporate service providers. They provided him with specialized services that helped him set up new companies offshore, expanding the new capital web he was now situated in. As long as he is able to generate dividends from his investments, he does not concern himself with the technicalities of the web. In fact, when I asked him if he's even met the company secretaries or lawyers involved in structuring some of his investments, he told me that he has not. He's left most of the work of managing those relationships to his financial advisors.

These follow-up conversations with Evan reveal the social character of these capital webs, illuminating the challenge of giving global capital a face. Like *Anelosimus eximius* spiders, U/HNWIs have formed armies of subordinates who cooperate in building out these massive and complex capital webs on their behalf—three-dimensional structures without clear beginning or end, challenging to reproduce or replicate, and challenging to trace.

Famine: Losing

The greatest risk so many investors articulated was the fear of losing everything as a result of the initial "gut feeling" that drove them to enter risky and incalculable markets. Broken capital webs are a manifestation of relationships of sabotage at best, or mutual destruction at worst. The experience of tremendous loss in this market has driven people to some of their lowest lows, even into despair. Indeed, when I spoke with those who were in the middle of such devastating losses, who hadn't had time to process those events, they could not imagine how they might recover or start anew.

While I do not have large-scale quantitative data to calculate how often people experienced feast versus famine, I do have rich qualitative data from those in a state of famine as they tried to make sense of their losses and the rupture in relationships that ensued. Spiderweb capitalism relies heavily on relational connections, and when those fall apart, investors experience more than just the material loss of money. These moments reshape their feelings about once-trusted partners, themselves, and even the place they came to identify closely with.

George and Damien each lost millions of dollars as a result of broken capital webs. The experience was both raw and incredibly traumatic as they described what they thought went wrong. For George, a breakdown in relations with the state resulted in colossal losses. For Damien, resistance on the part of local partners caused him and his foreign partners tremendous loss.

GEORGE

George had an entirely different experience than Larry in the mining and natural resources sector. George began his relationship with Vietnam after his first trip, in 1989, when a small group of investors came to Vietnam in search of "an El Dorado," as he called it, which later became the umbrella name he used to refer to all his companies. Because the mining sector in Vietnam is so small, I decided to anonymize not only the name of the mine, but even the mineral itself. For the purposes of this book, I use "vietranium" as a pseudonym for the real mineral.

At that time, George told me, "Your typical mining areas are often very well developed and tightly controlled and tightly owned. So, you are always looking for something where the chances of finding something are better, and the chances of finding something bigger are better." He was then working in Australia, where it was difficult to find good ground, because all of the major mines had already been explored with advanced technologies.

Vietnam was attractive to George and his team because it was just beginning to open up and had not been explored with modern technologies. George told me that in their own research, a look back in time showed that Vietnam was once a place that had been mined by explorers from all around the world. In one of their corporate presentations, which they used to raise capital, they had a slide that detailed the history dating back to 1850, when Chinese miners first discovered vietranium in Vietnam. Then, in the early 1900s, a major British development company mined small shallow pits with limited tunnels. Sometime between 1950 and 2000, a group from an unidentified country (possibly Thailand, based on our interview) dug a couple of tunnels and ended their development after concluding that the price of the mineral was too low, not worth their exploration, development, and extraction efforts.

From George's perspective, what made his group's investments in vietranium inherently risky was the complex relationships with the state. George felt that state officials he was dealing with did not understand "the modern business structure or the technology that would be required in the research and exploration phase." And at the same time, he sensed that the officials felt it would not be fair if George and his team took control over the mineral and it resulted in commercial success: vietranium was inherently a natural product of Vietnam, and therefore, any profits belonged to the Vietnamese people.

Like many of the other investors in this market, George worked a great deal with middlemen known as fixers or brokers who were key to helping him manage negotiations with government officials—an "ever-changing process," as he described it. The lack of clarity regarding regulations and legislation meant that every step of the process had to be negotiated. Moreover, because the people in positions of political power shift every couple of years, all these relationships had to be renegotiated with every new election, making it exceptionally challenging to develop long-term projections.

Given the sheer number of years that George had spent in Vietnam, one would think he might feel most confident about knowing how to navigate government relations. In fact, several other interviewees who invest in very different sectors of the economy told me that George was someone they often went to for advice on how to manage government relations. So, when I asked him how his strategies for government relations had evolved over the years, he said:

> This is the puzzle of Vietnam. I don't think you ever quite solve the puzzle, because the puzzle is constantly changing. . . . It's as if the communist system has been designed [so] that no one ever truly gets full decision making. It will always need the support of someone else. Those political alliances or allegiances are constantly changing, and they all have different political capital that they are using for different projects, and it is a constantly changing wind. You are constantly at a stage of wondering if you have enough support to keep a project moving.

George went on to describe how "70 percent of my time is [spent] dealing with government relations," and how for him the greatest risk and area of uncertainty has less to do with the actual mining processes of exploration, extraction, and production and much more to do with negotiating the dynamic relations with government officials. This kind of investment relies heavily on a relationship of mutual benefit between state officials and foreign investors, and when these relationships rupture in a tug-of-war over control and profits, it could mean the demise of the entire investment.

Over the course of thirty years, the project raised over $140 million from a variety of sources. When the relationships were well managed and things were going well, George explained, "[we] were flush with investment money, and everyone was getting paid."

From George's perspective, after years of successfully managing these ties, the state effectively shut them down by issuing a back tax bill once they discovered that the mine was commercially viable. This was an effort to push the foreign investors out. George explained:

> One day we woke up and the tax department said we owed them $15 million without any basis. They had done a similar thing to [a large company whose executives George was friends with], and I think there was another motor vehicle company, and it was just a shakedown. The grossly inefficient government departments are told by the Ministry of Finance that they need to raise more money, and just like in the old days when businesses were government owned, government business had to find more money and satisfy the state budget. . . .

George explained that it was hard to involve lawyers because neither local nor foreign law firms were very well established in Vietnam. They were dealing with a totally different set of laws that did not adhere to an international standard. Rule of law, he explained to me, was "not strength-based law, where the government is constantly putting out directives." Instead, he said, in his experience it was "mainly [a] negotiation," in which he must rely on his connections with someone in one department to work with a state official in another department. For example, George's company had closer relationships with deputies in the Ministry of Science, who understood the accuracy of their reports in the mineral exploration and processing phase and would make the case to the tax department that they should not be taxed the same way during the exploration phase as in the processing and distribution phases.

Nonetheless, with the $15 million back tax and no way to pay that amount, they came under a status of "tax coercion," which, George explained, means that tax authorities were constantly coming to take away their invoice book, creating an administrative nightmare that would effectively shut them down. To get around this, George and his team began an aggressive lobbying strategy through various law firms. However, many of those firms refused to take their case because it involved people at the highest levels of government whom George referred to as "very corrupt." Several firms told George that they "did [not] want to use their political capital" by representing George and his group. Instead, they suggested that George try to pay 10 percent (or the equivalent of USD$1.5 million) in bribes. However, paying such a large bribe was not possible because, as George explained to me, their parent company was listed on the Canadian and Australian stock exchanges under very strict securities laws, such that engagement in bribery could result in criminal charges and possible jail time.

From George's perspective, the lack of a clear rule of law with respect to taxes meant that the government could arbitrarily levy a $15 million back tax, which would place the investment in a status of noncompliance and affect their listing on the US, Canadian, and Australian stock exchanges. This status could force them into bankruptcy, effectively pushing them out of the country. Indeed, years later, when I was looking them up, I found court documents with their bankruptcy filing.

George also described how challenging it had been to get proper media attention to portray their side of the story. He compared Vietnam to Korea, telling me that "there are a smaller number of really powerful Vietnamese businessmen who are also politicians, who are trying to collect the full sweep of investments in the Korean way." Those politicians control the media and have ways to work against the foreign investor because, as he told me, "the Vietnamese [politicians and bureaucrats] are incredibly nationalistic and patriotic, almost xenophobic. They hate to see foreigners come in and mine natural resources and take profits out of the country." George was describing a tension that resonates across the region as local state elites work to push out foreign investors to keep the bulk of the profits from the mines within the country—an extension of anticolonialism. From the government's perspective, those resources belonged to the country, and were not something they would allow a foreign investor to easily exploit.

Although I was not able to formally interview the government officials linked to this specific project, several interviews and reports by journalists helped me to triangulate this case from the government's perspective. In an interview, the Director of the Department of Taxation told the press that "there were signs that these companies had sold their mineral to parent

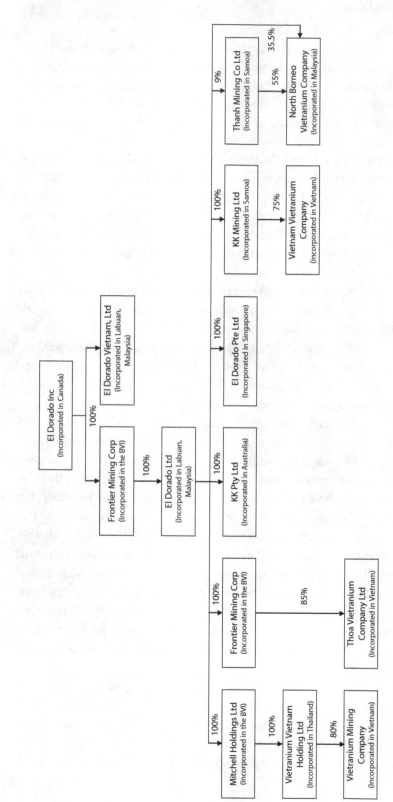

FIGURE 7.1. El Dorado Mining Company ownership structure (*Source:* Kimberly Kay Hoang)

companies at less than market prices, while materials were imported at higher prices to evade taxes." In the same report, the Deputy Prime Minister told local authorities that "tax debts must be collected for guarantees before the two [vietranium] mining companies are issued new licenses."[1] This back tax was assessed after the mining company reported cumulative losses of $30 million in 2014. What government officials are referring to here is the process through which investors book their liabilities onshore in Vietnam while declaring their profits offshore in another country. These tax avoidance strategies have long been attributed to foreign investors.

After reading the government officials' public statements, I searched through the court filings to find a detailed chart of the mining company's tax default as they worked to declare bankruptcy. The court documents revealed the complex ownership structure of the companies, which led the government to conclude that George and his team were trying to evade taxes onshore (see figure 7.1).

Figure 7.1 shows the legal offshore structures George and his team set up all around the world. The Vietnamese entities are subsidiaries of companies in Thailand and the British Virgin Islands, and the latter two are ultimately subsidiaries of a company incorporated in North America. Given the setup of this structure, it is not difficult to see why the government might conclude that George and his group were not being honest about their earnings.

After two years of unsuccessful negotiations over their tax bill, the Vietnamese government revoked their business registration certificate, forcing the mining company to stop all operations. Public reports stated that at the time of losing their business license, the mine had already racked up over $145 million in losses. In 2017, George and his firm announced its withdrawal from Vietnam and stated that the companies would be sold to finance their debts.

However, the buyers of the companies were two of the firm's former executives. As local advisors to the government began investigating, they told the press, "The biggest question is why a heavily indebted company can be sold. The buyers understand the problems with the companies, and therefore, it is a mystery why they bought such bad companies. Maybe the buyers have found the solutions to the companies' problems, *or* it is just a game played by foreign investors?" [emphasis added]

George insisted to me that all of this was a calculated ploy by the Vietnamese government to smear their image in the country. He maintained that they had been honest with their reporting and that they were good guys caught in a bad system, where everyone is believed to be underreporting their earnings. He said:

> We responded to [those reports] saying that we are an international company, and we are listed on reputable stock exchanges; we are audited by international auditors and we can't do that. But they had a mindset at the time—they weren't worldly, and they thought, "*We know auditors can be bought, everyone can be bought,*" and they didn't trust us. I don't know whether they truly believed that or not, or if there was a plan to squeeze us out, but the effect was that the pressure came from all directions, and very few people were willing to stand behind us.

> Quite frankly we cannot pay huge bribes; we cannot pay $200,000 here, $500,000 there, and $1 million over there. We can't do it.

George told me his theory of wealth creation in Vietnam: "I believe most of the wealth created in Vietnam is through corruption and comes from internal contracts . . . the building of infrastructure, roads, bridges, courts, airports. This is why, with the TPP [Trans-Pacific Partnership], they really insisted on private investors being able to sue the government. Americans had a similar problem in China because 97 percent of the economy was the government." Without the full backing of something like the TPP, investors like George had no way of working with state officials who had the power of the local laws behind them. In George's case, his companies could not renew their operating licenses, and when they went to the People's Committee, they were told that they would not be able to renew this license until they brought on a Vietnamese partner with a certain percent ownership. The government wanted the Vietnamese partner to be in control both of the mine and of the money flows.

With the press controlled by the state, they did not have room to finesse these tensions. George told me, "The press is controlled; when we said to the [People's Committee] that if you keep up the royalty then we will shut down, their response was, 'Don't threaten us.' . . . We are not threatening you, it's a fact! We cannot afford to pay it, and they would say we are cheap. . . . We are captive. No one will buy this project; Vietnam is a pariah. . . . No one will put in more money."

What George was describing is a showdown and a relationship of sabotage between El Dorado mining and the Vietnamese government. Neither party trusted the other; both felt that they were fundamentally being cheated somehow. The tension escalated as El Dorado mining solicited help from foreign embassies and governments, but Vietnam's unwillingness to back down led George and his group to begin financially engineering the sale and transfer of the company within the same group of people. This was a sketchy move, from the perspective of government officials. After over two years of being in a standoff with the government, however, George sold their stake in the firm to a group of other executives. Shortly after that, they declared bankruptcy and left Vietnam for good. In my last follow-up conversation with him, they were pursuing legal advice and public relations consulting in London, but did not feel hopeful that they would reach any kind of resolution with the Vietnamese government.

The kind of loss that George described is very difficult, because nearly thirty years of nonstop negotiations led to a government takeover of their business. This kind of loss is precisely what makes these markets risky and unpredictable. During our final conversation George was in London, and after pleading with multiple heads of state from Europe, Australia, and Canada to put pressure on the Vietnamese government to resolve these relationships, George and his firm divested all of their interests from Vietnam. Since this dissolution, George has been on a roadshow all around the world, trying to undermine the Vietnamese state by cautioning potential new investors about the risks of negotiating relations in these frontiers.

DAMIEN

Just as local state elites have the power to sabotage an investment project, private-sector partners also engage in their own modes of resistance and sabotage in their joint ventures with foreign partners. Much of the literature on foreign entrepreneurs living in frontier markets focuses primarily on the "weapons of the weak" used by those most disenfranchised by these investments, and operates on the assumption that all people in Third World economies occupy positions of inferiority, subordination, or weakness in relation to foreigners from First World states. This binary does not reflect an emergent friction in relations of sabotage between spiders in different parts of the web.

In contrast to Evan, Damien, a Russian national based in Singapore who also makes investments in the technology sector, described his exit using war metaphors to characterize the "guerilla-like tactics" of his local partner in a "hostage takeover of the investee company." I met Damien in a cigar bar. Our conversation lasted more than five hours over whisky, and it was perhaps one of the most memorable I had. Damien told me the story as a drama in five acts, with such vivid imagery and detail that I almost felt like I was right there with him as he relived the experience all over again.

Damien is the founder of a venture capital firm that specializes in what he calls "under-invested emerging digital markets." They make investments all around the world, with portfolio companies not just in Southeast Asia but also in the Middle East, Africa, and Latin America. Most of their investments focus on the digital technology space that provides e-commerce services. He referred to his business strategy as "spray and pay," which involves "forming shallow relationships with a bunch of different companies, with a bunch of people who work in a language you don't understand, knowing that the majority of the investments will result in a loss while hoping that a small number will generate enough returns to compensate for the entire portfolio." Their strategy was to enter at a very early stage when the local companies have a valuation of USD$3–4 million, with the intention of helping the local company reach a valuation of $15–20 million.

In this early phase, he says, "I would not tell my own investors [this], but we have absolutely no control over rogue entrepreneurs." This is the kind of work where relationships really matter. Outside investors have to place a great deal of trust in the local investee company to take on the role of dealing with the local bureaucracy and "doing what they need to do to play in the gray." As Damien pointed out, "As long as they tell us exactly how many stacks of books [accounting books] they have, we don't force them to be directly honest with us. Our objective is capital appreciation."

In 2008, an investor from Germany approached Damien, looking for a target company in Vietnam to invest in. He seeded an idea for an e-commerce platform for 500,000 euros. The company took off, and together they decided to gather more funds from investors from Germany, Russia, and Singapore to invest a total of USD$10 million. This would be their first major deal in Southeast Asia, so they felt enormous pressure for it to succeed.

A year or two into the investment, trouble started to brew with their local partner, Tuan. As Damien described it, Tuan "did not know how to scale up the company and how to grow with a larger team of engineers and C-suite professionals charged with professionalizing their operations." There was a great deal of tension, because his local partner did not like having more-senior and experienced people around him reporting his cash flow to investors. The company suffered over $800,000 in losses over four months. At first, "no one suspected that Tuan was stealing money, because they all thought that he would want to grow the business to hit $50 million pre-IPO," when he stood to earn massive returns.

When they all agreed to hire a competent chief financial officer, Tuan became defensive. The new person started to raise concerns about Tuan mixing personal expenses with company expenses. After several questions arose over why the company had suffered such losses, Tuan decided to let go of the C-suite executives brought in by outside investors and instead hired subpar people who were "controllable." Damien called this group a "cast of fantastic characters." The new head of cash collection was Tuan's cousin, the head of procurement and merchandising was his mother, and the new accountant was his aunt, whom Damien described as "the scariest lady I have encountered in my entire life."

This was when the foreign investors decided to take drastic action. They flew to Vietnam to "stir up some shit" in an effort to remove Tuan from the company. They offered him a deal. He would keep all of his shares and get $1 million to walk away, become a chairman, and maintain his reputation and status as a star in the Vietnamese ecosystem. That someone could get a promotion and a million-dollar private settlement after blatantly stealing from the company was revealing, not only of how commonplace theft was, but that the investors did not even think twice about finding a way for Tuan to exit with both money and dignity.

But Tuan was not about to leave easily. He felt that "this position was his sovereign right, that the company was his, and that someone giving him money does not put obligations on him." Over the phone, Tuan agreed to step aside. So the foreign investors all flew back to Vietnam, thinking that they were about to sign new documents that aligned with the new solutions they'd agreed upon over the phone.

This was when Tuan's tactics of sabotage emerged.

When the team of foreign investors arrived, they were crammed into a tiny room with no air conditioning. The foreign investors were expecting to meet five or six key employees to sign the documents. Instead, there were fifty people crammed into this room, and things got very awkward. With all of the people in the room, Tuan entered and said, "You need to sit down and listen." As he's telling me this story, Damien laughs uncomfortably, "That's when the first member of the team stands up and starts reading a proclamation from a piece of paper in Vietnamese with Tuan as the translator, saying, 'This is our father and our founder and our cherished leader. We shall never be managed by traitors, foreigners installed by a bunch of investors, and the suppression of socialist da, da, da.' Then the second, and a third and fourth person" read similar proclamations.

Tuan, with a very theatrical gesture, says, "Guys, I would have stepped down. Believe me. But the team revolted. Without their support nothing would happen; you see I have to stay and carry on this burden." This turned into a form of nationalist resistance on the part of Damien's local elite partner.

Furious, the investors left the country and sent a message telling Tuan they were onto his tricks and that he needed to step down, otherwise a list of legal measures would be brought to bear on him. Damien goes on, "So what was Tuan's response? He turned around and fired the board."

What ensued after this was "mutual destruction," Damien told me. They approach several foreign embassies in Vietnam to try to stop Tuan in any way that might be possible. They froze Tuan's access to bank accounts in Singapore. And they turned to the Vietnamese government and police to try to block Tuan from entering the office. The appeals to Vietnamese state officials did not work. Damien laughs and says, "Funnily enough, everybody north of the captain in every branch of the Vietnamese police synchronously went on vacation and stopped [answering their phones]."

After about a month of pushing the Vietnamese government to intervene, Tuan left the country, leaving his aunt with all of the licenses and the company seal. Damien describes the ensuing interaction with her as unforgettable:

> So, then this 70-year-old Vietnamese lady was a little fireball. We asked her to sit down and talk to us and basically explain documents, stamps, money, things you need to run the company.
>
> [She] faces down a room full of angry lawyers and investors, ignores them, and takes out a little elegant phone. She calls her son, the cousin of the CEO who was the head of cash collection, and says something to him in Vietnamese that was roughly translated to us as, 'I am being held hostage! Save me!"

Twenty minutes later, Damien told me, 200 people were crowded outside the gates of the offices. Some of them were wearing company uniforms. Many of these people were the company's delivery guys, who are not afraid of anyone. That group also brought their friends, and so right there on the street was a massive scene of what looked like protestors. To outsiders, it looked like there was going to be a riot on the street, as the crowd was trying to break down the gates of the office. All the while, one of the managers took the lead among the crowd and started chanting, "We're all brothers, we're all friends, we're all Vietnamese."

The theatrics invoked by Tuan's extended family felt like an emotional grenade launched at the group of foreign investors. They were not prepared for the guerilla war–like tactics that did not involve actual weapons, but rather, emotional tools of manipulation. Damien and his group of foreign investors did not know how to respond. They all understood that Tuan could take the entire company down with him if he did not exit gracefully. That would not only result in huge financial losses, but it would be hard for them to even rebuild the company without an army of employees who had walked out as a result of their loyalty to Tuan, their old boss.

It did not stop there. When pressed for access to the company documents and passwords, the 70-year-old aunt tells everyone that she has forgotten all of the passwords, misplaced the company stamp, that there was no money left, and she did not know what bank housed the accounts. In addition, the back-end engineers shut down all of the systems in the data center by infecting it with a virus.

In short, the guerilla-like tactics—the old aunt holding the company seal and bank accounts hostage, followed by a staged protest—were all intimidation tactics in this local space, meant to make the foreign investors and their lawyers feel outnumbered and ill-equipped to fight back. What Tuan and his family were probably hoping was that the investors would feel so emotionally exhausted from all of the back-and-forth that they would just give up and leave the country, thereby allowing Tuan and his family to maintain control of the firm and operations onshore in Vietnam.

Damien told me that he could not deal with the "Vietnamese guerilla war–like tactics" that transcended the business ties. The drama, which involved not only Tuan's family members but all of the local employees, forced Damien to make an exit from the investment by selling their shares in the Singapore-based entity to another investor, who might be better equipped to deal with the drama onshore. Following this exit, Damien and his group moved away from Vietnam altogether. Tuan's attempt to sabotage his foreign partners ended with the destruction of this entire capital and relational web, leaving Damien no choice but to exit this market.

Socio-emotional Experiences of Feast and Famine

In his book *Someone To Talk To,* sociologist Mario Luis Small highlights the abundant evidence in medicine, psychology, and sociology demonstrating that when people confide in others during difficult times in their lives, it improves their mental and physical health. Small asks an important question: When people need someone to talk to about a personal difficulty, how do they decide whom to talk to? What he finds is that we are "far more willing . . . than common sense suggests" to confide in those we are *not* close to, because we are "less deliberative, more sensitive to expectations, less attached to the past, and more responsive to context" than we think.[2] While Small looks primarily at those in situations of "famine," this is an important question to examine also among those experiencing "feast." Who do people talk to when they experience not only failure, but also extraordinary success?

NO ONE TO TALK TO

What I found was incredibly ironic. The people who made millions as a result of their exits felt like they had *no one to talk to*. Their newfound wealth made them feel paranoid and skeptical of everyone around them. I only came to understand this sense of loneliness when I asked them a simple question: "How did you celebrate this massive accomplishment?" Evan told me that he had a drink alone at the hotel bar. Evan was wary of telling anyone because he felt like so many people were already coming to find him. Everyone from bankers, to lawyers, to private wealth managers—have reached out to him, offering their professional services.

When I pressed him about how he would celebrate with friends or family members, Evan told me that he never even shared the details of his earnings with his wife. She knew that he had sold the company, but she never knew how much exactly he took home in his personal bank account. When I asked Evan why he chose to keep this a secret, he said to me, "Money changes people. It changes relationships." When I tried to probe deeper to get at the question of whether he was trying to hide the money from her, he pushed back, telling me that his wife is not a numbers person. As long as he is able to provide for the family—take care of all the household expenses, buy her nice gifts for special holidays, and take care of the kids' private school tuition—she does not care. To celebrate, he splurged on a USD$43,000 Van Cleef & Arpels diamond bracelet for her and took the family on a vacation to the Maldives, where they stayed at a Four Seasons Resort. That, according to him, made her happy. In a follow-up text chat over WhatsApp, he explained to me that their relationship was more traditional. His money was their money, while her money was her money—meaning that he was responsible for covering all of their monthly household and childcare expenses. However, his wife was a working professional as a

teacher trainer. All of the money she made was earmarked for her to spend
however she chose.

   When I asked Larry how he celebrated his wins, the first thing he said to
me was, "No one tells you this, but it can be lonely at the top." Like Evan, he
did not have anyone to celebrate with because he did not want to brag about
the sudden increase of the dollars in his bank account. Like Evan, Larry did
not really have any one to talk with. At the time, Larry was dating a local
Vietnamese woman, and he showed me a beautiful yellow canary diamond
ring that he had purchased for his upcoming proposal to her. It was a stun-
ning 6 carats. Coy about the price, he would only tell me that it was in the
six figures. Larry's fiancée similarly did not know how much he had made in
his final exit or where any of the money was located offshore. But according
to him, she was happy as long as he could manage their household expenses
and plan a few vacations here and there. She was an artist, and being with
him allowed her to find the space to work on perfecting her craft.

   With no one close to talk to, Larry and Evan both described going
through a bout of intense loneliness in the initial months after their exits.
Suddenly, the community of people they had been in touch with every day
for work dissipated as people moved on to other ventures. They did not have
a community of people in their networks who they could talk with about
how to reinvent themselves in the market, or how to stay relevant. Larry
describes an acute moment of "looking up" at all the people on the list of
Forbes magazine who were far wealthier than he was and wanting to expand
his network of mentors to some of those people. Some came to him as "tire
kickers" looking to explore a new Southeast Asian frontier, but were still
reluctant to invest their money. However, there were plenty of others whom
he did not know, and figuring out how to penetrate those webs was a new
goal for him in his search for people to talk to.

SOMEONE TO TALK TO

The experience of famine in this market came with an incredibly complex
set of emotions and cast of characters. No two interviewees in this category
dealt with the experience of famine in the same way. However, all of them,
ironically, had confidants who they could talk with; these confidants were
often complete strangers, sometimes from all around the world. Those in a
state of economic famine turned to their lawyers, public relations agents, and
company secretaries to lend an ear. Some also found therapists with whom
they carried out virtual sessions online, while others sought out temporary

comfort among women in hostess bars who provided them with a brief refuge from reality.

Eve, a tech entrepreneur who was the founder of a large startup company in Myanmar, lost everything after she formed a partnership with Ethan, a foreign investor turned Chief Financial Officer based out of Singapore, who not only stole the company that she founded but made it insolvent. Once they started to raise money, Ethan engaged in a hostage takeover of the company by having the company secretary write him more shares to dilute Eve's and her early investors' equity. By diluting the shares of his partners, he made sure all the other stakeholders controlled less than 49 percent of the company. This was part of Ethan's ploy to push Eve and her investors out before their initial public offering.

Eve explained to me that this was all part of a scam, whereby Ethan wanted to list the company—which did not yet have a business or even revenue—on a public stock exchange. She said, "There was nothing, no substance . . . especially on the AIM [alternative investment market]", which is the secondary market of London. At the beginning she tried to stay quiet to keep things civilized, because she really wanted to protect her reputation and protect the shareholders. But almost overnight, she became ensnared in a legal battle with what she described as "a lot of conflicting noise" from investors and friends whom she respected.

Describing this experience Eve told me, "It takes a lot out of you. Especially that first year. It takes a lot out of you." During this time of crisis, she leaned a great deal on her close friends, including the former Chief Technology Officer, as well as her siblings. She also talked through much of this loss with a therapist based out of Australia, whom she met with regularly online, because access to professional therapy was nonexistent in Southeast Asia. All of these people were key to helping her find clarity, acceptance, and the courage to launch a new company with a new set of local investors who knew her full story and believed in her ability to get the company off the ground. In multiple follow-up conversations with her, nearly two years after our first interview, she told me that these experiences helped her focus on a strategy of feasting that does not come at the cost of famine for others—especially those who trust her with their money, and who have made significant investments in her reputation as a founder for the quality of the companies she builds.

Like Eve, George also had a network of people he leaned on in times of trouble. I spent several hours talking with George over Skype, phone, and messaging during the two years in the aftermath of his failed investment.

Even though George's brothers were in the same industry as he was, he felt bad discussing his personal struggles with them, because they all had problems of their own. During the years that he was thriving in Vietnam, so many of the people I interviewed pointed to George as "their person to talk to" about how to finesse their unique and complex webs. But when George was in trouble, he did not turn to any of those people. As someone who was first in the market and in deep, he did not feel like they would be able to help. None of those people had the kinds of relationships or connections that could help George's case locally.

What I found surprising was that George relied heavily on people who were weaker ties in his network for emotional support, as Mario Small's work also suggests. The two people with whom George grew extremely close were one of his lawyers based out of London, who managed the case through international courts, and the public relations agent he hired, based out of Singapore, who helped him manage media reports and press releases in all other countries outside of Vietnam. George kindly introduced me to both. While I did not get much out of his lawyer after I told her that I could not serve as an expert witness on his case, I did manage to have an interesting discussion with Dani, his public relations agent.

Dani explained to me that her job was all about crisis management. People unfortunately engage her firm when they are in a crisis, and they need to have a trusted team in place to help them figure out how to manage it. "We ask them to tell us almost everything, because they don't always know how to capitalize on a crisis." The work she is doing with George is all about finding ways to put international pressure on local and state officials by controlling and framing the narrative on the outside. The local media will always side with the state, and so people like George have to find ways to engage an international audience.

George did not have a therapist. But he had Dani, who saw herself basically as a kind of therapist to him. In his view, she was brilliant at her job and easy to talk with. What made her good at her job, according to him, was that she was always there to listen, but she was "fair" about her billable hours and did not overcharge him for these conversations. Dani's firm came up with a plan for how they would address El Dorado's complex tax issues directly on the company website in an effort to appear most transparent to their shareholders, thereby making this failed investment appear as a failure on the part of the state, not of the investment team managing the project onshore.

At the end of the day, having someone to talk to was crucial for those in a state of material and psychological famine. People found relational connections not among those close to them, "in their corner," but rather among those with whom they felt understood, who had also experienced the context and the shame associated with losing so much. The weak ties, it turns out, were key for all of them to find ways to recover and reinvent themselves, either in new industries or in new markets in other countries.

———

Feast and famine are the two extreme ends of an exit that involves winning or losing everything. Winning and losing are not simply about executing on a solid business plan. These markets depend so much on the power of relationships and on access to inside information or preferential treatment. Thus a key component that drives these different outcomes has to do with relationships either of coordination, which leads to mutual profit, or of sabotage, which results either in one winner and another loser or in a relationship of mutual destruction.

As we've seen, the experience of feast comes with a momentary feeling of relief and economic security before it evolves into a feeling of paranoia and concern about how to stay relevant in the market. The experience of winning also ironically comes with the downside of feeling like there is "no one to talk to" to share in the success and the win, not even those with whom people share their most intimate and personal spaces.

The experience of famine, on the other hand, is often the outcome of relations involving sabotage that destroy the already frayed relational strands holding this web together. Yet those who lost it all found someone to talk to. Those people were not close friends or even business partners. Instead, they were people in an outer circle, such as lawyers, public relations agents, and hostess workers—all people who were key to helping them find ways to become resilient and bounce back from devastating losses.

Regardless of the emotional highs and lows that come with experiences of feast and famine, everyone eventually exits from their investments. No deal lasts forever. And, as they all exit this market, new players will enter with new sources of capital and different webbed networks, all hoping that they will be the next to feast in this game of roulette.

Conclusion

UNRAVELING CHAOTIC AND
TANGLED WEBS

For the past four years (2017–2021), as I wrestled with the different pieces of the puzzle and the evolving themes that constitute spiderweb capitalism and the craft of playing in the gray, I have had the privilege of presenting some of my preliminary findings to over thirty different academic audiences and a handful of closed-door meetings inside a few of the private firms where I carried out interviews. The question that I almost always get asked by students concerned with widening global inequality is how we can unravel these chaotic and tangled spiderwebs. As I have reflected on that question, the answer, to me, seems to be in the response that I have received in the closed-door presentations among global elites themselves. That is: these webs are structurally so massive and involve so many people working on different layers that there is no one villain to go after. Not a single person I interviewed described a feeling of personal responsibility for the ways that these global webs contribute to even wider forms of inequality, even if they themselves purport that they do not want to live in a world of massive inequality. In fact, spiderweb capitalism is designed to hide the consequences of individuals' actions in producing inequality.

This problem with spiderweb capitalism is systemic.

To put this into context, the 2008 global financial crisis gave rise to a social movement in the United States known as Occupy Wall Street. People occupied a public space—Zuccotti Park in New York's financial district—in massive protest against corporate greed and widespread economic inequality. Wall Street outsiders called into question the bonus payouts that financial executives reaped as a result of their reckless speculation in the housing market, which took a massive toll on Main Street individuals who lost not only their homes but also their largest investments. The public was furious. The villains of that story were financial executives like Countrywide's Angelo Mozilo, who made $470 million between 2003 and 2008, and Stanley O'Neal, the former chairman and CEO of Merrill Lynch who received $90 million in 2006 and 2007.[1] These bonuses were not products of the profits they helped their firms make, but rather of years of unproductive speculative trading.

Occupy Wall Street may have raised public awareness of inequality and changed the way we talk about inequality, but the fact of the matter is that it has not changed the political and economic structures that create this inequality.[2] These protests failed to effect systemic change both at home and abroad. In fact, nearly ten years after heightened public critique of widening inequality, news of the global heist that took up to $12 billion from Malaysian national wealth fund 1MDB circled the globe. There were massive protests in Malaysia. Former Prime Minister of Malaysia Najib Razak received a 12-year prison sentence in Malaysia, and two of his co-conspirators, Khadem al Qubaisi and Mohammed Badawy al Husseiny, were also sentenced to prison in Abu Dhabi. But the rest of the world was silent, and Jho Low, the big spider in that web, is in hiding. Some suspect Low is hiding in China, while others suspect he is in Europe.[3] The point is that no one can locate him, and there is a network of people not only protecting him and his stolen money but also taking the fall for him.

Moreover, nearly five years after the explosion of the Panama Papers, ICIJ journalists have opened up Pandora's box in the "Pandora Papers," a trove of 12 million leaked confidential financial records that reveal how wealthy and powerful political figures from around the world have found ways to conceal their money. The Pandora Papers include information on over 300 politicians and public officials across 90 countries, illustrating how little anything has changed after the explosion of the Panama Papers in 2016.[4]

How was this possible, and why can't we fix this? Much of the answer lies in the fact that the boundary between legal and illegal activity is very gray. And even in cases of outright criminal theft, it is often extremely difficult to locate the dominant spider in these massive, complex webs. As far as I know, not a single person in my study has been charged with any criminal activity. In fact, massive spiderwebs hide in plain sight, as offshoring is part of the mundane, everyday, and, most importantly, legal way that firms cut costs.[5]

United States: Home to the World's Biggest Offshore Jurisdiction

Spiderweb capitalism is not a story about what happens somewhere "over there" in small countries like Malaysia, Vietnam, or Myanmar. All of this ultimately connects back to the United States and Western Europe—places with an image of transparency, clear rule of law, and lower levels of corruption or tax evasion. In fact, as my colleague and business school professor Hal Weitzman finds, the United States is home to one of the largest "domestic tax havens" for US companies and wealthy individuals and an "offshore jurisdiction" for those outside of the United States.[6] This may come as a surprise, as the US has been the most aggressive with regulations that require American citizens to report their bank account balances and earnings overseas. The US also subjects foreign financial institutions to enormous fines if they do not comply with the Foreign Account Tax Compliance Act (known as FATCA), which requires them to report on the foreign assets held by their US account holders.

Nonetheless, the deputy director of the FACT (Financial Accountability and Corporate Transparency) Coalition, Clark Gascoigne, argues that "right now, the United States is the easiest place in the world to set up an anonymous shell company."[7] The ICIJ reports highlight high-profile examples of the embeddedness between political officials and private financial actors that goes all the way up to the highest levels of office. For example, President Donald Trump's personal attorney Michael Cohen used a shell company registered in Delaware to receive payments from a firm linked to a Russian oligarch.[8] To be clear, this is not a partisan issue. Penny Pritzker, the former US Secretary of Commerce under the Obama Administration and longtime backer of Obama, has her own set of shell companies offshore.[9] Pritzker's investments in the two Bermuda-based firms were included in a federal ethics filing in which Pritzker pledged to sell investments to avoid conflicts of interest.[10] Federal ethics law limits Cabinet members' ability to participate "personally and substantially" in government matters that could affect their financial interests. But documents show that in June of 2013 Pritzker transferred shares to a Delaware-registered DRBIT Investors LLC, which is "owned by trusts that are for the benefit of Penny Pritzker's children."[11] Delaware is one of the top places for US (offshore) hedge funds due to their trading strategies or investor bases.[12]

At the same time, Delaware, Wyoming, Nevada, and increasingly Florida, Texas, and South Dakota are home for the shell companies of foreign owners who do not reside in the United States. While the United States requires US citizens to disclose their assets and bank accounts overseas for tax purposes, the US—a co-founder of the Organization for Economic Cooperation and Development (OECD)—is not a participant in its common reporting standard (CRS), an automatic exchange of information between tax authorities on a global level. In fact, the US has also refused to cooperate with developing country governments looking to trace private savings by those who are using places like Delaware as tax shelters to evade paying taxes in their countries of citizenship.

Delaware is a prime example of how the boundaries between legal and illegal or licit and illicit are unclear. As French-Canadian author Alain Deneault writes, "expert wordsmiths in tax matters presented a highly nuanced defense of the democratic virtues of Delaware in order to distinguish it from gangster offshore jurisdictions such as Bermuda and the Seychelles."[13] As several of my interviewees remarked when I pressed them on their offshore structures, "The biggest gangsters on the block are in the United States." In fact, the Obama administration provided legal tax breaks to foreign companies that created jobs in the United States under the ruse that "the accumulation of private wealth derived from . . . labor" would benefit the mass of wage earners.[14] For non–US citizens, Delaware serves as an offshore tax haven that guarantees banking secrecy, minimal taxes, and a favorable tax location for those coming from China, with Mandarin as a secondary language.[15]

Delaware in particular serves as a prime example of how the very definition of onshore/offshore varies not simply by sovereign nations, but by people's national citizenship. This place raises a bigger question around activity that is technically legal but morally reprehensible, as wordsmiths engage in the game of legalizing practices that widen inequality and legitimize capital accumulation.

Regulating the Regulators

The most aggressive solution to the problem of the hidden wealth of nations, proposed by French economist and UC Berkeley Professor Gabriel Zucman, is a global asset registry. Zucman makes a strong and convincing case that the United States could thoroughly reform its corporate taxation system without much international cooperation by unilaterally abandoning arm's-length pricing, taxing corporations on their global profits, raising the personal dividend tax rate, and crediting corporate taxes to shareholders.[16]

This aggressive solution, if adopted by the United States and Europe, Zucman argues, would account for close to 50 percent of the world GDP and would therefore have a significant impact on reducing the tax gap between the rich and poor.

However, as Zucman notes himself, and as my book reveals, global wealth generated in countries such as China, Russia, the Middle East, and Southeast Asia all use these or similar offshore structures. At the same time, we no longer live in a world where the United States and Europe write the rules of the road for everyone else. If we account for the 50 percent of the world's GDP that now exists outside of the US and Europe, in countries where political and economic power not only overlap but co-constitute each other, spiderweb capitalism has other places to flourish. Thus, solving the problem of global inequality would necessitate a structure in which the countries harboring the world's wealthiest people took part in this global wealth registry. This would require coordination between regulators not only in the United States and Europe, but also in China, Russia, the Middle East, and Southeast Asia, to name a few. This kind of coordination is unlikely given the geopolitical tensions at play between these countries. On the one hand, the US is working to secure its global hegemony, while on the other, the rapid ascent of other world powers means that other nations are also competing and coordinating to dismantle all forms of Western hegemony around the world.

Even many of the non-Western countries listed above are places where political power and economic power are so deeply entangled that these webs will continue to flourish all around the world. Both in and outside of the United States and Europe, the problem, then, is a systemic one of asking the regulators to regulate themselves. However, in countries where political and economic power not only overlap but co-constitute each other, this system feels virtually impossible to dismantle. To complicate matters further, among the global elites from the United States and Europe whom I interviewed, the fear is that taxing them will make them less competitive than their peers in China, Russia, and so on, where state regulators are not only not cracking down on offshore systems, but are instead reaping massive profits from them.

There is no systematic mechanism for regulating the regulators. The fact of the matter is that there also is no way to publicly shame regulators who abuse their positions for personal profit. For example, one limitation of this book has been my inability to study, in any kind of systematic way, state regulators who themselves play in the gray. I found it most challenging to convince state officials to sit down with me for a formal interview in which I would ask questions about their role in systemic corruption, or even about offshore structures they might be involved in. As the same time, Article 38 of China's new national security law in Hong Kong, which states that individuals can face lengthy prison sentences if their academic work is deemed subversive by Chinese authorities, has created a chilling effect of self-censorship. Fear of the state in these places feels very real and palpable, so I have tiptoed around it in ways that limits our ability to dig even deeper into the layers of the web I have outlined in this book. As I come to the end of this book project, I still do not have a clear answer of how to systematically study the state in Vietnam, Myanmar, Hong Kong, or even Singapore.

Theorizing "The Global"

The examples throughout this book that highlight the embedded ties between regulators and private financial actors in a coordinated web across different sovereignties forces all of us to confront a big question: "What is 'the global'?" Currently there are different conceptions of the global. They include world systems, world order, and global cities frameworks, as I have laid out in the introduction and chapter 1. However, if all these financial webs are part of one ecosystem, how might we think of innovative ways to unravel these webs? Zucman's approach is predicated on creating a global bureaucracy, which I would argue is almost like Max Weber's principles of bureaucracy (i.e. formalized rules, specialization, hierarchy, etc.) on steroids. For example, even though this is not how Zucman articulates it, his solution posits a global bureaucratic state that involves coordination and the sharing of information across sovereignties. I would argue that a global bureaucracy is a powerful thought concept even if no one has been able to conceive of the mechanisms to make it a reality. Merely suggesting this as a possibility is a major contribution and an important step to solving the problem of spiderweb capitalism enabled by gray economies.

In thinking outside of the box, Zucman introduces another way of conceiving of the global. To continue tackling this problem, future work must interrogate the question, "What is the global?" which will require sustained creative, collaborative, and true interdisciplinary scholarly engagement. To develop solutions to this problem we need to build an equally elaborate global network of movements, organizations, and research aimed at trying to reconstitute the relationships between peoples and nation-states and their relationship to land and capital.

History teaches us that nothing ever gets dismantled; the current relationships between peoples, nation-states, land, and capital that make up spiderweb capitalism will undergo a transformation, and this new form will require a different conception of what constitutes the "the global" beyond national boundaries. For example, the rise of new cryptocurrencies points to the possibility of a viable alternative to the hegemony of the US dollar. The quick exchange of money that supersedes national currencies is a sign that we are moving in the direction of a new global order that supersedes sovereignties. It remains to be seen what new political structure will emerge in response to the rise of alternative currencies and the decline of national currencies. Regardless, the point is that people who are pushing cryptocurrencies are already trying to reconstitute the relationship between currencies and nation-states. These are precisely the kinds of thinking that are required to really approach the problem of spiderweb capitalism. Regardless of one's political ideology or slant, any response to this global structure of spiderweb capitalism requires innovative thinking and action on the global level, and the examples of Zucman and cryptocurrencies show that we are on our way there.

A Fork in the Road

The geopolitical conflicts and cooperation between global superpowers have extraordinary ripple effects in smaller countries around the world. I planned to return to Vietnam and Myanmar in the summers of 2020 and 2021, but both trips were put off as a result of the COVID-19 global pandemic. However, as I reconnect with people via Zoom, Whatsapp, LinkedIn, Facebook, and Instagram, I cannot help but wonder how this spiderweb will ultimately reconfigure itself.

On February 1, 2021, the military seized control of Myanmar following a general election which Aung San Suu Kyi and members of her National League for Democracy (NLD) won by a landslide. The armed forces claimed widespread election fraud and arrested Aung San Suu Kyi, accusing her of manipulating the election results. As unrest gripped Myanmar, with protestors taking to the streets, the military has responded with brute force, leaving more than 600 dead.[17] The coup moved Myanmar back to being a country under full military rule. The military seized control over broadcast networks, telephone, and internet access, leaving hundreds of people lined up outside of closed banks to withdraw their deposits. Many of the foreign expats that I kept in close contact with fled the country because of the coup.

In my follow-up conversations with Tin Aung, the deputy chairman of an investment firm in Myanmar, he told me, "Myanmar is tragic. The coup set the country back at least a decade." With COVID surging and an already weak healthcare system there will be more deaths and suffering, with no solution in sight. Sein Win, the CEO of a Singapore based investment firm that spearheaded several investments in Myanmar, told me that the picture is very bleak in the short and medium term. He is extremely concerned that the "xenophobic military government will not be conducive for transparent foreign investment" and will be more inclined to take "shady investments from China." Without much hope, he explained that while "Myanmar is strategically located, resource rich," it also has a large population, a massive need to upgrade its infrastructure, and a government that, following the coup, will only attract foreign capital from places used to dealing in contexts with a complete lack of transparency.

Foreign investors face three choices in Myanmar: leave, suspend their operations, or stay and work with the new military regime.[18] Among the small group from my study that I was able to touch base with, nearly all are selling their Myanmar subsidiaries. Those in manufacturing have suspended operations to send a signal to the military state. Others are opting to stay but remain silent while they watch and wait to see how this will affect their investments. In an interview with Nikkei Asia's *DealStreetAsia*, Field Pickering, chief operations officer at early-stage investor Seed Myanmar, told the paper, "The country will be untouchable for foreign investors for at least the year of the state of emergency. . . . Any company in Myanmar who had fundraising plans for 2021 and was able to persevere through a tough 2020 due to COVID-19 is in for a one-two punch, and we are likely to see a number of casualties due to a dearth in fundraising."[19]

As Myanmar turns inward, the writing seems to be on the wall that there will be a return to a form of crony capitalism that enriches the ruling class as well as the generals, with deeply entrenched ties between big business and politicians.[20] As a small group with military ties dominates the country's natural resources, the overwhelming majority of the population will dive deeper into poverty. Following the coup, Myanmar's military regime has publicly stood with China—now its biggest supplier, and donor of coronavirus vaccines.[21] At the same time, China announced a new trade route through Myanmar, which is designed to link Yangon port on the Indian Ocean to the Chinese border province of Yunnan, thereby boosting trade and increasing Beijing's influence in Myanmar.[22]

In contrast to Myanmar, Vietnam emerged as a key world leader that has not only effectively managed the COVID-19 crisis by keeping cases and deaths low compared to more-developed countries, but has also proven a leader in the manufacture and supply of personal protection equipment (PPE) for the rest of the world. Vietnam's manufacturers exported almost 1.2 billion masks through December 2020 to North America, Europe, and around Asia.[23] Mimi Vu, a partner at Raise Partners, took part in a tour for US Embassy Hanoi staff to visit two factories outside of Hanoi, where members of the Embassy's Marine Security Detachment joined political and economic officers to see how cotton was spun into face masks. In a news report following that meeting, a Vietnamese reporter highlighted Vietnam's effort in donating millions of facemasks to several neighboring countries, as well as shipping huge orders of PPE equipment and gloves to the United States.[24] Notably, these face masks produced for the US Marine Corps were worn during President Joe Biden's inauguration in January 2021. During this global crisis, Cushman & Wakefield assessed that Vietnam is now the second most cost-competitive manufacturing hub in the world following China. As the US-China trade war has escalated, there has been a shift to trade with Vietnam, a place with a tech-savvy population of 97 million, fast-growing regions linked by infrastructure planning, and tax incentives in the Economic Zones.[25]

The tale of two countries—Vietnam and Myanmar—in a key geopolitical position between the US and China is a story of retreat and protectionism in Myanmar, on the one hand, and state-managed capitalism steamrolling ahead in Vietnam, on the other. Nonetheless, both countries are positioned as key places for the United States and China to continue to vie for influence in the region. The strategic competition was out on full display during Vice President Kamala Harris's visit to Vietnam in August of 2021, when she urged Vietnam to join the US in opposing China's "bullying" actions in the South China Sea.[26] Harris brought the announcement of a 1 million–dose COVID-19 vaccine donation, but when her plane was delayed China quickly sent an envoy to one-up the US with a pledge of 2 million doses.[27] While some would argue the more vaccines that get to the people of Vietnam the better, we cannot ignore the tensions building between two big brothers/ sisters—the United States and China—and smaller countries in Southeast Asia. The rivalry between China and the United States as both countries work to position themselves as global hegemons means that coordinating how to dismantle the vast financial structures of spiderweb capitalism is probably one of the most important thought projects of the twenty-first century.

The Prey: Caught in the Web

While the focus of this book has been on how global elites exploit frontier markets, what I have left largely unexplored is the prey caught in these massive webs. The prey, I would argue, is everyone else—the people outside of these political and economic power webs whose lives are deeply impacted by the power plays of spiders and their associates.

One consequence of these massive webs is the growing economic inequality between the rich and poor globally. There is plenty of evidence that heightened concentrations of wealth in the hands of a small group of spiders will result in higher levels of poverty; an increase in crime as a consequence of competition for scarce resources; poor access to social services like public health and education; and the far greater power of wealthy citizens to influence regulators and political power holders, compared with the poor.[28]

As I wrapped up this book, I could not help but reflect on the dizzying journey around the world it took me on. I spent most of my time inside: cars with tinted windows, the lobbies of luxury hotels, on the top floors of office buildings with the most seductive views—all of this away from the people. Like the elites I studied, I got a small glimpse of the view from up in the air and of the strategies and moral dilemmas involved with exploiting frontier markets. However, that physical distance from the grime of the street and the consequences of these actions meant that dominant spiders are way out of touch with the harsh reality of how their investments affect the everyday lives of those who have no power.

For example, in Vietnam thousands of people lost their jobs as a result of the government shutdown of the vietranium mine. And during the time that I was carrying out my research, hundreds of local Vietnamese fisherman lost their entire livelihoods in the wake of economic and environmental damage wrought by Taiwan's Formosa corporation, which allegedly discharged toxic waste through a pipeline into the ocean, leaving 70 tons of dead fish washed up onshore.[29] Andrew Le, an environmental sociologist, argues that such environmental disasters have triggered a mass outmigration of people who are compelled to leave as the Vietnamese state prioritizes the interests of foreign investors over its own citizens.[30] Similar outmigration patterns are also occurring in Myanmar as a result of the religious and ethnic violence that is ongoing there.[31] At the same time, since the 2021 coup, those working for foreign companies in Myanmar live in a state of worry over whether they will still have jobs as foreign firms withdraw their investments. This is just a small list of the often-devastating consequences for the lives of everyday people caught in capital webs over which they have no control.

These structural webs produce intersecting consequences, including poverty, climate change and environmental damage, and the outmigration of people. These problems are so massive that they will require a collective effort on the part of civil society to demand what Nobel Prize economist Joseph Stiglitz calls a new social contract. This new social contract starts with a vision of greater balance between government, markets, and civil society, and pushes back against the legal but morally reprehensible behavior of people and institutions.[32] On a global scale, I would argue that this requires greater coordination and will of the people to fix corrupt and broken political and economic systems.

This book takes only one step towards unraveling the spiders' tangled financial webs and exposing the ways they profit from playing in the gray. However, because spiderweb capitalism is global and systemic, it will take a creative, interdisciplinary, and collective effort to begin to unravel these webs and replace them with a world where the rich and poor do not live in parallel universes, or, as journalist Nelson Schwartz puts it, on opposite sides of a velvet rope.[33] Future generations must have the creative will to build a society with policies and protections in place to save our planet, reduce inequality, and prevent most people from becoming trapped, drained, and lost in these massive spiderwebs. After all, those who do not have the financial power or resources to build their own webs are, in this tangled system, ultimately prey.

The Gendered Paradox
of Studying Elites

This book has given me the privilege to go on an incredible journey of social scientific discovery. As with most ethnographies, the questions I began with evolved over time as I uncovered new layers that would eventually become the heart of this book. In my effort to move from data collection to analysis and the presentation of my preliminary findings, I received many questions about how I got access to study such a hard-to-reach population all over the world. In this appendix, I reflect on what it meant to "study up" by studying elites. However, this book also "scales up ethnography" by engaging in a kind of fieldwork that was not grounded in any one place, but instead took me all around the world. In piecing together a global web, I worked to qualitatively unpack not only how different nodes in a network were connected, but the substantive material that held them together.

The first part of the appendix outlines the evolution of my project from its conception between 2009 and 2015 to the intensive data collection period between 2016 and 2017 and follow-up interviews from 2017 to 2020. I describe how my questions shifted, not only as a result of new data, but also in the dialectical process of moving between data and existing literatures. I draw on insights from this data to weigh in on the ongoing debates within the broader academy around data transparency and data replicability. I argue that efforts to double down on transparency by using real names of people not only would have made this project impossible, but neglects the value of subjectivity in qualitative research, which aims for theoretical generalizability without the goals of replication. I also outline how I got access to study this group of elites, and the process by which I analyzed the data. Epistemological insights allowed me to transform barriers into opportunities that pushed me down new paths, which enabled me to revise my core empirical puzzle and the theoretical framework that followed.

In the second part of this appendix, I reflect on my unique social position as the child of Vietnamese immigrants, a woman, and a professor associated with one of the most elite universities in the world, whose highly publicized first book, *Dealing in Desire*, is banned in Vietnam. I focus on what I call the *gendered paradox*: despite being a female professor at an elite institution, my status as a woman in a male-dominated world enabled me to access an economy of free or highly discounted things. At the same time, being a woman also came with the personal cost of public chastisement at best and incessant harassment at worst. Most of my research participants found me non-threatening and were therefore far more forthcoming in many instances than I think they would have been around male researchers. As a result, the best insights in this book came during the time I spent with people outside the office: in bars, during short and long plane rides, and in restaurants. While some of these settings were not ideal for me, as I was often the only woman among a group of men, these were also the places where men could let down their guard and be simultaneously angry, honest, and vulnerable.

The Empirical Puzzle

Inspiration for this book project grew out of some unanswered questions left after I completed my first monograph, *Dealing in Desire: Asian Ascendancy, Western Decline, and the Hidden Currencies of Global Sex Work*, in which I illustrate how the illicit activity in the global sex industry helps to shape flows of capital, by providing foreign investors, local entrepreneurs, and political officials with a space to establish relationships of trust inside high-end hostess bars. The findings for the first book came out of extensive fieldwork done while embedded working as a hostess in these bars for twelve or more hours a day. This left me with a limited view of the deals brokered outside of the bars, or the alternative strategies that Westerners or women might have engaged in to carry out deals.

In the summer and winter months between 2012 and 2015 I carried out preliminary research to test the feasibility of this project for potential external funding opportunities. I spent two years, 2014–2016, drafting research proposals and applying for external research funding to return to Southeast Asia to answer some of those questions. The initial proposals set up a fairly simple puzzle: How do Western and East/Southeast Asian investors embed themselves in newly emerging markets where there is a great deal of speculation and where *social non-contractual relationships* are key to negotiating *legal contracts*? Does Westerners' need to establish enforceable *legal contracts* and adhere to the Foreign Corrupt Practices Act to broker capital deals limit their participation in the social practices of East/Southeast Asian investors who are used to finessing corrupt markets?

While I spent nearly ten years in and out of Vietnam between 2005 and 2015 at the start of the preliminary research for my first book, the truth is that I did not have many leads from the first project to answer these new research questions. The field had changed. In Vietnam, there was a new Prime Minister and new players looking to seize their relationship with the new person in power. Several key players I met in 2009 had left the market after either losing large sums of money on deals gone bad or making a great deal of money and investing those funds in a diverse portfolio outside Vietnam. A small group had ventured into Myanmar, which brought me there for the first time in 2014 to see a new crop of investors who had capitalized on Vietnam's move to chase a new frontier.

As I describe in the introduction, I began to gain access to this world by serving as the personal assistant for two different chief executive officers of two Vietnamese investment management and real estate development firms with diverse portfolios in real estate and manufacturing projects. By following up with investors five years after my initial meeting with them, I have been able to examine how Western investors altered their investment strategies after struggling to gain access to key political officials who were crucial to closing investment deals. This access enabled me to collect ethnographic data on deals between the firms and their investors who originate from Western and East/Southeast Asian contexts.

Within the firms, I worked mostly on real estate transactions as a translator and note taker in meetings with foreign investors. This position enabled me to observe interactions between local firms and their partnerships with foreign investors. However, I did not learn nearly as much in the back office as I did in other spaces, such as coffee shops, restaurants, and spaces of leisure (bars, golf courses, etc.), where foreign investors could partake in some form of entertainment—crucial to a business style where brokers established personal relationships prior to discussing business deals. I wrote ethnographic field notes of my observations in these settings. The debates around ethnography, law, and data transparency fundamentally altered my research strategy.

ETHNOGRAPHY AND LAW: PROBLEMS WITH DEBATES AROUND DATA TRANSPARENCY AND REPLICATION

The standard economic, sociological, or political approach to studying flows of global capital involves quantitative analysis of cross-national data on gross or net capital flows, international reserves, and foreign direct investments (FDIs.) Largely absent from these studies is a qualitative approach that considers the *people* who broker capital deals.

To intervene in this literature, I built upon the work of two economic anthropologists, Karen Ho and Caitlin Zaloom, who have used qualitative methods to uncover how the world's leading financial institutions in New York, Chicago, and London have transformed economic cultures through the craft of speculation.[1] Through an in-depth study inside firms, both scholars describe how investment bankers, traders, business managers, financial analysts, and software engineers collaborate to build new markets. I set out to extend their theoretical and empirical approaches with a qualitative study, at first of real estate investments in Southeast Asia.

The work with these firms would have provided me with greater depth, similar to that captured in Ho's and Zaloom's studies. However, two barriers to staying in the firms emerged as I became privy to common practices in Vietnam and Myanmar that were considered illegal or corrupt by US FCPA standards.

First, the entire academy was embroiled in a public debate about data transparency and replication in the aftermath of the rapid rise and fall of Alice Goffman and her research for her book *On the Run*.[2] She was accused of being an accessory to criminal activity and of fabricating her data. To be frank, while I have been critical of her scholarship, the gendered witch hunt against her work was extreme as she became the scapegoat for a broader, ill-informed debate about the merits of qualitative research.

It was this ethnographic debate that led me to consult the University of Chicago's Social and Behavioral Sciences Institutional Review Board [IRB] for human subjects. There I learned that that the IRB's main concern rightly involves the protection of research subjects rather than the researcher herself. I was advised to consult with the University of Chicago's lawyers. After consulting with the lawyers as well as my University IRB administrators, I decided to pull out of an ethnography within one or two firms and instead only carry out interviews.

This is because US laws around the Foreign Corrupt Practices Act [FCPA] limit participation in any kind of illicit activity—translating emails, sitting on in meetings, potentially witnessing a subtle bribe—that would effectively make me an accessory to criminal activity. However, I was advised that if my research participants told me about such activities or practices, I was not mandated to report it.

The advice I received raises a number of questions that I would like to outline here, because certainly neither I nor Alice Goffman were the first researchers to study a group of people engaged in illicit activity. Criminologists and gender scholars of sex work have led this charge for many years.[3]

Notably, the implementation of the IRB in 1974 and the rise of feminist epistemologies beginning in the 1980s created an academic environment that was friendlier to researchers belonging to marginalized groups. Before the IRB, researchers were solely at the mercy of their peers' evaluation of their ethics according to informal, culturally implicit taboos. This was particularly important for women researchers because of the well-documented informal double standards for the ethical conduct of women in contrast to men in twentieth-century America. The National Research Act of 1974 provided a degree of institutional support against informal attacks on women researchers who, even if their peers continued to cast suspicion on their field ethics, could point to their original IRB clearance in defense of their work.[4] At the same time, feminist epistemologies helped scientifically legitimize the work of diverse scholars by emphasizing the need in social science for researchers occupying multiple and different standpoints.[5]

However, it was in the context of a new sensitivity to researcher positionality—awakened by feminist epistemology—that the self-proclaimed "rogue sociologist" emerged, reopening basic questions about the position of the self both in the field and in academic presentation. According to Sudhir Venkatesh, his unusually high level of participation in the gang he researched for *Gang Leader for a Day* pushed "the boundaries of mainstream sociology ... [which are] stuffy and losing relevance daily in the academic and public eye" while achieving equally ethical and exceedingly rigorous science.[6]

The debate resurfaced in 2015 when several journalists and law professor Steven Lubet accused Alice Goffman of making up her data, and argued that the difficulty of fact-checking some of her claims was symptomatic of a broader problem of accountability in ethnography. Lubet also claimed that Goffman's activities in the field made her an accessory to criminal activity. At a 2016 conference at Northwestern University, hosted by Gary Alan Fine, on the topic of "Ethnography and Law," Lubet cautioned all of us against studying illicit activity. His argument was that if it implicates a researcher in criminal activity, one should not study it.

To resolve some of these critiques around data replicability, the editors of *Contexts* magazine ran a forum on "How to Do Ethnography Right." In that special issue, Alexandra Murphy and Colin Jerolmack call on sociologists to get rid of anonymity altogether. They argue that "our default practice should be to name names and places, unless there are specific case-by-case reasons not to." There are two problems with this approach of doubling down on transparency. First, these arguments completely miss the point that qualitative research prioritizes researcher subjectivity. It is virtually impossible for two researchers to go into the same field site and emerge with the same data. Our positionality, subject position, and unique relationships in the field shape not only who we gain access to but also the kinds of information people are willing to share. When I teach courses on ethnographic field methods and send students to the same site, naturally their field notes all look very different, based on the unique concerns that they each have going in.

Second, while Murphy and Jerolmack illustrate with case-by-case reasons not to anonymize, it makes me wonder how this would apply to Alice Goffman's case. If they were advocating de-anonymization in her case, what would make my case different? Her research subjects were in a far more vulnerable position than my research subjects would ever be, and, in fact, revealing identities would have had more-severe consequences for Goffman's research subjects.

Still, I found myself asking, if the market that I'm studying is riddled with corruption, why should I, as a researcher, risk exposing the people willing to open up to me, and open me up to trying to understand the broader forces and practices at play in their actions? Moreover, how do we actually uncover illicit, illegal, or criminal behavior while also doing our job of protecting our research subjects? What are the limits to studies that involve illegal or illicit activity?

Surely this book raises more questions than answers.

In an international setting there are several conflicting issues that arise with respect to IRB research ethics. For example, a number of less-developed countries do not have IRBs, and the task of getting "IRB Approval" or "Institutional Affiliation Abroad" can be extremely arduous as one navigates multiple levels of bureaucracy. For example, in Myanmar, universities and nonprofit organizations are not allowed to sponsor visas for research scholars. To enter the country as a researcher, I had to draw on my status as a Fulbright Scholar, and therefore a US government–funded researcher, to get a diplomatic note from the US Embassy in Myanmar, which then helped me request permission from the Ministry of Foreign Affairs to enter the country as a known researcher. Similarly, in Vietnam, I had to get the approval of the president of Vietnam National University after a proposal was passed through multiple offices: from the office of international cooperation to the dean's office to the president's office. These processes took six to nine months to complete, and none of these offices had an institutional ethics department. What seemed to matter was censorship over my research activities, more than the protection of human subjects.

At the same time, being in both Vietnam and Myanmar taught me that the question of what is legal or illegal is a socially constructed question that varies greatly from one jurisdiction to another. This leaves open a host of questions for a US researcher seeking to study business practices in foreign contexts where corruption is rampant and part of the everyday course of doing business. Moreover, uneven enforcement of the law makes the prohibition of some activities toothless in the view of many who practice them. If bribery is part of the common practice—how do we open up these social black holes to uncover how *real people* move money around the world, and how they deal with the complex challenges they face when navigating diverse institutional contexts?

I certainly do not claim to have all of the right answers and am open to revising my methods for future work. However, while navigating this complex web in real time, I decided to resolve this problem through multiple approaches. First, I decided to leave the firms, knowing that I would be sacrificing depth for breadth. Fortunately for me, at the time of my research Brooke Harrington published her book *Capital without Borders*, which looked at private wealth managers all around the world.[7] This provided me with a distinctly new model for how to carry out a multi-site global research project. In the end, the choice was not mine to make. It seems that the academy and lawyers decided that implicating myself in criminal activity was not worth the risk for the data I might have been able to gather.

I decided not to write about the firms where I worked because of the risks around maintaining research confidentiality. However, I realized that to keep going forward with this project, I needed to expand the scope of my research to include more sectors of the economy than just real estate and manufacturing—which was what I initially proposed—because (a) after 75 interviews I reached a saturation in the real estate market, and after publishing one article[8] I realized there was no way I could write a whole book without sacrificing the anonymity I had promised my study participants; (b) most of the investors I interviewed were making investments

in incredibly diverse sectors of the economy; and (c) I purposefully interviewed over 300 research subjects so that I could not remember the intimate
details of any one person off the top of my head. In fact, at this point, I know
them more by their pseudonyms than by their real names, and when I see them
casually during follow-up visits to Southeast Asia, I am often embarrassed by
accidently referring to them by their fake names rather than their real names.
Lastly, I purposefully do not trace one deal from beginning to end, and instead
draw on multiple cases to triangulate a broader set of practices.

These methodological choices fundamentally altered the course of my
research and the questions I could ask. I shifted from a focus grounded in
two countries to one inherently global in nature. I stumbled into the world
of offshoring practices without even looking for it as the new kinds of data
emerged, and I felt that I had to revise my research questions. The new questions motivating this book were about how to connect these intricate webs
to map out and reveal a much larger system. Maximizing the strengths of
qualitive research, I was also interested in the substantive matter that held
two nodes in a network so closely together: What flowed between them,
and why?

Funding, Access, Recruitment, Data Analysis and Presentation

FUNDING

Compared to most ethnographies, this project was extremely costly. It would
not have been possible without the external funds I received for data collection from the Fulbright Global Scholar Award and the Social Science
Research Council Transregional Scholar Award. In addition, the University of Chicago backstopped much of this research by funding a full year's
research leave so that I could use all of the research funds from SSRC and
Fulbright to pay for the costs of airfare, hotels, and meals while abroad.
I also received research support from the Center for International Social
Science Research and the Center for the Study of Gender and Sexuality as
well as in-kind support from the University of Chicago through the Jeff Met-
calf Internship Program, a small Albion Small research grant, and a David
Hoeft Award for Newly Tenured Faculty to fund the undergraduate research
assistants that worked on the project at various stages. The vast majority of
the funds were spent on airplane tickets, heavily discounted hotels that I
was able to get through many of my research participants' corporate contacts, and meals. I rented cheap apartments that were at times extremely

uncomfortable, but it was the only way I could afford the travel and hotels. I was obsessive in the field, trying to interview as many people as possible and to take every opportunity offered to me to travel to various sites where investors were raising money and where they were sourcing deals to invest that money. The time spent traveling together was incredibly generative, as I got to know them better and was able to ask follow-up questions along the way.

ACCESS

The questions that I almost always get when I present these findings to academic audiences are: How did I gain access to such a large group of powerful people? And: How was I able to get them to talk about some of the most private, intimate details of how they navigate these markets? Two key factors, I believed, greatly enabled my access to ultra-wealthy elites, financial professionals, and their world of offshoring and overseas investments.

First was my status as a professor at the University of Chicago. I actually began to conceptualize this project while I was an assistant professor at Boston College. During that time, I visited both Vietnam and Myanmar and had an incredibly challenging time gaining access to people working in asset management firms. The emails, LinkedIn messages, and Facebook messages that I sent to potential interviewees often went unanswered. I was able to carry out the first 35–40 interviews through snowball sampling and introductions through UC Berkeley and Stanford University alumni networks that hosted social gatherings and dinners in Ho Chi Minh City.

But my move to the University of Chicago fundamentally helped get this project off the ground. I quickly learned that in the world of international finance, Harvard and Wharton MBAs were known to dominate local asset management firms worldwide. Alumni networks were crucial not only for recruiting financial professionals and executives, but also for raising capital. The University of Chicago, on the other hand, had a reputation for espousing free market economics globally. Many of the people I met saw the UChicago Economics Department and the Booth School of Business as two places where theory and intellectual rigor meet global finance. The dominant reputation of these two departments and schools often clouded my status as a "lefty sociologist" critical of elites, which had made me suspect when I was coming from Boston College, an institution well known for its social justice orientation.

In addition, my move to the University of Chicago in 2015 came on the heels of the launch of my first book, *Dealing in Desire*. The book had won several awards, which put me on the map of the UChicago Alumni office. In

2016, I was invited to give six Harper Lectures for UChicago Alumni groups in Hong Kong, Singapore, Beijing, Shanghai, Delhi, and Mumbai. There I met mostly UChicago Booth alumni who were working in banks, law firms, and asset management firms, and who were key to making introductions for me all around the world. As alumni who valued the power of intellectual rigor and debate, they were most empathetic to a project that was trying to understand broader processes and practices, and they trusted that I was not looking to write an exposé on any one firm or individual. These networks placed incredibly high levels of trust in the UChicago IRB and ethics process, which place great emphasis on the protection of research subjects and their anonymity.

The second factor that helped me gain access was that my new book was, at the time, trending in Vietnam. The book was featured in a seven-part series in a Vietnamese newspaper, *Zing News* (zing.vn). The articles featured a short interview with me after a public lecture at the US Embassy in Ho Chi Minh City. These pieces garnered such high levels of publicity that most of the research subjects I contacted in Vietnam had already heard about me in the media and knew about the work I did for my first book. To my surprise, many were curious to meet me and learn more about the backstory of my research, so our meetings were mutually informative.

At the same time, I was studying a group of highly educated professionals who almost always carried out their due diligence on me before agreeing to sit down for an interview. To my surprise, most of them had read the introduction of my book that was available online for free. So, when we sat down for an interview, the kind of work I thought I needed to do to build rapport or warm them up was not as hard as I expected. Many were impressed by my ability to tell a broad story, which they felt to be true based on their own experiences, while also carefully anonymizing all my sources. So most often the first thing people would say to me would be, "I know you know how this business works, so what do you want to know?" They wanted me to cut to the chase far more quickly. I found this almost shocking at first, but it was crucial to helping me generate incredibly rich data.

THE RECRUITMENT PROCESS AND TRAVEL

I trained a team of thirteen undergraduate research assistants to accompany me on interviews, write narrative summaries, transcribe, conduct news runs, code data, and manage an archive of *Vietnam Economic Times* articles. The interviews lasted anywhere between one and seven hours. Our longest transcript was 35,000 words, which could be a case study all by itself.

During 2016–2017, I worked with a team of five of those undergraduate research assistants from the University of Chicago: three accompanied me in Vietnam and two in Hong Kong. This team helped me organize 11 years of the *Vietnam Economic Times* (2006–2016) and 4 years of *DealStreetAsia* (2014–2017) and *Frontier Myanmar* (2016–2018) to analyze newspaper articles related to real estate investments. From the newspaper articles, we identified several key informants to solicit for interviews. We contacted some people through personal introductions from the networks, but we also contacted several people through LinkedIn without any personal introductions. Following each interview, we asked the respondent for the contact information of other people to interview from our list of ideal interview subjects and from people they knew who they thought would be informative to the project. I went to every interview, and the students took turns accompanying me on interviews. They never went alone because I felt it was important for me to be there, to know when to probe the interview subjects at the appropriate points and to quickly familiarize myself with my own data.

To their credit, the three students who were with me in Vietnam played one of the most important roles in helping me get this project off the ground. They were fearless and had far more energy than anyone I had ever seen. In fact, during our pre-departure meetings, I often worried about them going out to bars or getting in trouble while I was their only chaperone overseas. However, they proved quite the opposite. All of them worked tirelessly by my side and were aggressive with their recruitment strategies. When I ran low on steam, their excitement, energy, and sheer intellectual curiosity kept me going. Our shared experiences and mutual surprise over much of the data also helped me begin to think through emergent themes from the data.

After the first 75 or so interviews, I realized that recruitment through newspapers and magazines revealed only part of the story. Through a snowball referral process, we came to learn that many of the deals I was studying never actually appeared in the news. This is because many people were concerned that media coverage of the deals would result in unwanted attention and the possible issuance of government back tax bills. Therefore, no matter how systematic our analysis of the newspapers, it would leave a lot of gaping holes too big to fill. Among the deals that we studied that had made it into the papers, most had undergone a process of professionalization and were gearing up for a possible IPO. To capture investments at all stages of the deal cycle, we relied far more heavily on interviews through snowball sampling.

I conducted roughly 181 interviews between Vietnam and Myanmar, and through that network I asked for introductions to law firms, banks, company secretary offices, and family offices that managed investments offshore. I then moved to Singapore and Hong Kong, where I made each city my home base for six months to follow the money and carry out more interviews. Importantly, while based in Vietnam, Myanmar, Hong Kong, and Singapore, I made several local trips with investors to project sites as they were sourcing deals to deploy money, and several international trips all around the world while they were raising capital.

The experience felt akin to a sort of global whiplash, as I would often wake up in random hotel rooms forgetting which city I was in or where I would be headed next. My schedule was often dictated by last-minute invitations to travel alongside different groups of financial professionals. The deeply discounted hotels I stayed in were far more luxurious than the four-story walkup I rented in Yangon or the 12th-floor apartment I rented in Ho Chi Minh City for less than USD$700 a month, which reminded me of my lifestyle as a graduate student carrying out fieldwork while I was living in Vietnam in 2009–2010.

By the end of the project I had conducted a total of 302 interviews. However, only 49 percent of the research subjects gave me permission to audio-record our interviews. For those who did not allow me to record their interviews, I took extensive field notes; if a student accompanied me, he or she did the same, so that I had two sets of notes for each interview.

To protect my research subjects and grant them the anonymity promised in my interviews, I do not use the real names of the people, the businesses, or even, in some cases, the natural resource. Strategic minerals like gold or tungsten, as well as oil and gas, were too difficult to disguise, because there are only two or three major mining projects in the country. The same is true for oil and gas companies. Therefore, naming the strategic resource would make it impossible to anonymize research subjects. In addition, in some instances, I created a composite case by bringing multiple cases with similar investors together into one, so as to de-identify all of the people I spoke with. In addition, when possible I triangulate interview data with legal documents, press releases, and media interviews to gain some perspective outside that of the protagonist (my interviewee), who leads the story from the interviews.

DATA ANALYSIS AND PRESENTATION

Back in Chicago, I employed another team of eight research assistants, who transcribed recorded interviews and worked with me to analyze the data. Even though the research subjects consented before I turned on the recorder and their full names were never mentioned on the recordings. I had students code names so that none of them had interviewees' real name or the master list with real names. However, there were so many intimate details in the interviews themselves that I grew nervous as the very talented undergraduates curiously tried to identify the real names of one or two research subjects. While I never confirmed any of their queries, this fundamentally altered my approach to data sharing with the students.

In light of this, I purposefully mixed up the interviews so that no student had access to the full group of interviews or to ones that might be connected to one another in a social network. Thus each student had no more than 6 percent of the full dataset of audio recordings. While I plan to destroy the audio recordings after the completion of this project, I do not plan to publicly share any of the interview transcripts because of the identifying information in them, which includes company names, former employers, relationships with banks and company secretary offices, and details about deals that are not publicized.

With the transcripts, the students also wrote a narrative summary of each interview, which helped me develop the initial set of codes. These narrative summaries were crucial in helping me to develop a narrative arc for the book and determine the themes that would become the chapters of the book. From there, I coded the data in NVivo. In the primary coding rounds, I noticed that every research subject described two distinct processes: (1) their network of people from all around the world whom they relied on to raise capital and structure their investment deals, and (2) their varying relationships to local government officials, which either facilitated or impeded their investment projects.

Although I had not set out to analyze the complex networks around the world or even proximity to government officials, after noticing the high frequency with which investors discussed government ties, I developed secondary codes to capture (1) the structure of offshoring, (2) the barriers and opportunities investors experienced in their efforts to access government officials, and (3) the practices investors engaged in to embed themselves in close networks of political elites, or to create both physical and symbolic boundaries between themselves and political elites.

After the first round of coding, I returned to the literature on offshoring and new geographies of capital, law and corruption, and moral markets in order to think through some of the emerging themes from the data. Through a dialectical process of moving between my data and the literature, I began the process of theory building from this case study. By engaging in a creative inferential process of theory building based on surprising research observations, I developed a new set of questions about the interconnected spiderweb I was uncovering, which then led me to follow the data with new interviews in other countries.[9]

In addition, where possible, I triangulated interview transcripts with media reports, legal documents, handbooks, and presentations which were publicly available online through Google searches. These documents helped to fill out portions of the story that were not covered in the interview data.

In July of 2019, I hosted a book workshop with Jennifer Carlson, Sida Liu, and Greta Krippner, who each read the first full draft of this book's manuscript. In that draft, the story was strong, but the theorization and conceptualization were weak. Together they spent a day talking through my data with me and helping me to think through a new architecture for the book. I spent a year revising with their comments in mind and then held a second book workshop with my University of Chicago colleagues Geoff Wodtke, Amanda Sharkey, and Patrick Bergmann, who each provided substantive feedback that helped me sharpen the theoretical contributions of this book to continue with the revisions. In addition, I had the privilege of receiving critically engaged feedback from Andrew Abbott, Terence Halliday, and Hannah Appel, who pushed my theorizing in the final round of revisions.

The Gendered Paradox of Studying Elite Men

In any field site, every ethnographer's subjective sense of self inevitably shapes the kind of data they get access to. Yet, all ethnographers are multidimensional individuals with different selves, which we activate based on the relational context we are in. The person I am on campus at the University of Chicago is not always the same self that comes out in the field as I was living abroad and collecting data all around the world. The ability to move between and navigate uniquely different social spaces was key to this project. For example, in Southeast Asia, different parts of my identity mattered more than others, including being an American-born daughter of Vietnamese war refugees with family members who were on both sides of that war; being a professor from the University of Chicago; and being a woman who was often non-threatening in a male-dominated world. These all uniquely shaped not only the kind of people I was able to access, but also the kinds of things they were willing to share over the course of my ethnography.

Ninety percent of the interviews I carried out were with men. This is not surprising for many, given the gendered divisions on Wall Street and in finance broadly.[10] However, this meant that on all of the travels to project sites or to raise money, I was often the only woman traveling in an entourage of men. Looking back, there were many moments that left me feeling extremely uncomfortable. I often got into cars with complete strangers in order to access hard-to-reach project sites off of unpaved roads. I also got into planes without a clear sense of where we were ultimately headed. These kinds of split-second choices made while I was carrying out fieldwork were ones that I often look back upon and wonder if I could have negotiated them differently.

In the course of my interviews with mostly men, over drinks and in bars, some of the men hit on me incessantly the same way they would on bartenders and hostesses. To them, women are objects who all have a price and could easily be bought with fancy dinners or extravagant gifts. While more powerful women in my field sites were able to ward off some of these advances, I was not one of them. That division between wealthy, high-powered women—who have the ability to draw on other women's labor to entertain potential investors and male partners—and myself was huge. Those women could outright refuse advances or walk away from men who were too aggressive because they had something those men wanted in a business deal. I, on the other hand, possessed nothing of value to most of these men.

In this world, I had no power, so I often put up with it and kept quiet while also carefully finding ways to duck out of situations that made me uncomfortable. For example, one evening I was out with a group of five men—three were foreign investors from South Korea, one was an overseas Vietnamese who had been working in Vietnam for over fifteen years, another a local Vietnamese partner. We had dinner together before moving to a Skydeck bar with 360-degree views of Ho Chi Minh City for some fancy cocktails. From there we moved to a night club. In each venue, I watched as the men collectively courted tables of single women—no one knew whether they were hostesses/sex workers or just cute partygoers. But as the night wore on, we all ended up at a party in a private home. By 3:00 a.m., it was clear that this party was starting to grow intimate and in no time would soon turn into an orgy party.

As I made my way to the door to escape the party scene, two women blocked the front door, saying in Vietnamese, "*Chị ơi chị ơi đừng bỏ em ở đây* (Big sister, big sister, please don't leave us here)!" I looked them straight in the face and told them that I was walking out this door and they were welcome to come with me. I left, but they pouted and chose to stay. In truth, I will never know what compelled them to stay. I never got the women's names, and if I were to see them again, I am not sure that I would even recognize them.

The following morning, I had to sit through a two-hour interview with the clients from South Korea, who went into great detail describing the scene after I left the party and the group sex they had together with women who were so inebriated that they were unconscious. While I listened without much probing, it was an incredible personal challenge for me to keep a straight face while trying to appear nonjudgmental. While I was not at all interested in a play-by-play of the party, I had to listen to these gruesome details in order to get information on the details of the deal. Yet, even as I tried extremely hard to ignore them, hearing these kinds of stories multiple times made me realize how important these experiences were for men's homosocial bonding, which shapes part of the argument of this book.

In this way, I became somewhat akin to a therapist as several people opened up to me about the moral mazes that they felt they had to navigate. Oftentimes, interviews lasted much longer than anticipated, and interviewees often shared a great deal of personal detail without much probing from me. What was striking was that when I asked these men if they had friends or close confidants whom they trusted to talk with when navigating morally compromising situations, the vast majority of them told me that they didn't, because they feared that it would taint their reputation or that other people could use that information to inflict harm on them. As an aside, I often wondered why people were willing to be so open with me with respect to things about them that were socially undesirable, but I rarely asked them to reflect on that with me, in part because I was afraid that it might prompt them to stop sharing. Near the end of my research, however, I finally had the courage to ask Eric, one man who confided in me multiple times about engaging in morally suspect behavior, and he said to me, "I suppose it's because you're a woman, who's non-threatening, because it's your job to maintain confidentiality. There's nothing you can do to inflict harm on me, and at the end of the day it's not like these countries are swarming with therapists."

In the field, I made it very clear that I was married, and was very conscious about wearing my wedding rings while I was out and about. However, this did not seem to deter many of the men, and I found myself having to do what many women do on a daily basis: ducking, diving, and finagling my way out of uncomfortable situations. On several occasions, I got the best interview data from conversations that were set up over long and multiple-course dinners. These men introduced me to some of the world's finest restaurants. For me, they were the perfect setting for intimate interviews because the ambience was often quiet, and if I was allowed to record our conversation, there was not a ton of background noise. The tables were usually large enough for me to take notes either on my phone or in a small notebook; I jotted down details and key phrases to help jog my memory of the conversation that unfolded. However, at the end of each dinner I made sure to pay the bill in order to draw clear boundaries and leave nothing open to interpretation after a long meal. This was not a date. It was an interview.

While I was fortunate to get to work with several undergraduate research assistants, for some reason the advertisements attracted economics or public policy majors more than they did sociology majors. In the field, four out of the five research assistants were young men between the ages of 18 and 20. My students always dressed professionally for the interviews, wearing at least button-up shirts, if not ties and a blazer. Whenever we would walk up to an office space, or while we waited for the interviewee in coffeeshops or restaurants, most everyone mistook the students for the professor and me for the students' research assistant, leading to a confusing set of introductions off the bat, for both student and interviewee. While being a University of Chicago professor certainly got us in the door for interviews, it was clear that the majority of the men I spent time around found me non-threatening. The extremely talented research assistants were invited out to hostess bars by many of the men I studied as a way of including them in the same kinds of male homosocial bonding experiences I write up throughout this book. In addition, they were aggressively recruited by the people we studied to take more-lucrative internships in local firms.

While being a petite Asian-American woman in this setting did not garner much in the way of respect, and in some instances brought on harassment and vitriol that I had to swallow in front of my students, there was a huge advantage. Possessing virtually no power meant that I could ask seemingly stupid questions that yielded incredibly detailed insights. Oftentimes I did not even realize this until I was coding the transcripts and analyzing the data weeks after an interview.

While students transcribing the data often expressed a level of discomfort with having to listen to and transcribe audio recordings of men screaming at me about how women are nothing in finance, or berating my lack of understanding of basic economics, I had to remind the students that those moments afforded me priceless opportunities to probe and dig deeper for details that in the end yielded far richer insights.

In truth, care and control are two sides of the same coin. It was precisely my subject position as a woman, or a poor teacher, an immigrant child with working-class origins, that shaped my entry into this world without anyone feeling threatened by my presence. In truth, there was no way I could afford to spend time in these spaces without access to their corporate discounts for plane tickets, hotels, and an economy of free and heavily discounted things. At the outset, both my research subjects and their wives shaped my wardrobe choices to help me fit into these spaces. It started with hand-me-down designer clothes from wives' stuff that was brand-new, with tags on them, so that I did not stand out in the group during our travels. Some of these research subjects owned franchises of luxury brands globally, providing me with access to luxury handbags, shoes, and clothing, with the deepest discount running at 90 percent off. By the end of this project, my entire wardrobe had transformed, and, in truth, so too did my tastes in clothing, food, travel, and a seductive world that I would have never otherwise had access to.

It is this gendered paradox—being a highly educated professor from one of the most elite universities in the world while also being a woman in a male-dominated world—that shaped the analytical frames and theories that emerged from this book. My multi-dimensional subject position in the field not only transformed the argument, but ultimately transformed my own sense of self, and for that I am also deeply grateful to those who not only opened up their private worlds to me, but gave me the tools to navigate their social and capital webs.

Prologue

1. All names of interviewees are pseudonyms to protect the anonymity of my research participants.

2. The description of UHNWIs as being "nowhere and everywhere" comes from Palan and Nesvetailova (2014).

Introduction

1. Porteous and Menkes (2013). The International Consortium of Investigative Journalists have been able to identify offshore funds linked to the close relatives of China's top leaders President Xi Jinping and former Premier Wen Jiabao. These secretive offshore accounts shroud the wealth of the Communist elite.

In addition, Russian President Vladimir Putin's close friend Sergey Roldugin allegedly operates a hidden network of associates who shuffled at least $2 billion through banks and offshore companies. Bernstein et al. (2016).

2. US Department of Justice (2020).

3. Wright and Hope (2018).

4. Piketty (2014), Zucman (2015).

5. Ho (2009).

6. Knuth and Potts (2016).

7. For more on shifting legal geographies see Potts (2020).

8. Palan, Murphy, and Chavagneux (2009).

9. In her book *Uneasy Street*, Rachel Sherman (2017) was only able to interview 50 people in 42 different households with a focus on how they thought about their wealth rather than on how they made their money. Justin Farrell (2020) also describes the challenges of interviewing elites in his book *Billionaire Wilderness*.

10. See Pistor (2019) for works on writing legal code; Potts (2018), Potts (2016) on shifting legal geographies.

11. Acemoglu and Robinson (2012), North (1990). On elites and prestige see Mills ([1956] 2000).

12. Veblen (1921, 4–5). On crony capitalism see Evans (1995), Kang (2002).

13. See Dharmapala (2017), Dharmapala (2019) for work on profit-shifting methods and taxation.

14. For instance, political scientists and sociologists alike look primarily at states' capacity to shape markets (see for example Panitch and Gindin [2012], Armijo and Katada [2015]). In this vein, nation-states are the primary focus, with offshore jurisdictions as another sovereignty that offers competitive tax rates, drawing U/HNWIs to send their money (see Panitch and

Gindin [2012, 1]). Theories in the Varieties of Capitalism literature frame Third World countries as weak predatory states without a relational legal bureaucracy, where the state has an unconstrained capacity to extract resources from civil society (see Evans [1995]). In this framework, nation-states are primarily responsible for creating the conditions conducive to capital accumulation, with the legal profession playing a dominant role in writing law that is backed by the coercive powers of the state. (See Weber [(1922) 1978] for argument on the state's monopoly over legitimate violence. See also Pistor [2019].) Countries with democratic and inclusive economic institutions will experience prosperity and growth, while extractive economies that concentrate power narrowly in the hands of the elite impede and even block economic growth. (See Acemoglu and Robinson [2012].)

15. Sassen (2000).

16. Sassen (2001).

17. Sassen (2001).

18. Sassen (2001). The focus on the practices that constitute economic globalization in command centers looks primarily at *production* and the specialized services necessary for running dispersed networks of factories, offices, and service outlets. But the focus on *production* fails to account for the complex ownership structures, and thereby the very connections between global cities and offshore sovereignties.

19. Reich (1983).

20. Palan and Nesvetailova (2014).

21. Piketty (2015, viii).

22. Zucman (2015).

23. Shaxson (2011).

24. Palan, Murphy, and Chavagneux (2010, 51). See also Fichtner (2015, 1); Palan and Nesvetailova (2014) (as cited in Akhtar and Grondona [2019, 1]).

25. Young (2018, 59).

26. Young (2018, 59–60).

27. As Ronen Palan and Anastasia Nesvetailova explain, the financial system has gone through a number of transformative phases since World War II, leading to the "emergence and persistent growth of new legal or quasi-legal spaces and financial innovations which were either aimed at and/or resulted in the avoidance or minimization of state regulations" (Palan and Nesvetailova [2014, 2]). Building on this work, Shaina Potts rightly points out that "these financial geographies remain inextricably entangled not only with business actors, but with legal and political actors as well [because] law anchors economic geographies in state spaces and (often contradictory) state interests at a variety of scales" (Potts [2018, 1–2]).

28. Krippner (2017).

29. Sherman (2017), Mears (2020), Farrell (2020).

30. Tsing (2005), Harms (2016).

31. Mills ([1956] 2000).

32. For the licit life of capitalism see Appel (2019).

33. For sabotage see Veblen (1921); for coordination see Mills ([1956] 2000).

34. For other examples of global ethnographies see: Block-Lieb and Halliday (2017), Burawoy et al. (2000).

35. Freeland (2012).

36. For studies on elites see: Cousin, Khan, and Mears (2018), Sherman (2017), Mears (2020), Freeland (2012), Atkinson and Piketty (2007), Bourdieu (1984).

37. Cousin, Khan, and Mears (2018).

38. *Forbes* (2021).

39. Freeland (2012, 48).

40. Forbes (2019).

41. Mills ([1956] 2000), Cousin, Khan, and Mears (2018).

42. This framing emerged out of conversations with Benjamin Cornwell.

43. Zarroli (2016).

44. See methodological appendix.

45. Hoang (2015).

46. Sassen (2001).

47. Ong (2011).

48. Ong (2011), Koolhaas (2004).

49. Nam (2012, 2011), Hoang (2015).

50. Zoellick (2010), World Bank (2012).

51. Merrill Lynch and Capgemini (2011).

52. Ahmed (2014).

53. O'Neill (2013).

54. Gray (2017).

55. Esteva and Prakash (1998). (For a deeper evaluation of One-Third/Two-Thirds Worlds in one connected economic system, see also Mohanty [2002]).

Chapter 1

1. Goldman (2016).

2. Richkoff (2018).

3. Smith (1986).

4. In his book *Treasure Islands* Nicholas Shaxson introduces the concept of a spiderweb to refer to offshore financial structures and the ways that businesses artificially manipulate financial paper trails across borders. Shaxson points out that there is a real route of capital flow accompanied by an artificial paper trail, set up by accountants, which is a layered hub-and-spoke array of tax havens, in his case centered on the city of London (Shaxson [2011, 13–17]). In Shaxson's frame there are three main rings. The inner ring consists of Britain's three Crown Dependencies: Jersey, Guernsey, and the Isle of Man. The next ring involves Britain's 14 overseas territories. The third, outermost ring is made up of a more diverse array of havens like Hong Kong and the Bahamas. What links these three rings is a history of empire and colonialism ([2011], 17–18). Importantly, the "spiderweb lets the City get involved in businesses that might be forbidden in Britain, giving the financiers in London sufficient distance from wrongdoing to allow plausible deniability . . . [so that b]y the time the money gets to London . . . it has been washed clean" ([2011, 18–19]). This empirical illustration is what I build on to theorize spiderweb capitalism. However, while Shaxson's account has a clear center (in his case either the United States or Britain), my theoretical framework argues that this is a global phenomenon without a clear center or ring. In other words, there isn't simply a "British spiderweb" or a "US spiderweb"; rather, spiderweb capitalism accounts for a global web with no clear center or anchor.

5. Names of firms associated with the people I interviewed have been fictionalized.

6. Piketty (2014).

7. "A strategic action field is a meso-level social order where actors (who can be individual or collective) interact with knowledge of one another under a set of common understandings about the purposes of the field, the relationships in the field (who has power and why), and the field's rules. . . . When they interact in a larger political, social, or economic field, that field also becomes an SAF." Fligstein and McAdam (2011, 3).

8. For more on "what is at stake," see Bourdieu and Wacquant (1992) as cited in Fligstein and McAdam (2011, 3–5).

9. Fligstein and McAdam (2011, 11).

10. Harrington (2016).

11. Leigh, Frayman, and Ball (2012).

12. Beginning in the 1920s following the first World War, governments increased taxes to pay for their respective war efforts. Those who wanted to escape new tax hikes took their money to Switzerland.

13. Lane and Milesi-Ferretti (2017, 9).

14. McCoy (2016).

15. Treanor (2017).

16. Shields and Franklin (2015).

17. Harrington (2016, 13).

18. Bruner (2016).

19. Zucman (2015, 25).

20. USTR (2016).

21. Baker (2012).

22. Pennington (2016).

23. Swanson (2018).

24. Lee (2018).

25. O'Neill (2013).

26. World Bank (2018).

27. South China Morning Post (2017).

28. Bahree (2015).

29. Witt and Redding (2013).

30. Beresford (2008), Kerkvliet (2001), Gillen (2010).

31. Nguyen, T. P. (2014, 100).

32. Malesky, McCulloch, and Nhat (2015, 681).

33. Kim (2017).

34. Koolhaas (2004), Ong (2011), Hoang (2018).

35. Nam (2011).

36. Kim (2017).

37. *Regulatory opacity* involves the practices of state agencies and urban developers, as they negotiate a multitude of urban development regulations at both urban and national levels. *Regulatory transparency,* in contrast, *underscores* the work of the state, in concert with multilateral institutions, to address the problem of state corruption in urban development. Kim (2017).

38. Hoang (2018).

39. The British ruled Burma from 1824 to 1948. In the years leading up to Burma's independence, Japan invaded and occupied it in 1942. Britain then helped to liberate Burma from Japanese occupation with assistance from the Anti-Fascist People's Freedom League (AFPFL), led by Aung San. But in 1947, Aung San and six members of his interim government were assassinated by his political opponents and rival U Nu. In 1948, Burma became independent, with U Nu as its Prime Minister. In the late 1950s, the AFPFL split into two factions, and Chief of Staff General Ne Win led a military coup in 1962 that ousted Prime Minister U Nu from power.

40. Turnell (2009).

41. In 1988, Aung San Suu Kyi emerged as the leader promoting democracy in Burma. To quell a democratic social movement, the government arrested and killed hundreds of democracy activists. An internal military coup led to the rise of the State Law and Order Restoration Council (SLORC), which announced the country's name change from Burma to Myanmar. (For more historical context see Turnell [2009].)

42. Turnell (2011).

43. Jones (2014).

44. Jones (2014).

45. Turnell (2009).

46. Jones (2014).

47. Szep and Marshall (2012).

48. ISEAS – Yusof Ishak Institute (2010).

49. ISEAS – Yusof Ishak Institute (2010).

50. Szep and Marshall (2012).

51. See Hoang (2018, 2015), Hoang, Cobb, and Lei (2017).

52. Harrington (2016, 19).

53. Aung (2017).

54. Pritzker's family is known for their businesses in the Hyatt Hotel chain. He has an estimated personal net worth of 3.5 billion.

55. Shaxson (2011) cites *The Economist* magazine to point out that Rupert Murdoch's "News Corporation paid a tax rate of just 6 percent—compared with 31 percent for its competitor Disney" (7). See also "Rupert Laid Bare," *The Economist*, March 18, 1999.

56. Block-Lieb and Halliday (2017).

Chapter 2

1. Khanna and Palepu (2010).

2. Bussell (2013), North (1990), Rose-Ackerman (1999).

3. This chapter draws inspiration from Viviana Zelizer's (2012) concept of relational work to theorize the process of relational capitalism in the public domain. Her work shows how deal brokering in markets with very little data often involves personal relationships, which provide investors with some kinds of assurances as well as an intimate "gut feeling" to take big risks in new frontier markets.

4. For more on relational work see Zelizer (2012).

5. Hoang (2015, 2020).

6. Mills ([1956] 2000, 98). Key to the accumulation of wealth are the ways that wealthy individuals have been able to exploit corruptible political systems and employ lawyers to carry out the legal footwork, as did the robber barons of the nineteenth century, who then freely "exploited national resources, waged economic wars among themselves . . . [and] made private capital out of the public domain." Mills ([1956] 2000, 95).

7. Homoerotic triangles bridge the work of C. Wright Mills and Eve Sedgwick, to show how women are used as props in trust-building exercises between men with political and economic power. I put C. Wright Mills's ([1956] 2000) concept of the power elite—or the idea of an interlocking directorate between political and economic elites—into conversation with Eve Sedgwick's (1985) concept of the erotic triangle to advance a theory of gendered relations in deal brokering. To advance this framework, I empirically examine how public officials and private investors do trust and/or establish relationships of mutual hostage over women's bodies.

8. René Girard (1966) and Eve Sedgwick (1985).

9. Sedgwick argues, "We can go further than that, to say that in any male-dominated society, there is a special relationship between male homosocial (including homosexual) desire and the structures for maintaining and transmitting patriarchal power" (Sedgwick [1985, 25]). See also: Hoang (2020) for a deeper theoretical engagement of homoerotic triangles.

10. Cooley, Heathershaw, and Sharman (2018).

11. On cultural matching see Rivera (2012).

Chapter 3

1. Osburg (2018, S149) asks the question, "How does a state fight corruption in a context in which corrupt practices are not only ubiquitous but more or less institutionalized as the 'unwritten' rules of the game?" Advancing his work, I flip this question so that the focus is not on how states fight corruption but rather on how investors finesse this local context.

2. Aguilera and Vadera (2008), Rose-Ackerman (2010)

3. Gorsira, Denkers, and Huisman (2018).

4. Irrawaddy (2021b).

5. My research subjects call this playing to the "white of the gray" vs. the "black of the gray." I realize that for some this has racist connotations of light/white being clean and black/dark being dirty. So rather than invoke the colors white vs. black, I chose the words "lighter vs. darker" to better capture the process.

6. See: 15 U.S.C. § 78dd-2(B) and Deming (2011).

7. Spalding (2015).

8. "*Gift exchange* delays reciprocity and reframes exchanges as expressions of friendship. . . . For gift exchange to be accomplished, interpersonal trust or socialization must be present. . . . *Bundling* uses cross-subsidization across multiple innocuous exchanges to synthesize a taboo exchange. . . . Bundling makes . . . disreputable commensuration appear to be a set of reputable [exchanges]" so that "actors can . . . maintain the pretext that there is no [impropriety] about their exchange. . . . *Brokerage* finds a third party to accept responsibility for exchange." Rossman (2014, 43, 48, 53).

9. Rossman (2014).

10. Mauss (1990).

11. Lainer-Vos (2013).

12. Lee (2016).

13. Stovel and Shaw (2012, 140).

14. Stovel and Shaw (2012).

15. Sanyal (2012).

16. Rossman (2014).

17. US Department of Justice (2016).

18. This idea of "exporting corruption" was one that Jeffrey Kidder at Northern Illinois University brought up as an insightful analysis after a talk I gave in the Sociology Department's colloquia. Prof. Kidder brought this up in the context of developed countries like the United States exporting pollution to other countries with looser regulatory structures, and asked if there were parallels to exporting corruption. I thank Jeffrey for this insight.

Chapter 4

1. There is a notable gap in the literature theorizing taxation, which is surprising given that scholars of the economy as early as Marx, Schumpeter, Elias, Bourdieu, and Simmel reflected on the social and economic significance of taxation (Aalbers [2017]).

2. Sayer (2015).

3. For an argument on the blurry line between legal and illegal tax strategies, see also Braithwaite (2009b), Maurer (2008).

4. Shen (2010).

5. De Mooij and Ederveen (2008).

6. Zelizer (2005).

7. Shen (2010).

8. See also Harrington (2016) for Chinese example.

9. Shen (2010, 212).

10. Shen (2010, 212).

11. Zhao (2014).

12. Gleckman (2013). In this article Gleckman also cites the work of Harvard professor Steve Shay, who refers to this money as "ocean income," or "revenue that simply disappears into the deep blue."

13. See, for example, Desai, Foley, and Hines Jr. (2006), Desai, Foley, and Hines Jr. (2004).

14. Desai, Foley, and Hines Jr. (2004, 2730).

15. It was not until 2016 that China even established a set of transfer pricing rules (Bell [2017]).

16. Nguyen (2017).

17. The TMF Group outlined some key features of the new law. Under the new (Vietnamese) Decree 20:

- The ownership threshold increased to 25% from 20%
- Two entities with mutual transactions more than 50% of sales/purchases are no longer treated as related parties
- The dossier must include identifying related-party transaction prices and benchmarks on data sources.
- TP documentation now includes a master dossier on global group information and a local dossier and country-by-country profit report.

18. Vu (2017). (The quoted interview is no longer online, but a contemporaneous interview with Joseph Vu is accessible on the PricewaterhouseCoopers transfer pricing podcast, *TP Talks*.)

19. Klassen, Lisowksy, and Mescall (2017).

20. Le (2018).

21. Tu and Le (2018).

22. Le (2018).

23. Few scholars look at the varied strategies of different players in the market and how they collaborate with one another. Economic sociologists and sociologists of law do not pay much attention to tax as an important variable in global capital flows. Much of the work on tax is carried out by economists and legal scholars, who employ large datasets without attention to people or relationships, or they use single case studies as their unit of analysis. There are fragments of the discipline that look at tax as it relates to the sociology of professions (see Halliday [1987]), theories of the state (see Tilly [2007]), socio-legal scholarship on defiance of tax (see Braithwaite [2009a, b]), and work on transnational legal orders (see Genschel and Rixen [2015]).

24. Worstall (2016).

Chapter 5

1. Wright and Hope (2018, 9).

2. DaCosta (2010).

3. Gunasegaram (2018).

Chapter 6

1. Young (2004).

2. Lamont (1992).

3. On the sacred and profane see Durkheim (1995); on the way money pollutes society, see Douglas (1966); on the way money corrupts see Zelizer ([1979] 2017), Friedman and McNeill (2013).

4. On the transformation of the social moral order, see Polanyi ([1944] 2001). On the social moral order see Weber ([1922] 1978).

5. For more on homoerotic subplots see: Sedgwick (1985).

6. A Korean chaebol is a large industrial conglomerate that is run and controlled by an owner or family.

7. Halliday and Carruthers (1996).

Chapter 7

1. *Vietnam Economic Times* 2016 article, not attached here to maintain anonymity of research subjects.

2. Small (2017, 6).

Conclusion

1. Ferguson (2010).

2. For more on changing public perceptions as a result of the Occupy Wall Street social movements, see Gaby and Caren (2016).

3. Dhanoa (2020).

4. Gladstone (2021).

5. Lewin and Peeters (2006).

6. Weitzman (forthcoming).

7. Woodman (2018a).

8. Woodman (2018a).

9. Woodman (2018b).

10. Woodman (2018b).

11. ICIJ (2017).

12. Fagetan (2021).

13. Deneault (2011, 92–93).

14. Deneault (2011, 83).

15. See: *https://corpfiles.delaware.gov/whyDE_chinese.pdf*, as cited by Deneault (2011).

16. Zucman (2014).

17. Goldman (2021).

18. Agence France-Presse (2021).

19. Nguyen (2021b).

20. Coyle (2021).

21. The *Irrawaddy* (2021).

22. Zhou (2021), Davies (2021).

23. Davis (2021).

24. Nguyen (2021a).

25. Tonkes (2020).

26. Lee (2021).

27. Mahtani (2021).

28. Birdsong (2015).

29. Sands (2016).

30. Le (2020).

31. For Rohingya Crisis in Myanmar see: BBC News (2020); for Buddhist-Muslim conflicts see: Gonzalez (2020).

32. Stiglitz (2019).

33. Schwartz (2020).

Methodological Appendix

1. Zaloom (2006), Ho (2009).

2. Goffman (2014).

3. See for example Bernstein (2007), Bourgois (1996), Contreras (2013), Ralph (2014), Vargas (2016), Stuart (2016).

4. The link between the National Research Act of 1974 and feminist methodologies was first noted by Elizabeth Long (Professor Emerita of Sociology at Rice University) in an unpublished co-authored paper I worked on with Long titled "Why is Rogue in Vogue? Ethnographies on Gangs, Drugs, and Sex Work." The paper, titled "Feminist Epistemology and Gendered Careers in Sociology," was presented at the American Sociological Association Annual Meeting in Montréal, Canada, in August 2017, on a panel titled *Qualitative Methodology I: Epistemology and Ethnography.*

5. Doucet (2018).

6. Venkatesh (2008).

7. Harrington (2016).

8. Hoang (2018).

9. See also Tavory and Timmermans (2014) for a more extensive framework on abductive theory building.

10. See Bear et al. (2015), Mears (2020).

REFERENCES

Aalbers, Manuel B. 2017. "Financial Geography I: Geographies of Tax." *Progress in Human Geography* 42 (6): 916–27. https://doi.org/10.1177/0309132517731253.

Acemoglu, Daron, and James A. Robinson. 2012. *Why Nations Fail: The Origins of Power, Prosperity, and Poverty.* New York: Crown.

Agence France-Presse. 2017. "Vietnamese Banker Sentenced to Death in Fraud Saga That Exposed Deeply Rooted Corruption in Financial System." *South China Morning Post,* September 29, 2017.

Agence France-Presse. 2021. "Leave, Suspend, Or Stay: The Choices Of Foreign Investors In Myanmar." *Barron's,* July 8, 2021. https://www.barrons.com/news/leave-suspend-or-stay-the -choices-of-foreign-investors-in-myanmar-01625751007.

Aguilera, Ruth V., and Abhijeet K. Vadera. 2008. "The Dark Side of Authority: Antecedents, Mechanisms, and Outcomes of Organizational Corruption." *Journal of Business Ethics* 77 (4): 431–49.

Ahmed, Kamal. 2014. "Twenty-Four European Banks Fail EBA 'Stress Test.'" *British Broadcasting Corporation,* October 26, 2014.

Akhtar, Jahanzeb, and Verónica Grondona. 2019. "Tax Haven Listing in Multiple Hues: Blind, Winking, or Conniving." Research Paper no. 94. Geneva, Switzerland: South Centre.

Appel, Hannah. 2019. *The Licit Life of Capitalism: US Oil in Equatorial Guinea.* Durham, NC: Duke University Press.

Armijo, Leslie Elliott, and Saori N. Katada. 2015. "Theorizing the Financial Statecraft of Emerging Powers." *New Political Economy* 20 (1):42–62.

Atkinson, A. B., and Thomas Piketty, eds. 2007. *Top Incomes over the 20th Century: A Contrast between European and English-Speaking Countries.* Oxford, UK: Oxford University Press.

Aung, Myo, and Michael Peel. 2017. "Myanmar: The Military-Commerical Complex." *The Financial Times,* February 1, 2017. *https://www.researchgate.net/publication/313249258_Myanmar _the_military-commercial_complex.*

Bahree, Megha. 2015. "Military, Political and Business Cronyism at Heart of Land Seizures in Myanmar." *Forbes Asia,* March 30, 2015.

Baker, Peter. 2012. "Obama to Visit Myanmar as Part of First Postelection Overseas Trip to Asia." *New York Times,* November 8, 2012. *https://www.nytimes.com/2012/11/09/world/asia/obama -to-visit-myanmar.html.*

BBC News. 2020. "Myanmar Rohingya: What You Need to Know about the Crisis." *BBC,* January 23, 2020. *https://www.bbc.com/news/world-asia-41566561.*

Bear, Laura, Karen Ho, Anna Lowenhaupt Tsing, and Sylvia Yanagisako. 2015. "Gens: A Feminist Manifesto for the Study of Capitalism." *Theorizing the Contemporary* (Fieldsites). doi: *https:// culanth.org/fieldsights/gens-a-feminist-manifesto-for-the-study-of-capitalism.*

Bell, Kevin. 2017. "China's New Transfer Pricing Rules Keep Arm's Length Approach." *Offshore News Flash,* April 5, 2017. (Possibly reprinted from Bloomberg BNA *Tax Management*

Transfer Pricing Report.) http://www.offshorenewsflash.com/2017/04/05/chinas-new-transfer-pricing-rules-keep-arms-length-approach/.

Beresford, Melanie. 2008. *"Doi Moi* in Review: The Challenges of Building Market Socialism in Vietnam." *Journal of Contemporary Asia* 38 (2): 221–43.

Bernstein, Elizabeth. 2007. *Temporarily Yours: Intimacy, Authenticity, and the Commerce of Sex.* Chicago, IL: University of Chicago Press.

Bernstein, Jake, Petra Blum, Oliver Zihlmann, David Thompson, Frederik Obermaier, and Bastian Obermayer. 2016. "All Putin's Men: Secret Records Reveal Money Network Tied to Russian Leader." International Consortium of Investigative Journalists (ICIJ), April 3, 2016. *https://www.icij.org/investigations/panama-papers/20160403-putin-russia-offshore-network/*.

Birdsong, Nicholas. 2015. *The Consequences of Economic Inequality.* Kansas City, MO: Seven Pillars Institute.

Block-Lieb, Susan, and Terence C. Halliday. 2017. *Global Lawmakers: International Organizations in the Crafting of World Markets.* New York: Cambridge University Press.

Bourdieu, Pierre. 1984. *Distinction: A Social Critique of the Judgment of Taste.* Cambridge: Harvard University Press.

Bourdieu, Pierre, and Loïc J. D. Wacquant. 1992. *An Invitation to Reflexive Sociology.* Chicago, IL: The University of Chicago Press.

Bourgois, Philippe. 1996. *In Search of Respect: Selling Cark in El Barrio.* Cambridge, UK: Cambridge University Press.

Braithwaite, Valerie. 2009a. *Defiance in Taxation and Governance: Resisting and Dismissing Authority in a Democracy.* Northampton, MA: Edward Elgar Publishing.

Braithwaite, Valerie. 2009b. "Tax Evasion." In *Oxford Handbook of Crime and Public Policy,* edited by Michael Tonry, 381–405. Oxford, UK: Oxford University Press.

Bruner, Christopher. 2016. *Re-Imagining Offshore Finance.* New York: Oxford University Press.

Burawoy, Michael, Joseph A. Blum, Sheba George, Zsuzsa Gille, Teresa Gowan, Lynne Haney, Maren Klawiter, Stephen H. Lopez, Seán Ó Riain, and Millie Thayer. 2000. *Global Ethnography: Forces, Connections, and Imaginations in a Postmodern World.* Berkeley: University of California Press.

Bussell, Jennifer. 2013. "Varieties of Corruption: The Organization of Rent-Seeking in India." Westminster Model of Democracy in Crisis? Conference at Harvard University.

Čihák, Martin, Aslı Demirgüç-Kunt, Erik Feyen, and Ross Levine. 2012. Global Financial Development Database. In *Benchmarking Financial Systems Around the World.* Policy Research Working Paper 6175. Washington, DC: World Bank. *https://openknowledge.worldbank.org/bitstream/handle/10986/12031/wps6175.pdf?sequence=1&isAllowed=y*.

Contreras, Randol. 2013. *The Stickup Kids: Race, Drugs, Violence, and the American Dream.* Berkeley: University of California Press.

Cooley, Alexander, John Heathershaw, and J. C. Sharman. 2018. "The Rise of Kleptocracy: Laundering Cash, Whitewashing Reputations." *Journal of Democracy* 29 (1): 39–53.

Cousin, Bruno, Shamus Khan, and Ashley Mears. 2018. "Theoretical and Methodological Pathways for Research on Elites." *Socio-Economic Review* 16 (2): 225–49.

Coyle, Kenny. 2021. "Burma's Communists Say Military Coup a Symptom of Myanmar's Crony Capitalism." *People's World,* April 26, 2021. https://www.peoplesworld.org/article/burmas-communists-say-military-coup-a-symptom-of-myanmars-crony-capitalism/.

Credit Suisse Group AG. 2017. *Annual Report 2017.*

Credit Suisse Research Institute. 2011. "The Base of the Wealth Pyramid." In *Global Wealth Report 2011.*

DaCosta, Gene. 2010. "Cayman Islands Companies: The Asia Connection." Conyers Dill & Pearman, December 2010.

Davies, Ed. 2021. "China Envoy Visits Myanmar as New Route to Indian Ocean Opened." *Reuters*, September 1, 2021. *https://www.reuters.com/world/china/china-envoy-visits-myanmar-new-route-indian-ocean-opened-2021-09-01/*.

Davis, Brett. 2021. "Vietnam's Textile Industry Combats Pandemic With PPE Switch." *Forbes*, March 24, 2021. *https://www.forbes.com/sites/davisbrett/2021/03/24/vietnams-textile-industry-combats-pandemic-with-ppe-switch/?sh=10fa2ccb5b4f*.

Deming, Stuart H. 2011. *The Foreign Corrupt Practices Act and the New International Norms*. 2nd ed. International Practitioner's Deskbook Series. Chicago: American Bar Association.

De Mooij, Ruud A., and Sjef Ederveen. 2008. "Corporate Tax Elasticities: A Reader's Guide to Empirical Findings." *Oxford Review of Economic Policy* 24 (4):680–97.

Deneault, Alain. 2011. *Offshore: Tax Havens and the Rule of Global Crime*. Translated by George Holoch. New York: The New Press.

Desai, Mihir A., C. Fritz Foley, and James R. Hines Jr. 2004. "Foreign Direct Investment in a World of Multiple Taxes." *Journal of Public Economics* 88 (12): 2727–44.

Desai, Mihir A., C. Fritz Foley, and James R. Hines Jr. 2006. "The Demand for Tax Haven Operations." *Journal of Public Economics* 90 (3): 513–31.

Dhanoa, Sandeep. 2020. "The Hunt for Jho Low: Where is Low Laying Low? Where is Whaley?" *Unreserved*, January 9, 2020. *https://www.unreservedmedia.com/the-hunt-for-jho-low/*.

Dharmapala, Dhammika. 2017. *The Economics of Tax Avoidance and Evasion*. International Library of Critical Writings in Economics 334. Cheltenham, UK: Edward Elgar Publishing.

Dharmapala, Dhammika. 2019. "Profit Shiting in a Globalized World." *American Economic Association Papers and Proceedings* 109: 488–92.

Doucet, Andrea. 2018. "Feminist Epistemologies and Ethics: Ecological Thinking, Situated Knowledges, and Epistemic Responsibilities " In *The SAGE Handbook of Qualitative Research Ethics*, edited by Ron Iphofen and Martin Tolich. London: SAGE Publishing.

Douglas, Mary. 1966. *Purity and Danger: An Analysis of the Concepts of Pollution and Taboo*. New York: Routledge.

Durkheim, Èmile. 1995. *The Elementary Forms of Religious Life*. Edited by Karen E. Fields. New York: The Free Press.

Esteva, Gustavo, and Madhu Suri Prakash. 1998. *Grassroots Post-Modernism: Remaking the Soil of Cultures*. London: Zed Press.

Evans, Peter. 1995. *Embedded Autonomy: States and Industrial Transformation*. Princeton: Princeton University Press.

Fagetan, Ana Maria. 2021. "The Non Regulation of Hedge Funds in Offshore Jurisdictions: Cayman Islands, British Virgin Islands, Mauritius, and Delaware." In Fagetan, *The Regulation of Hedge Funds: A Global Perspective*, 283–331.London: Palgrave Macmillan.

Farrell, Justin. 2020. *Billionaire Wilderness: The Ultra-Wealthy and the Remaking of the American West*. Princeton, NJ: Princeton University Press.

Ferguson, Charles. 2010. Inside Job. United States: Sony Pictures Classics.

Fichtner, Jan. 2015. The Offshore-Intensity Ratio: Identifying the Strongest Magnets for Foreign Capital. London: City Political Economy Research Centre, City University London.

Fligstein, Neil, and Doug McAdam. 2011. "Toward a General Theory of Strategic Action Fields." *Sociological Theory* 29 (1):1–26.

Forbes. 2019. "Billionaires: The Richest People in the World." *Forbes*, March 5, 2019.

Fourcade, Marion, and Kieran Healy. 2007. "Moral Views of a Market Society." *Annual Review of Sociology* 33: 285–311.

Freeland, Chrystia. 2012. *Plutocrats: The Rise of the New Global Super-Rich and The Fall of Everyone Else*. New York: Penguin Books.

Friedman, Daniel, and Daniel McNeill. 2013. *Morals and Markets: The Dangerous Balance*. New York: Palgrave Macmillan.

Gaby, Sarah, and Neal Caren. 2016. "The Rise of Inequality: How social movements shape discursive fields." *Mobilization: An International Quarterly* 21 (4): 413–29.

Genschel, Philipp, and Thomas Rixen. 2015. "Settling and Unsettling the Transnational Legal Order of International Taxation." In *Transnational Legal Orders*, edited by Terence C. Halliday and Gregory Shaffer. New York: Cambridge University Press.

Gillen, Jamie. 2010. "An Examination of Entrepreneurial Relationships Between the State and Nonstate in Ho Chi Minh City, Vietnam." *Urban Geography* 31 (1): 90–113.

Girard, René. 1966. *Deceit, Desire, and the Novel: Self and Other in Literary Structure*. Translated by Yvonne Freccero. Baltimore: John Hopkins University Press.

Gladstone, Rick. 2021. "Pandora Papers: A Money Bomb With Political Ripples." *The New York Times*, October 4, 2021. *https://www.nytimes.com/2021/10/04/world/pandora-papers.html*.

Gleckman, Howard. 2013. "The Real Story on Apple's Tax Avoidance: How Ordinary It Is." *Forbes*, May 21. *https://www.forbes.com/sites/beltway/2013/05/21/the-real-story-about-apples-tax -avoidance-how-ordinary-it-is/?sh=335819546523*.

Goffman, Alice. 2014. *On the Run: Fugitive Life in an American City*. Chicago: University of Chicago Press.

Goldman, Jason G. 2016. "Meet the Spiders That Have Formed Armies 50,000 Strong." *https:// web.archive.org/web/20160124034948/http://www.bbc.com/earth/story/20160122-meet-the -spiders-that-have-formed-armies-50000-strong*.

Goldman, Russell. 2021. "Myanmar's Coup and Violence, Explained." *New York Times*, May 29, 2021. *https://www.nytimes.com/article/myanmar-news-protests-coup.html*.

Gonzalez, Nathaniel James. 2020. "Living with Violence: The Causes and Consequences of Recurrent Buddhist-Muslim Violence in Myanmar." Doctoral Dissertation, Sociology, University of Chicago.

Gorsira, Madelijine, Adriaan Denkers, and Wim Huisman. 2018. "Both Sides of the Coin: Motives for Corruption Among Public Officials and Business Employees." *Journal of Business Ethics* 151 (1): 179–94.

Gray, Alex. 2017. "These Are the World's Fastest-Growing Economies in 2017." *World Economic Forum*, June 9, 2017. *https://www.weforum.org/agenda/2017/06/these-are-the-world-s-fastest -growing-economies-in-2017-2/*.

Gunasegaram, P. 2018. *1MDB: The Scandal that Brought Down a Government: a Prime Minister, a Whizz and the Biggest Kleptocracy the World Has Ever Known*. Petaling Jaya, Malaysia: Strategic Information and Research Development Centre.

Halliday, Terence C. 1987. *Beyond Monopoly: Lawyers, State Crises, and Professional Empowerment*. Chicago: University of Chicago Press.

Halliday, Terence C., and Bruce G. Carruthers. 1996. "The Moral Regulation of Markets: Professions, Privatization and the English Insolvency Act 1986." *Accounting, Organizations and Society* 21 (4): 371–413.

Harms, Erik. 2016. *Luxury and Rubble: Civility and Dispossession in the New Saigon*. Asia: Local Studies / Global Themes 32. Oakland: University of California Press.

Harrington, Brooke. 2016. *Capital Without Borders: Wealth Managers and the One Percent*. Cambridge, MA: Harvard University Press.

Ho, Karen. 2009. *Liquidated: An Ethnography of Wall Street*. Durham, NC: Duke University Press.

Hoang, Kimberly Kay. 2015. *Dealing in Desire: Asian Ascendancy, Western Decline, and the Hidden Currencies of Global Sex Work*. Oakland, CA: University of California Press.

Hoang, Kimberly Kay. 2018. "Risky Investments: How Local and Foreign Investors Finesse Corruption-Rife Emerging Markets." *American Sociological Review* 83 (4): 657–85.

Hoang, Kimberly Kay. 2020. "Engendering Global Capital: How Homoerotic Triangles Facilitate Foreign Investments into Risky Markets." *Gender & Society* 34 (4): 547–72.

Hoang, Kimberly Kay, Jessica Cobb, and Ya-Wen Lei. 2017. "Guest Editors Introduction: Inter-Asian Capital Circulations, Cultural Transformations, and Methodological Positions." *positions: asia critique* 25 (4): 633–44.

ICIJ. 2016. "Giant Leak of Offshore Financial Records Exposes Global Array of Crime and Corruption: Overview of the Panama Papers." Organized Crime and Corruption Reporting Project, April 3, 2016. *https://www.occrp.org/en/panamapapers/overview/intro/*.

ICIJ. 2017. ICIJ Offshore Leaks Database: Power Players: Former Secretary of Commerce, US (2013–2017) Penny Pritzker. Washington, DC: International Consortium of Investigative Journalists. *https://offshoreleaks.icij.org/stories/penny-pritzker*.

ISEAS—Yusof Ishak Institute. 2010. "Timeline: US-Burma/Myanmar Relations." *Contemporary Southeast Asia* 32 (3): 434–36.

Jones, Lee. 2014. "The Political Economy of Myanmar's Transition." *Journal of Contemporary Asia* 44 (1): 144–170.

Kang, David C. 2002. *Crony Capitalism: Corruption and Development in South Korea and the Philippines*. New York: Cambridge University Press.

Kerkvliet, Benedict J. Tria. 2001. "An Approach for Analysing State-Society Relations in Vietnam." *Sojourn: Journal of Social Issues in Southeast Asia* 16 (2): 238–78.

Khanna, Tarun, and Krishna G. Palepu. 2010. *Winning in Emerging Markets: A Road Map for Strategy and Execution*. Boston, MA: Harvard Business Press.

Kim, Hun. 2017. "Capturing World-Class Urbanism Through Modal Governance in Saigon." *positions: asia critique* 25 (4): 669–92.

Klassen, Kenneth J., Petro Lisowsky, and Devan Mescall. 2017. "Transfer Pricing: Strategies, Practices, and Tax Minimization." *Contemporary Accounting Research* 14 (1): 455–93.

Knuth, Sarah, and Shaina Potts. 2016. "Legal Geographies of Finance: Editors' Introduction." *Environment and Planning A* 48 (3): 458–64.

Koolhaas, Rem. 2004. "Beijing Manifesto." *Wired*, August 1, 2004. *https://www.wired.com/2004/08/beijing/*.

Krippner, Greta R. 2017. "Unbounding the Economy." *Socio-Economic Review* 15 (3): 686–90.

Lainer-Vos, Dan. 2013. "The Practical Organization of Moral Transactions: Gift Giving, Market Exchange, Credit, and the Making of Diaspora Bonds." *Sociological Theory* 31 (2): 145–67.

Lane, Philip R., and Gian Maria Milesi-Ferretti. 2017. "International Financial Integration in the Aftermath of the Global Financial Crisis." Washington, D.C.: SSRN. *https://papers.ssrn.com/sol3/papers.cfm?abstract_id=2978676*.

Le, Andrew N. 2020. "The Quest for Mobility: The Constraints of Privatized Migration Control, Opportunistic Brokerage, and Migrant Resistance in Vietnam " Doctoral Dissertation, Sociology, University of California, Los Angeles (publication no. 20040).

Le, Thanh. 2018. "Grab Refuses to Release Details of Uber Buy-Out to Vietnam's Tax Man." *VnExpress International*, April 19, 2018. *https://e.vnexpress.net/news/business/grab-refuses-to-release-details-of-uber-buy-out-to-vietnam-s-tax-man-3738911.html*.

Lee, Cheol-Sung. 2016. *When Solidarity Works: Labor-Civic Networks and Welfare States in the Market Reform Era*. New York: Cambridge University Press.

Lee, Yen Nee. 2018. "Vietnam Unseats Singapore as Largest IPO Fundraiser in Southeast Asia." *CNBC*, December 26, 2018. *https://www.cnbc.com/2018/12/27/vietnam-unseats-singapore-as-largest-ipo-fundraiser-in-southeast-asia.html*.

Lee, Yen Nee. 2021. "Kamala Harris Kicks Off Vietnam Visit by Calling Out China's 'Bullying' Tactics." August 25, 2021. *https://www.cnbc.com/2021/08/25/vp-kamala-harris-talks-south-china-sea-in-vietnam-amid-us-china-rivalry.html*.

Leigh, David, Harold Frayman, and James Ball. 2012. "The Offshore Trick: How BVI 'Nominee Director' System Works." *The Guardian*, November 25, 2012. *https://www.theguardian.com /uk/2012/nov/25/offshore-trick-bvi-nominee-director*.

Lewin, Arie Y., and Carine Peeters. 2006. "The Top-Line Allure of Offshoring." *Harvard Business Review*. *https://hbr.org/2006/03/the-top-line-allure-of-offshoring*.

Mahtani, Shibani. 2021. "Harris, in Vietnam, Gets a Dose of China's Challenge to the U.S." *The Washington Post: Asia & Pacific*, August 25, 2021. *https://www.washingtonpost.com/world /asia_pacific/kamala-harris-vietnam-china-coronavirus/2021/08/25/77e51efa-0564-11ec-b3c4 -c462b1edcfc8_story.html*.

Malesky, Edmund J., Neil McCulloch, and Nguyen Duc Nhat. 2015. "The Impact of Governance and Transparency on Firm Investment in Vietnam." *Economics of Transition* 23 (4): 677–715.

Maurer, Bill. 2008. "Re-Regulating Offshore Finance?" *Geography Compass* 2 (1): 155–75.

Mauss, Marcel. 1990. *The Gift: The Form and Reason for Exchange in Archaic Societies*. New York: Routledge.

McCoy, Kevin. 2016. "U.S. Slaps $1.3B in Penalties on Swiss Banks." *USA Today*, January 27, 2016.

Mears, Ashley. 2020. *Very Important People: Status and Beauty in the Global Party Circuit*. Princeton, NJ: Princeton University Press.

Merrill Lynch Global Wealth Management and Capgemini. 2011. *2011 Asia-Pacific Wealth Report*. *https://www.capgemini.com/us-en/wp-content/uploads/sites/4/2017/08/Asia-Pacific_Wealth _Report_2011____English_Version.pdf*.

Mills, C. Wright. [1956] 2000. *The Power Elite*. New York: Oxford Unviersity Press.

Mohanty, Chandra Talpade. 2002. "'Under Western Eyes' Revisited: Feminist Solidarity through Anticapitalist Struggles." *Signs: Journal of Women in Culture and Society* 28 (2): 499–535.

Nam, Sylvia. 2011. "Phnom Penh: From the Politics of Ruin to the Possibilities of Return." *Traditional Dwellings and Settlements Review* 23 (1): 55–68.

Nam, Sylvia. 2012. "Speculative Urbanism: The Remaking of Phnom Penh." PhD Dissertation, Department of City and Regional Planning, University of California, Berkeley.

Nguyen, Duy. 2021a. "Vietnam Produces Face Masks for US Marine Corps." *Hanoi Times*, February 8, 2021. *http://hanoitimes.vn/vietnam-produces-face-masks-for-us-marine-corps-316217.html*.

Nguyen, Thi Bich Ngoc. 2021b. "Investors Slam on Brakes in Myanmar in Wake of Coup: Country 'Untouchable' during State of Emergency, Says Venture Capitalist." *DealStreetAsia*, Nikkei Asia, February 6, 2021.

Nguyen, Thi Thanh Thuy. 2017. Updates on Transfer Pricing in Vietnam. TMF Group Regulatory Update, June 8, 2017.

Nguyen, Tu Phuong. 2014. "Rethinking State-Society Relations in Vietnam: The Case of Business Associations in Ho Chi Minh City." *Asian Studies Review* 38 (1): 87–106.

North, Douglass. 1990. *Institutions, Institutional Change and Economic Performance*. Cambridge, UK: Cambridge University Press.

O'Neill, Jim. 2013. *The Growth Map: Economic Opportunity in the BRICs and Beyond*. London: Penguin Books.

Ong, Aihwa. 2011. "Introduction: Worlding Cities, or the Art of Being Global." In *Worlding Cities: Asian Experiments and the Art of Being Global*, edited by Ananya Roy and Aihwa Ong. Oxford: Blackwell Publishing Limited.

Osburg, John. 2018. "Making Business Personal: Corruption, Anti-corruption, and Elite Networks in Post-Mao China." *Current Anthropology* 59: S18, S149–59.

Palan, Ronen, Richard Murphy, and Christian Chavagneux. 2009. *Tax Havens: How Globalization Really Works*. Ithaca: Cornell University Press.

Palan, Ronen, and Anastasia Nesvetailova. 2014. "Elsewhere, Ideally Nowhere: Shadow Banking and Offshore Finance." CITYPERC Working Paper No. 2014-01. London: City Political Economy Research Centre, City University London.

Panitch, Leo, and Sam Gindin. 2012. *The Making of Global Capitalism: The Political Economy of American Empire*. New York: Verso.

Pennington, Matthew. 2016. "Obama Orders U.S. Economic Sanctions on Myanmar Lifted." Associated Press, October 7, 2016. *https://www.pbs.org/newshour/world/myanmar-economic -sanctions-lifted*.

Piketty, Thomas. 2014. *Capital in the Twenty-First Century*. Translated by Arthur Goldhammer. Cambridge, MA: The Belknap Press of Harvard University Press.

Piketty, Thomas. 2015. Foreword to *The Hidden Wealth of Nations: The Scourge of Tax Havens*, by Gabriel Zucman. Translated by Teresa Lavender Fagan. Chicago: University of Chicago Press.

Pistor, Katharina. 2019. *The Code of Capital: How the Law Creates Wealth and Inequality* Princeton, NJ: Princeton University Press.

Polanyi, Karl. [1944] 2001. *The Great Transformation: The Political and Economic Origins of Our Time*. Boston: Beacon Press.

Porteous, Kimberley, and Emily Menkes. 2013. "Highlights of Offshore Leaks So Far." International Consortium of Investigative Journalists (ICIJ), April 4, 2013. *https://www.icij.org/inside-icij /2013/04/highlights-offshore-leaks-so-far/*.

Potts, Shaina. 2016. "Reterritorializing Economic Governance: Contracts, Space, and Law in Transborder Economic Geographies." *Environment and Planning A: Economy and Space* 48 (3): 523–39.

Potts, Shaina. 2020. "(Re-)Writing Markets: Law and Contested Payment Geographies." *Environment and Planning A: Economy and Space* 52 (1): 46–65. First published online April 5, 2018. *https://doi.org/10.1177/0308518X18768286*.

Ralph, Laurence. 2014. *Renegade Dreams: Living through Injury in Gangland Chicago*. Chicago: University of Chicago Press.

Reich, Robert. 1983. "The Next American Frontier." *The Atlantic Monthly*, 43–58.

Richkoff, Cheryl Adams. 2018. "All About Social Spiders, the Spiders That Live Together In Enormous Webs." Weird Nature, *Ranker*, updated September 23, 2021. *https://www.ranker.com /list/what-are-social-spiders/cheryl-adams-richkoff*.

Rivera, Lauren. 2012. "Hiring as Cultural Matching: The Case of Elite Professional Service Firms." *American Sociological Review* 77 (6): 999–1022.

Rose-Ackerman, Susan. 1999. *Corruption and Government: Causes, Consequences, and Reform*. Cambridge, UK: Cambridge University Press.

Rose-Ackerman, Susan. 2010. "The Law and Economics of Bribery and Extortion." *Annual Review of Law and Social Science* 6 (1): 217–38.

Rossman, Gabriel. 2014. "Obfuscatory Relational Work and Disreputable Exchange." *Sociological Theory* 32 (1): 43–63.

Sands, Gary. 2016. "Vietnam's Growing Environmental Activism: Another Act of Civil Disobedience Shows that Ordinary Vietnamese Are Becoming More Vocal." *The Diplomat*, October 29, 2016. *https://thediplomat.com/2016/10/vietnams-growing-environmental-activism/*.

Sanyal, Rajib. 2012. "Patterns in International Bribery: Violations of the Foreign Corrupt Practices Act." *Thunderbird International Business Review* 54 (3): 299–309.

Sassen, Saskia. 2000. *Cities in a World Economy*. Thousand Oaks, CA: Pine Forge Press.

Sassen, Saskia. 2001. *The Global City: New York, London, Tokyo*. Princeton, NJ: Princeton University Press.

Sayer, Andrew. 2015. *Why We Can't Afford the Rich*. Bristol, UK: Policy Press.

Schwartz, Nelson D. 2020. *The Velvet Rope Economy: How Inequality Became Big Business*. New York: Doubleday.

Sedgwick, Eve Kosofsky. 1985. *Between Men: English Literature and Male Homosocial Desire*. New York: Columbia University Press.

Shaxson, Nicholas. 2011. *Treasure Islands: Uncovering the Damage of Offshore Banking and Tax Havens*. New York: St. Martin's Griffin.

Sherman, Rachel. 2017. *Uneasy Street: The Anxieties of Affluence*. Princeton, NJ: Princeton University Press.

Shields, Michael, and Joshua Franklin. 2015. "Credit Suisse Will Sell Its US Private Bank." *Reuters*, September 13, 2015. *https://www.businessinsider.com/r-credit-suisse-plans-to-sell-us-private-bank-newspaper-2015-9*.

Small, Mario Luis. 2017. *Someone To Talk To*. New York: Oxford University Press.

Smith, Deborah R. R. 1986. "Population Genetics of *Anelosimus eximius* (Araneae, Theridiidae)." *Journal of Arachnology* 14 (2): 201–17.

Spalding, Andy. 2015. "Notes from IACA, Part Three (concl.): A Facilitation Payments Question We Could Not Answer." *The FCPA Blog*, August 5, 2015. *http://www.fcpablog.com/blog/2015/8/5/notes-from-iaca-part-three-concl-a-facilitation-payments-que.html*.

Stiglitz, Joesph. 2019. *People, Power, and Profits: Progressive Capitalism for an Age of Discontent*. New York: W. W. Norton & Company.

Stovel, Katherine, and Lynette Shaw. 2012. "Brokerage." *Annual Review of Sociology* 38 (1): 139–158.

Stuart, Forrest. 2016. *Down, Out, and Under Arrest: Policing and Everyday Life in Skid Row*. Chicago: University of Chicago Press.

Swanson, Ana. 2018. "Trump Proposes Rejoining Trans-Pacific Partnership." *New York Times*, April 12, 2018. *https://www.nytimes.com/2018/04/12/us/politics/trump-trans-pacific-partnership.html*.

Szep, Jason, and Andrew R. C. Marshall. 2012. "Special Report: An image makeover for Myanmar Inc." *Reuters*, April 13, 2012. *https://www.reuters.com/article/us-myanmar-cronies-image-idUSBRE83B0YU20120413*.

Tavory, Iddo, and Stefan Timmermans. 2014. *Abductive Analysis: Theorizing Qualitative Research*. Chicago: Chicago University Press.

The Irrawaddy. 2021a. "Myanmar Junta Backs Beijing in Spat With US Over Origins of Coronavirus." *The Irrawaddy*, September 3, 2021. https://www.irrawaddy.com/news/burma/myanmar-junta-backs-beijing-in-spat-with-us-over-origins-of-coronavirus.html.

The Irrawaddy. 2021b. "Over 50 Top Officials from Myanmar's Ousted NLD Govt Face Long Jail Terms." *The Irrawaddy*, November 30, 2021. https://www.irrawaddy.com/news/burma/over-50-top-officials-from-myanmars-ousted-nld-govt-face-long-jail-terms.html.

Tilly, Charles. 2007. *Democracy*. Cambridge, UK: Cambridge University Press.

Tonkes, Paul. 2020. "Covid-19 a Catalyst for Vietnam Manufactoring." *Business Times*, updated October 26, 2020. *https://www.businesstimes.com.sg/asean-business/covid-19-a-catalyst-for-vietnam-manufacturing*.

Treanor, Jill. 2017. "US Authorities Lift Threat to Prosecute HSBC." *The Guardian*, December 11, 2017. *https://www.hitc.com/en-gb/2017/12/12/us-authorities-lift-threat-to-prosecute-hsbc/*.

Tsing, Anna Loewenhaupt. 2005. *Friction: An Ethnography of Global Connection*. Princeton, NJ: Princeton University Press.

Tu, Anh, and Chi Le. 2018. "Grab Says It Will Not Pay Any Back Taxes Owed by Uber in Vietnam." *VnExpress*, April 6, 2018. *https://e.vnexpress.net/news/business/grab-says-it-will-not-pay-any-back-taxes-owed-by-uber-in-vietnam-3732953.html*.

Turnell, Sean. 2009. *Fiery Dragons: Banks, Moneylenders, and Microfinance in Burma*. Copenhagen, Denmark: NIAS (Nordic Institute of Asian Studies) Press.

Turnell, Sean. 2011. "Myanmar in 2010: Doors Open, Doors Close." *Asian Survey* 51 (1):148–54.

US Department of Justice. 2016. "Hamburg Man Extradited from Vietnam on Fraud Charges." News release. Buffalo, NY: US Attorney's Office, Western District of New York, December 9, 2016. *https://www.justice.gov/usao-wdny/pr/hamburg-man-extradited-vietnam-fraud-charges*.

US Department of Justice. 2020. "Goldman Sachs Charged in Foreign Bribery Case and Agrees to Pay Over $2.9 Billion." News release. Washington, DC: US Department of Justice Office of Public Affairs, October 22, 2020. *https://www.justice.gov/opa/pr/goldman-sachs-charged -foreign-bribery-case-and-agrees-pay-over-29-billion.*

USTR: The Office of the United States Trade Representative. n.d. "The Trans-Pacific Partnership." *https://ustr.gov/sites/default/files/TPP-Strategic-Importance-of-TPP-Fact-Sheet.pdf.*

Vargas, Robert. 2016. *Wounded City: Turf Wars in a Violent Chicago Barrio.* New York: Oxford University Press.

Veblen, Thorstein. 1921. *The Engineers and the Price System.* New York: B. W. Huebsch, Inc.

Venkatesh, Sudhir. 2008. *Gang Leader for a Day: A Rogue Sociologist Takes to the Streets.* New York: Penguin Press.

Vu, Joseph. 2017. "Recent Changes to Vietnam's Transfer Pricing Regulations." *TP Talks*—PwC's Global Transfer Pricing Podcast. Episode 12. April 12, 2017. https://www.pwc.com/gx/en /services/tax/transfer-pricing/podcasts/episode-12.html.

Weber, Max. [1922] 1978. *Economy and Society.* Berkeley: University of California Press.

Wei, Shen. 2010. "China's Dilemma: How Can a Weak Company Law Regime Support a Strong Market for International Private Equity Investments? A Real 'Piggybacking' Case." *Business Law International* 11 (3): 195–224.

Weitzman, Hal. 2022. *What's the Matter with Delaware? How the First State Has Favored the Rich, Powerful, and Criminal—and How It Costs Us All.* Princeton, NJ: Princeton University Press.

White House: President Barack Obama. 2016. "The Trans-Pacific Partnership: What You Need to Know about President Obama's Trade Agreement." *https://obamawhitehouse.archives.gov /issues/economy/trade.*

Witt, Michael A., and Gordon Redding. 2013. "Asian Business Systems: Institutional Comparison, Clusters and Implications for Varieties of Capitalism and Business Systems Theory." *Socio-Economic Review* 11 (2): 265–300.

Woodman, Spencer. 2018a. "Michael Cohen Scandal a Reminder That the U.S. is a Tax Secrecy Paradise." International Consortium of Investigative Journalists (ICIJ), May 21, 2018. *https:// www.icij.org/inside-icij/2018/05/michael-cohen-scandal-a-reminder-that-the-u-s-is-a-tax -secrecy-paradise/.*

Woodman, Spencer. 2018b. "Paradise Papers Helps Reveal Illinois Governor Candidate's Offshore." International Consortium of Investigative Journalists (ICIJ), March 15, 2018. *https://www.icij.org /investigations/paradise-papers/paradise-papers-help-reveal-jb-pritzkers-offshore-connections/.*

World Bank Group. 2018. Economy Profile of Vietnam. Doing Business 2019. Washington, DC: World Bank. *https://openknowledge.worldbank.org/bitstream/handle/10986/30827/131869-WP -DB2019-PUBLIC-Vietnam.pdf?sequence=1&isAllowed=y.*

Worstall, Tim. 2016. "What Facebook and Apple Can Teach You about Transfer Pricing." *Forbes,* July 29, 2016.

Wright, Tom, and Bradley Hope. 2018. *Billion Dollar Whale: The Man Who Fooled Wall Street, Hollywood, and the World.* New York: Hachette Books.

Young, Alford A. Jr. 2004. *The Minds of Marginalized Black Men: Making Sense of Mobility, Opportunity, and Future Life Chances.* Princeton Studies in Cultural Sociology. Princeton, NJ: Princeton University Press.

Young, Cristobal. 2018. *The Myth of Millionaire Tax Flight: How Place Still Matters for the Rich.* Stanford, CA: Stanford University Press.

Zaloom, Caitlin. 2006. *Out of the Pits: Traders and Technology from Chicago to London.* Chicago: University of Chicago Press.

Zarroli, Jim. 2016. "JPMorgan Chase Agreees to Pay $264 Million in Chinese Bribery Scheme." News segment, *All Things Considered.* Washington, DC: National Public Radio, November 17, 2016.

Zelizer, Viviana A. Rotman. [1979] 2017. *Morals and Markets: The Development of Life Insurance in the United States*. New York: Columbia University Press.

Zelizer, Viviana A. 2005. *The Purchase of Intimacy*. Princeton, NJ: Princeton University Press.

Zelizer, Viviana A. 2012. "How I Became a Relational Economic Sociologist and What Does That Mean?" *Politics and Society* 40 (2): 145–74.

Zhao, Grace. 2014. "Transfer Pricing Lands Apple, Starbucks, and Fiat in Hot Water." *Global Financial Integrity*, June 18, 2014. *https://gfintegrity.org/transfer-pricing-apple-starbucks-fiat -hot-water/*.

Zhou, Laura. 2021. "China Announces New Myanmar Trade Route as It Seeks to Bolster Ties with Military Junta." *South China Morning Post*, September 5, 2021. *https://www.scmp.com /news/china/diplomacy/article/3147583/china-announces-new-myanmar-trade-route-it-seeks -bolster-ties*.

Zoellick, Robert B. 2010. "The End of the Third World? Modernizing Multilateralism for a Multipolar World." Delivered at the Woodrow Wilson Center for International Scholars, Washington, DC, April 14, 2010. Washington, DC: World Bank.

Zucman, Gabriel. 2014. "Taxing across Borders: Tracking Personal Wealth and Corporate Profits." *Journal of Economic Perspectives* 28 (4): 121–48. *https://pubs.aeaweb.org/doi/pdfplus/10.1257 /jep.28.4.121*.

Zucman, Gabriel. 2015. *The Hidden Wealth of Nations: The Scourge of Tax Havens*. Translated by Teresa Lavender Fagan. Chicago: University of Chicago Press.

INDEX

Abbott, Andrew, 236
accountants/auditors: as subordinate spiders, 30–31; tax certainty, offering services that strive for, 142–44
accounting practices: arm's-length prices, calculating, 142; manipulation of, 129; multiple books, operating with, 128, 141; round-tripping, 126; theft through, 121; transfer pricing, 126, 139–42
anti-corrupters, 91–98
Anti-Fascist People's Freedom League (AFPFL), 244n39
Appel, Hannah, 10, 236
Apple, 138–39
Asian Infrastructure Investment Bank (AIIB), 36
asset protection trusts (ATPs), 52
Aung San, 244n39

banks and banking: bankers as subordinate spiders, 31–32; "know your customer/client" (KYC) regulations, 34; setting up an account for an SPV, 162–63; weak local banking institutions and offshore banking, 49–50
Bergmann, Patrick, 236
bribes and bribery, 90–91, 122–24; to avoid enforcement of taxation, 127–28, 130; avoiding "pay to play," 82–87; blurring practices, 107; comfort of East/Southeast Asian investors with, 40; examples of, 153–55; facilitation payments made by greasers, 91, 98–104; graft engaged in by bribers, 91; necessity of in Vietnam, 78–79, 173, 177–78; obfuscation strategies, 104; obfuscation strategies: brokerage, 112–20; obfuscation strategies: bundling, 107–12; obfuscation strategies: gift-giving, 104–7; paid through nominee accounts in OFCs, 36; rationalization of, 114–15; special purpose vehicle set

up for the purpose of, 159, 162. *See also* corruption
BRIC (Brazil, Russia, India, and China) countries, 37
British Virgin Islands (BVI), 156–57, 159–60, 191
brokerage, 112–20. *See also* bribes and bribery; fixers
bundling, 107–12
Burma. *See* Myanmar
Burmese Freedom and Democracy Act (BFDA), 41
"Burmese Way to Socialism," 40
Bush, George W., 41

capital: artificial flows of, 45; raising through offshore roadshows, 56–65; raising through onshore investor trips, 66–73; real people and global, 9; stealth, 155
capitalism: crony (*see* crony capitalism); relational, homoerotic bonding and, 78–82; spiderweb (*see* spiderweb capitalism)
Carlson, Jennifer, 236
Carruthers, Bruce, 185
Cayman Islands, 35, 151–52, 156
Chase Private Client, 192
China: as BRIC country, 37; Myanmar and, 218; rivalry in Southeast Asia between the United States and, 36–37, 219
CITI-Fund Administrator, 26–27
Coca-Cola, 44
Cohen, Michael, 213
Coldwell Banker (CBRE), 71
company secretaries as subordinate spiders, 32
Convention on the Recognition and Enforcement of Arbitral Awards ("New York Convention"), 50
coordination: experiences of in successful exits, 187, 193; making markets through, 10

A NOTE ON THE TYPE

This book has been composed in Adobe Text and Gotham.
Adobe Text, designed by Robert Slimbach for Adobe,
bridges the gap between fifteenth- and sixteenth-century
calligraphic and eighteenth-century Modern styles.
Gotham, inspired by New York street signs, was designed
by Tobias Frere-Jones for Hoefler & Co.

9 780691 231259